To the Elephant Graveyard

TARQUIN HALL

JOHN MURRAY
Albemarle Street, London

First published in 2000
by John Murray (Publishers) Ltd,
50 Albemarle Street, London W1X 4BD

Paperback edition 2001

A catalogue record for this book is available from the British Library

ISBN 0–7195–6158 2

Typeset in 11/13pt Bembo

Printed and bound in Great Britain by
The Guernsey Press Company Ltd

For Dinesh Choudhury
in gratitude for his kindness and unfailing hospitality

Contents

Illustrations

All the photographs were taken by the author except Plate 11 which is reproduced courtesy of the Assam Forest Department.

The Place where Elephants Die

Hidden away from the haunts of men, west of a widespread lake,
Out of the scope of human ken, in tangled thicket and brake,
'Mid arching trees where a foetid breeze ruffles the ragged sky,
Is the sombre place where the vanishing race of the elephants come
    to die.

Cullen Gouldsbury, Songs out of Exile

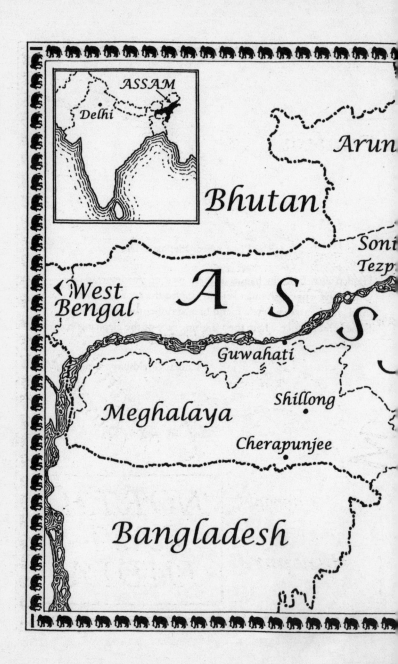

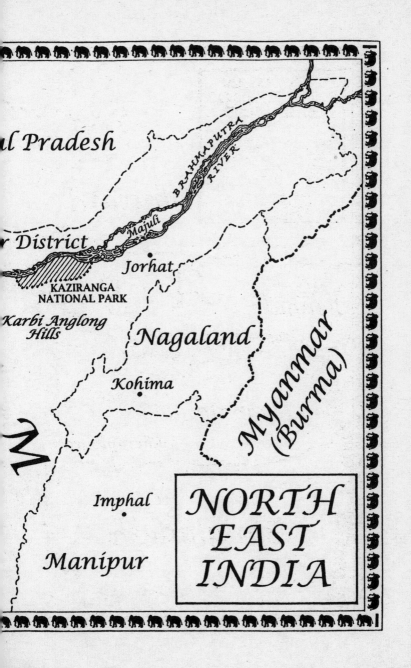

al Pradesh

BRAHMAPUTRA RIVER

Majuli

District

Jorhat

KAZIRANGA
NATIONAL PARK

Karbi Anglong
Hills

Nagaland

Kohima

Myanmar
(Burma)

Imphal

Manipur

NORTH
EAST
INDIA

I

The Hit

'Man and the higher animals, especially the primates, have some few instincts in common. All have the same senses, intuitions, and sensations, similar passions, affections, and emotions, even the complex ones such as jealousy, suspicion, emulation, gratitude and magnanimity; they practise deceit and are revengeful …'

Charles Darwin, *The Descent of Man*

THE ELEPHANT CAME in the dead of night. At first, he moved silently through the isolated hamlet, past the cottages, bungalows and huts where the inhabitants had long been fast asleep. Past the meeting-house, the fish-pond and the village shop. Past the cigarette stall, the water pump and the temple, dedicated to Hanuman, the monkey god.

The tusker crossed the rickety wooden bridge that spanned the village stream and turned east, following the sandy lane for several hundred yards. Here, he took a short cut over a field, breaking down one or two fences and trampling rows of cabbages underfoot. Soon, he passed another clutch of homes and a primary school.

For some unexplained reason, none of these buildings attracted his attention. Indeed his tracks, when examined the next morning, showed that he failed to stop even once along his chosen path. Instead, he continued to the edge of the settlement, strode straight up to a bamboo hut belonging to a local farmer called Shom, uttered a shrill trumpet and then launched his devastating attack.

Monimoy, a farmer from the same village, was a witness to what happened next. Now, two days later, he sat in the Assam Forest Department's public affairs office, telling his story to P. S. Das, the information officer whom I had come to meet soon after my arrival in Guwahati.

'I was making my way home after some drinking,' said Monimoy. 'I was walking in the lane when the elephant came. I watched what happened next with my own eyes!'

The farmer scratched at his nose with his index finger and glanced nervously around the gloomy office, sniffing the strong smell of kerosene emanating from a nearby petrol can. His hands shook like those of a junkie gone cold turkey.

'The elephant's eyes glowed red. Fire burned inside them. Flames and smoke shot out from his trunk. He was a monster – as big as a house, like one of the gods. His tusks were huge, like ...'

Das, sitting behind a desk positioned in front of the farmer, was tiring of the yokel's lengthy and highly coloured story. Impatiently he raised a hand to silence the excited farmer.

'Just tell us what happened.'

Monimoy fidgeted in his threadbare *dhoti*.

'Yes, yes, of course,' he stammered, 'I was just coming to that ...'

He swallowed hard, trying to calm himself, and then continued: 'The elephant charged at the hut, using his head like a battering ram. Time and again, he smashed into the walls. The timber creaked, snapped and gave way. He smashed at the door with his tusks, breaking it into little pieces. The elephant tugged at the supports with his trunk. Soon the roof caved in!'

Monimoy leaned forward in his chair, nursing his forehead in a manner that suggested he was suffering from a hangover.

'Inside, Shom's family screamed for help,' he continued. 'I could hear the terrified cries of his daughters. "Help us, help us," they pleaded. "The elephant is attacking us!"'

Monimoy had watched from the lane, drunk and helpless. Rather than going to the rescue, he remained frozen to the spot.

'I couldn't move,' he stammered, shaking his head from side to side regretfully. 'I couldn't do anything.'

It took the elephant only a few minutes to flatten the flimsy structure. Amidst the confusion, a lantern was knocked over, setting fire to the dry straw roof. Within seconds, the hut was engulfed in flames. Two of Shom's daughters escaped out of the back, running across the fields to the safety of a neighbour's cottage; another daughter and her mother hid in a nearby ditch. Sadly, Shom was not so fast on his feet.

'Shom was drunk. He stumbled out of the hut clutching a machete. I could see the terror on his face. He called out for someone to save him. This got the elephant's attention and he came after Shom.'

With shaking hands, Monimoy paused to pick up a mug of milky tea that stood on the desk before him.

'Shom tripped and fell on the ground. The elephant grabbed hold of him with his trunk. Shom struck out with his machete. The elephant knocked it from his hand.'

As he talked, Monimoy began to sweat openly. He shut his eyes tight as if the memory of what happened next was too much to bear.

'Shom was screaming and screaming. I can hear him now! He struggled to get free. The elephant held on to him and swung him around and then smashed him against a tree again and again.'

The elephant toyed with the local farmer, like a cat playing with a mouse, before dropping him on the ground. Remarkably, Shom was still conscious. He groaned in agony as blood seeped from his mouth and nose.

The triumphant beast stood over him, raised his trunk and trumpeted angrily. Then he prepared to finish off his victim.

'What happened next?' prompted Das impatiently.

Monimoy swallowed again.

'As I watched,' he said, 'the elephant knelt down and drove his right tusk straight through Shom's chest!'

Das grimaced. I shifted uneasily in my chair. Monimoy looked off into space, as if in a trance.

'For a moment, Shom writhed around. After that, he was still.'

The rogue elephant raised his tusk with the farmer still pinned to its end like a bug on the end of a needle.

'Then the elephant tossed him to one side and disappeared into the darkness, the blood dripping from his tusk.'

Two days earlier, on the morning of Shom's death, I had been reading the newspapers in my office at the New Delhi bureau of the Associated Press when the following article caught my eye:

RAMPAGING ROGUE FACES EXECUTION

Guwahati: The government of Assam today issued proclamation orders for the destruction of one wild rogue elephant, described as Tusker male, who is responsible for 38 deaths of humans in the Sonitpur district of Upper Assam.

The state Forest Department has therefore invited all hunters to come forward and bid for the contract worth 50,000 rupees.

The favoured candidate is one Dinesh Choudhury of Guwahati. In reply today to a question about whether he would accept the assignment, he said: 'It is a very dangerous thing. It will take some time before the elephant can be brought to task. We will have to travel on tamed elephants into the jungle areas and flush him out.'

The deadline for candidate application is tomorrow at 5:30 p.m.

*

Tearing the article from the paper, I reread it carefully. It sounded like one of the most promising stories I had come across for months. Who would have imagined, in this day and age, that the Indian authorities were hiring professional hunters to slaughter Asian elephants, which are more usually regarded as an endangered species? Surely, with modern tranquillizers, an elephant could be captured and placed in a zoo or, at the very least, driven into a game reserve? No doubt, I mused, corruption lay at the heart of the matter. If I had the chance to travel to Guwahati, the capital of the state of Assam, I sensed that I might be able to expose what sounded like an underhand business.

There was just one problem. The elephant was on the rampage in North-East India, an obscure part of the country rife with insurgency. The region was periodically off-limits to foreigners. In the past, I had been barred from going there. I decided to call Assam's representative in Delhi who made it clear that the regulations had been relaxed.

'I cannot guarantee your safety or offer any protection,' he said, 'but you are free to travel anywhere in the state, except military areas.'

That was good enough for me. I called my editor in London, sold him the story and explained that I might be away for as much as a fortnight. After that I booked myself on the next Indian Airlines flight to Guwahati.

Now, sitting in Das's office, I considered Monimoy's fantastic tale. It seemed implausible. Elephants do not breathe smoke and fire, they are not gods, and they certainly do not go around in the middle of the night knocking down people's homes and singling out particular human beings for premeditated murder. Elephants are kindly, intelligent, generally good-tempered creatures, like Babar or Dumbo. Monimoy, who had by his own admission been drinking at the time of the attack, was clearly prone to wild exaggeration. But could he also be lying?

My suspicions aroused, I questioned him carefully about his motives for travelling all the way from Sonitpur, a full day's bus ride, just to tell his story to the Forest Department.

'I have come on behalf of my village', he told me, 'to petition the government to shoot the elephant.'

He explained that his family, along with dozens of others, lived in constant fear. For weeks, the elephant had terrified their district, killing thirty-eight people.

'He is possessed! An evil god! He kills anyone who says bad things about him. That's why he murdered Shom. Only the day before, Shom said he hoped the elephant would be killed,' continued Monimoy. 'So, you see, by coming here and pleading with you to shoot the elephant, I am putting myself at great personal risk. When I return to my village, the elephant will surely come for me!'

His superstitious beliefs aside, Monimoy's motives seemed plausible and straightforward. Nevertheless, I had spent enough time in India to know that nothing in the subcontinent is ever clear-cut. There had to be more. Perhaps Monimoy, a shifty character if ever I'd seen one, had murdered Shom and blamed it on the elephant. Or maybe Monimoy was a poacher and had provoked the animal who, in turn, had killed his partner, and now the farmer was attempting some kind of cover-up. Or perhaps the elephant lived in a forest that Monimoy hoped to chop down and cultivate, and that was why he wanted the elephant removed.

Whatever the case, I found it very hard to believe that an elephant would deliberately hurt anyone, except perhaps in self-defence.

When Monimoy eventually left, I asked Das what he thought of the farmer's extraordinary story. The information officer shrugged his shoulders.

'You're right. Elephants are generally very gentle creatures.

Usually, they won't kill a living thing, although you do get the odd rotten apple.'

'Yes, but this farmer made the elephant sound like a crazed monster,' I said. 'It was sheer nonsense – all that stuff about him creeping through the village and picking out a single house to attack. That's unheard of. No animal behaves like that.'

Das tipped back in his chair.

'You have a romantic view of elephants,' he remarked. 'Genuine rogues are rare, but we do get them from time to time. There's no more dangerous or cunning an animal.'

That's what you would say, I thought to myself. Your department is the one that has issued the warrant for the rogue's destruction. But why, I asked him, didn't they capture the animal instead?

'The average Asian male elephant weighs seven tonnes, stands nine feet high, can run at twenty-five miles an hour and possesses a trunk that could pull your head right off your shoulders,' Das explained. 'You can't put such a rogue elephant in a cage, you can't tie him to a post, you can't pacify him or reason with him, and he can't be trained. He has to be killed or he will kill. It's as simple as that.'

He drew hard on his cigarette and continued: 'An elephant must kill at least twelve people before a destruction order is given. When that happens, we have to choose a hunter. Not just anyone is invited to come forward. He must own a .458 velocity rifle, be a trained marksman and, preferably, have experience of shooting elephants.'

Das went on to explain that a warrant is issued with a description of the elephant's height, approximate weight, colouring and any distinguishing features.

'The warrant has a time limit,' he added. 'It's usually fourteen days. If the elephant in question is not eliminated within that period, then all bets are off.'

'It sounds like a Mafioso hit,' I joked as I jotted down the details in my notebook.

'If you like,' said Das, unamused.

Just then, the old-fashioned bakelite telephone on the desk gave a loud, shrill ring. Das picked up the receiver.

The person on the other end talked rapidly, the line distorting his voice.

'Yes, I understand,' said Das.

The line squawked and then squawked again.

'Right. I will. Five minutes.'

Das remained calm and aloof. He replaced the receiver, stroking his right cheek like a poker player considering his hand.

'I have just been given the name of the hunter who has been assigned to the task.'

'Who is it?' I asked excitedly.

'He is Dinesh Choudhury, a Guwahati man and a trained marksman, the best there is.'

Dinesh Choudhury: the name I had seen in the newspaper article. I asked Das how I might get in touch with him. He wrote down the address on a piece of paper and slid it over to me. Then he stood up and showed me to the door.

'Don't be misled by the environmentalists. This elephant is a man-killer,' he said, squeezing my hand and looking me straight in the eye. 'You should be careful. Things are not always what they seem. Rogue tuskers don't distinguish between locals and white men. He hates us all equally.'

I asked him whether it was true that the victims' families had gone on hunger-strike, as I had heard that morning.

'That's another thing,' he cautioned. 'Don't believe everything you read in the newspapers. Our Indian journalists are all consummate liars.'

Outside in the street, I hailed a three-wheeled auto-rickshaw and handed the piece of paper to its Bengali driver.

'Paan Ba-zaar?' he asked, reading the address and seeking confirmation of my destination.

'Yes, please. Paan Bazaar,' I repeated.

'Okay, Sahib!'

He revved up his lawnmower-like engine and, with a jolt and a shotgun blast from the exhaust, we lurched off down the road, his dashboard shrine flashing with multicoloured disco lights. He slipped an audio cassette into his player and grating Bengali film music blared from the speakers. The yowling soon attracted the attention of a street dog who ran alongside the doorless vehicle, yapping frantically and snapping at our wheels. Despite our increasing speed, the dog managed to keep up with us for nearly fifty yards before receiving a well-aimed kick from the driver. As the whimpering hound fell far behind, the driver turned in his seat, cocked his head at me and smiled triumphantly.

Soon we took a right turn down a back road pitted with potholes as deep as bomb craters. Crouched in a foetal position in a vehicle obviously designed for dwarfs, I bumped up and down on the rock-hard seat. The vehicle reached its top speed and the driver zoomed over a sleeping policeman, causing the auto-rickshaw to do a rear-end wheely and slamming my head against the steel support bar in the roof. Next we took a sharp turn left and I only just prevented myself from being dumped on the road by throwing my arms around the neck of the driver who, temporarily blinded by my embrace, nearly drove into the back of a water buffalo.

Rather than becoming enraged, I felt strangely exhilarated. For weeks, I had been shackled to my desk in New Delhi, covering the latest developments in the arcane world of Indian politics. Now, with my mobile phone and pager locked away in a filing cabinet, I smiled to myself. Whatever the outcome, this was sure to be an adventure.

As the driver continued his manic passage towards Paan Bazaar I reflected on my interview with Das.

Why had he made the elephant sound so dangerous and menacing? I wondered. Surely that was all bluster, just to reinforce the story and to make the price they had put on the rogue's head sound legitimate. Das was up to no good. He had to be.

Given this, I wondered how best to approach Mr Choudhury. He was bound to be unreceptive, so perhaps cash would help my appeal. Or the prospect of fame and publicity. Failing that, I might try playing on his vanity. Had I not come at vast expense all the way from Delhi to interview him? That always worked. Even the most publicity-shy people like that kind of attention.

Suddenly turning into one of the city's main thoroughfares we were swept along in a whirlwind of Indian traffic. Bullock carts and sacred cows meandered across lanes of pollution-belching cars. Vespas buzzed past. Drivers overtook, undertook, did U-turns in the middle of moving traffic, reversed down one-way streets the wrong way, and honked their horns incessantly. Overloaded trucks accelerated and then slammed on their brakes. Motor-scooters slalomed. Battered buses cut across lanes at breakneck speed. It was as if every vehicle was being piloted by a circus clown.

I watched as a mother and her child tried to cross the street, the two terrified figures clinging to one another like passengers on the sinking *Titanic*. They took a step into a gap in the traffic and immediately a bus cut off their line of retreat. Gingerly they took another few steps forward as a Maruti hatchback ground to a halt inches away from them, the driver cursing. I could see a truck bearing down on them from the other direction and held my breath, certain they would be run over. But at the last second, to my astonishment, the driver swerved to the right, pushing two bicycle rickshaws off the road, as the mother and child ran safely to the other side.

Wherever I had travelled in the subcontinent – from the

southernmost tip of Tamil Nadu to the hill stations crouched in the foothills of the Himalayas – it had been impossible to escape this chaos. Even here on the North-East Frontier, a part of the world that has remained isolated for centuries, traffic madness had spread like a virus.

Guwahati, or Gauhati as the British referred to it, might have been a beautiful city had it not caught this debilitating disease. Instead, it has been reduced to a sprawling, filthy, polluted and congested mess. Hundreds of thousands of Bangladeshi immigrants, corrupt politicians, a burgeoning indigenous population and a stagnant economy have only compounded the problem.

Guwahati's saving grace is its position, built around rolling emerald-green hills along the southern bank of the Brahmaputra, the largest of India's rivers. Known to the Assamese as the Lohit, or Red River and to the Burmese as the Bhullambuthur, which means 'Making a gurgling sound', it rises in Tibet and flows for 1,800 miles before discharging an estimated 500,000 cubic feet of water per second into the Bay of Bengal. Off to the left, I caught my first glimpse of this massive waterway, which remained virtually uncharted by European explorers until the end of the nineteenth century. It was broad, dark and brooding, its fast-moving surface alive with whirlpools, eddies and rapids as if some Hindu god was churning it from beneath. Fishing boats and ferries chugged upstream, straining against the current. Two Christmas pudding-shaped islands sat in the middle of the river surrounded by brown and yellow sandbanks. On the far shore, soft afternoon light played across rolling hills thick with jungle, while downstream, car windows glistened as they passed over a high, mile-long suspension bridge.

We turned down a filthy side street, its gutters heaped with festering rubbish, a welcome playground for India's flourishing rodents and carrion. Over one shop entrance a sign announced: 'M/S D. CHOUDHURY & SONS'.

'Okay. *Bus*,' I cried out above the noisy engine. 'Stop! This is it!'

The auto-rickshaw came to an abrupt halt. I stumbled out, half dazed, and paid the driver. He seemed amazed when I handed him a tip. Clearly it was his first – who else but a crazy foreigner would reward such suicidal driving? He nodded gratefully before turning round and heading back in the direction we had come, the repetitive Bengali music still blaring from his speakers.

I approached Mr Choudhury's shop and pushed the door ajar. A wide desk dominated the otherwise sparsely furnished, dimly lit room, its surface littered with a collection of odds and ends – a can of lubricating oil, a telescopic sight, a used shotgun cartridge filled with paper clips, and half a dozen dusty back issues of *The Shooting Times*. Against the far wall stood a glass cabinet full of rifles with polished chestnut-coloured butts and shiny barrels. Next to it, I spied some fishing rods, nets and tackle. But there was no sign of the owner.

'Hello. Is anyone there?' I called out as I stepped inside.

'One moment, please,' came a voice from the back. 'Take a seat. I'll be with you shortly.'

I sat down in the chair in front of the desk as instructed, still taking in my surroundings. Half a dozen black-and-white pictures hung unevenly from the damp-stained wall. One showed a handsome young man with chiselled features sitting on top of a magnificent-looking male elephant with long, thick, white tusks. In a smaller print, the same youth was kneeling over the body of a dead leopard, rifle in hand.

'There used to be thousands of leopards in Assam,' came the same voice, now just a few feet behind me. 'We used to bag them quite regularly. Today, all we're allowed to shoot are rats and crows.'

Startled, I leapt up from my chair and found myself standing face to face with the same man who appeared in the photographs on the wall, or rather an older version with greying sideburns and sagging jowls. Dressed in camouflage fatigues and a Guwahati Rifle Association baseball cap, he looked every bit the hunter – right down to his glasses, which were square, concave and, for a trained marksman, surprisingly thick. They were custom-made bifocals and the lenses reached above his eyebrows so that from certain angles his eyes seemed to bulge like goldfish in a bowl.

'Hello, I'm Dinesh Choudhury,' he said in a soft voice.

'Tarquin Hall,' I replied, shaking his hand. 'Very pleased to meet you.'

For a moment or two, a self-conscious unease crept over me as I was gently appraised through narrowed eyes, rather as a hunter might watch an animal in the wild.

Mr Choudhury did not appear to be the menacing character I had built up in my mind. If anything, he seemed gentle, with a slightly quizzical air and a boyish charm. Yet at the same time, there was something supremely confident about the man. He had the considered, introspective look of someone who makes few mistakes, his prominent chin and set mouth suggestive of resolution, even of obstinacy.

Olive-skinned with brown eyes, he was unlike the other Assamese I had seen in the street, most of whom had distinct Mongoloid features. With his aquiline nose and arched forehead, he might have been mistaken for an Italian. Indeed, as I discovered later, he was of Aryan stock, a descendant of Hindu Rajasthani princes who had fled to Assam three hundred years earlier to escape the Mogul invasion.

'So what brings you to my little shop, Mr Hall?' he asked at last, playing absentmindedly with an empty brass bullet casing that lay on the desk.

'Well, I've flown all the way from Delhi to find you. In fact I've been travelling for several days to get here,' I began, trying to sound as enthusiastic as possible.

'And you are a journalist. Is that right?'

'Yes,' I answered, realizing that Das must have tipped him off. Either that or he had made a calculated guess. Whatever the case, hacks have a bad name the world over and I was keen to present myself in an altogether different light.

'My main interest in life is travel writing,' I explained, taking a copy of my first book from my backpack and handing it to him.

He inspected the bright cover, glancing at the publisher's blurb. Then, thumbing through the pages, he paused to look at some of the photographs. Encouraged by his apparent interest, I continued: 'That book's about some journeys I made when I was younger. In one chapter, I go rattlesnake-hunting in Texas,' I added, hoping to strike a chord.

'Very interesting,' he said, smiling at me. 'You've done a lot of things for someone so young – is it not so?'

My attempt to engage his interest was working, I thought. Now that he was primed, I felt confident of tackling him on the subject of the elephant hunt. Would he be leaving soon?

'Yes, I think so. Probably tonight.'

'Ah, right,' I said, feeling a tingle in my stomach as I formulated the next question in my mind. 'Well, I was wondering if you would allow me to tag along, so that I might write about it later?' I paused. 'I think it would make a fascinating book.'

'Yes, yes, sure,' replied the hunter. 'I'm quite happy for you to come up to Sonitpur.'

A wave of relief and excitement swept over me.

'Oh great! Thank you very much,' I said, amazed at how easy this was proving.

But then Mr Choudhury raised a finger and added the word 'However'. He crossed his arms and stiffened.

'However,' he repeated, sitting back in his chair and frowning, 'you understand that you will not be able to come with us when we hunt the elephant. You will have to stay in the camp.'

My skin went clammy and my stomach started to churn. Had I heard him correctly? He wasn't going to allow me on the hunt? Did that mean he suspected my motives? That he feared I wanted to expose him and the elephant-shooting racket? Was he being friendly just to lead me on?

All I could say was, 'Why can't I come?' in a feeble, child-like whine.

'Well, the tusker has already killed thirty-eight people,' explained Mr Choudhury. 'That makes him a formidable opponent and very dangerous. Also, we will be travelling in areas where there are insurgents who are fighting for an independent Assam. I couldn't be responsible for your safety.'

My chance of a great adventure was fading fast. I had not come all the way from Delhi to sit around in some crummy camp. For a split second, I felt like arguing my case but then thought better of it. The only thing to do was to accept Mr Choudhury's offer, drive up to Sonitpur, spend some time with him and try to wangle my way on to the hunt later. With this in mind, I took a deep breath and changed tack.

'I completely understand the dangers and I would hate to put you in a difficult position,' I said. 'At the very least, I'd like to come up to Sonitpur. After all, I have come all the way from Delhi to be here.'

The hunter nodded his head in agreement.

'By all means come,' he replied. 'It will be very educational for you. I must warn you, though, that it will be rough. You'll be sleeping outside, the food will be basic and you'll have to help out in the camp. Everyone mucks in. You will be required to cook and clean up, and you may even have to do some hard manual labour.'

Though Mr Choudhury didn't know it, this was exactly the kind of experience I was looking for. After years of eating junk food and sitting at a desk, some honest physical work would do me good. But I was taken aback when he asked me if I smoked.

'Just a few a day,' I said casually. 'I've cut down a lot recently and ...'

The hunter was shaking his head in disapproval.

'No smoking. Elephants have an acute sense of smell. They don't like cigarettes.'

'Right, no smoking,' I said, wondering how I would survive.

Did I drink?

'Well, one or two ... you know, just sometimes ... the odd glass of beer ...' I felt almost apologetic.

One look told me that I would be off the sauce for a while.

'Right, no drinking,' I sighed out loud.

'And one last thing, from now on, don't use any deodorant.'

No deodorant? Banning fags and booze was one thing, but surely my Right Guard was harmless stuff? Or perhaps he found my brand offensive. Did he, like an elephant, have an acute sense of smell?

'It's a small detail, but it could be your undoing. An elephant will pick up its scent a mile off,' he added. 'And it might attract the unwanted attention of the rogue. He would be less than friendly.'

Then Mr Choudhury stood up, muttering that he had lots to organize before his departure.

'That settles it then. I will pick you up at your hotel at eight o'clock tonight. Please bring as few belongings as possible.'

I thanked him for his time and turned towards the door. But just then, he called me back. Reaching into the drawer of his desk he pulled out a book, a reprint of P. D. Stracey's *Elephant Gold*, the standard work on the Asian elephant in Assam.

'Here, I would like to give you this,' he said, and with that, taking up his fountain pen, he wrote an inscription on the title page, which he attributed to the legendary fifth-century Assamese sage Palakapya, who is said to have been born from an elephant.

It read:

> Where there is duty, there is nobility.
> Where there are elephants, there is victory.

On my way back to the hotel, my head was spinning. How could someone like Mr Choudhury, who seemed so kindly, shoot elephants? Had he grown so used to hunting animals that one more didn't make any difference? Or did he just need the money? Judging by the state of his shop, the rifle and ammunition business was hardly booming. The bounty of 50,000 rupees, the equivalent of roughly six hundred pounds, would go a long way in Assam. And there was the ivory to consider. The two tusks would be worth a fortune on the world market if they could be smuggled out of India – enough to set someone up for life.

It took less than twenty minutes to reach my hotel. The foyer was packed with Congress Party politicians and workers holding their annual regional meeting. The bigwigs, those who professed to be carrying on the work of the Mahatma, were all dressed in white homespun pyjamas, a uniform that had once stood for humility in the days when India's freedom fighters had identified with the common man. Now, it was synonymous with corruption and was worn by pot-bellied men with generous double chins. Somehow, I found it hard to imagine these individuals putting the Mahatma's example of abstinence into practice.

The Congressmen jostled for the attention of the lone man behind the reception desk. He had been landed with the jobs of telephone operator, receptionist, concierge, occasional bellboy – he had helped me with my bags – and cashier. Looming over the Congressmen I successfully caught his attention. His name was Rishi. It said so on his name-tag.

'You had a call, sir,' he said, beaming at me as he pushed

my room key over the counter and tried to grapple with two telephones at the same time.

'Oh really, who from?'

He rummaged behind the desk, getting the lines twisted, and handed me a message. It was from a 'Mr Banerjee, Ministry of Sports'.

I licked my top lip as I studied the slip of paper, noticing that my first name had been spelt 'Fartquin'.

'What does he want, this Mr Banerjee?' I asked Rishi, as he tried to fend off an irate Congressman who was complaining that he didn't have a room with a view.

'He's heard that you are a professional goalkeeper and is coming to meet with you.'

'A goalkeeper!' I exclaimed. 'I'm not a …'

Then, with a sinking feeling, I suddenly remembered what had happened that morning.

Upon my arrival at Guwahati airport, I had been required to register myself at Passport Control. The aggressive bureaucrat behind the desk had handed me a form to complete that asked for all the usual details: passport number, date of birth, country of origin and so on.

As a foreigner in a land that thrives on paperwork and bureaucracy, I was forever filling in such forms. Indian hotels always wanted to know everything about me, usually in triplicate. Sometimes, to amuse myself, I would give a false name, and I often added an out-of-the-way occupation like 'Brain Surgeon' or 'Concert Pianist' for good measure.

On this occasion I had scrawled 'Goalkeeper' and had handed the completed form back to the man. He had examined it carefully, checking the facts with those in my passport.

'Goalkeeper?' he exclaimed. 'That is no occupation.'

I shrugged my shoulders.

'Yes it is. I'm a goalkeeper,' I replied, deadpan.

'You mean you are a player of soccer?'

'Yes,' I confirmed, and then I overstepped the mark. 'I play for Manchester United.'

He returned his attention to the form, crossed out 'Goalkeeper' and inserted 'Soccer Player, Manchester Unlimited'.

In the end, all the fuss was worth it. He soon produced an ink pad and banged an Assam entry stamp on to an empty page in my passport. This was an unexpected and welcome bonus and I thanked him heartily, leaving the airport delighted. I had a new addition to my visa collection, and a rare one at that.

Nevertheless, it seemed as if my bluff had been called. The bureaucrat at the airport had obviously rung the Ministry of Sports and tipped them off. Now this Mr Banerjee was coming to the hotel.

Perhaps the airport official was still suspicious and wanted someone to check my credentials. I imagined myself having to prove my mettle against an Assamese striker on some Guwahati football pitch. Or perhaps Mr Banerjee wanted me to come and coach his team or even play in a game. If that were to happen, I would be unmasked as a fraud and, in such a sensitive part of India, rife with insurgency and drug smuggling, my innocent joke might be interpreted as something more sinister.

Whatever the case, I felt certain of one thing: Mr Banerjee would want to talk about soccer and all I knew about the game was that England had only once won the World Cup. I couldn't even remember in which year.

Up in my room, I tried to decide the best course of action. I had three hours to kill. If I remained in the hotel, I was a sitting duck. After a quick shower I slipped out. With any luck, Mr Banerjee would call while I was out, and later that night I would get clean away.

*

Sitting at the back of a local tandoori restaurant, I ordered a late lunch. While I waited for the platter of food to come, I tugged a box-file from my backpack and flicked through its contents. Dog-eared and yellowed with age, they were a clutch of private letters written by my godfather Charles that I had inherited on his death in 1989. Since then, I hadn't delved deeper than the first two or three. But now I pored over each page, searching for references to the North-East Frontier, where Charles had been stationed during the Second World War.

As I soon discovered, in April 1944 he had fought at the battle of Kohima in Nagaland, only a few hours' drive from Guwahati. According to his own vivid description, Charles, along with several hundred Allied troops and local tribesmen, took on the Japanese army and won. During the battle, regarded as one of the most desperate of the war, Charles spent three weeks in a rat-infested trench on the edge of the British Governor's tennis court. Day after day, and night after night, he defended his position against waves of Japanese infantry. Miraculously, Charles was one of the few lucky enough to make it out alive.

Later letters revealed that after the battle, he spent six months travelling around India, indulging his greatest passion: hunting. Not far from Mysore, in the southern state of Karnataka, he took part in five elephant hunts, bagging himself two pairs of tusks.

'There's nothing quite as satisfying as shooting an elephant,' he wrote to his younger brother Jeffrey in January 1945. 'The shot – to the heart or the brain – is a tricky one to accomplish, especially when the beast is charging towards you. I cannot put into words the thrill of seeing such a large animal falling to one's gun. I'm afraid it makes beagling seem rather silly.'

It was clear from Charles's words that he, like most of his generation, had a different attitude towards hunting. In his time, there had been no such thing as an endangered species list, and even the largest animals were considered little more than vermin. But to someone of my generation the idea of killing such a fine animal was utterly abhorrent.

During his tour of India, Charles had also spent some time in Assam and had visited Guwahati's Kamakhya temple. 'A fascinating place,' he wrote. 'A centre of the black arts, where the most unspeakable acts have been performed.'

Having finished my lunch and with two hours still left to kill, I headed off in search of this mysterious site. The temple, one of the holiest in India, stands on Nilchal Hill, on the south bank of the Brahmaputra. As I arrived, pilgrims from across the subcontinent, some of whom had travelled for weeks to reach this spot, filed back and forth along the narrow pathway that winds upwards towards the temple complex. The new arrivals wore expressions of expectation and excitement as they took the last few steps towards the goal upon which they had set their hearts. By contrast, the devotees making their way down towards the car park were lost in quiet contemplation, their eyes filled with satisfaction.

Amongst them, I spotted a half-naked sadhu, a Hindu holy man. He was covered from head to toe in grey ash that gave him a deathly look and enhanced the whites of his eyes so that they looked hypnotic. His dreadlocks, which fell to his waist, rivalled those of a Rastafarian, the rope-like strands blackened by years of accumulated dirt and grease. His forehead was marked with three horizontal ochre lines made in holy ash. These proclaimed him to be a follower of Shiva, the Hindu god of destruction.

On my way up to the temple, I stopped at one of the many curio stalls dotted along the way. Neat lines of bronze-cast Hindu gods were positioned next to a clutch of carved wooden snakes. Some frightening-looking bullwhips – which would have been more in place in an S&M shop – hung from hooks above the stallkeeper's head, together with garlands of glazed cowry shells strung with bright plastic beads. A dozen alarm clocks, fashioned like temples complete with lotus-shaped bells, sat on a shelf. The deluxe version, which was painted a gaudy red and gold, was made out of 'GENUINE PLASTIC' and claimed to play six different mantras.

The next stall sold everything a pious Hindu might want or need in the way of religious offerings. Coconuts, garlands of marigolds and boxes of incense-sticks were all on offer, together with bags of sugar balls and bunches of green bananas – the essentials for *puja*, or prayers. The man behind the stall, who wore a Chicago gangster-style hat, offered me a package deal. One hundred and fifty rupees would buy me everything I needed to take inside the temple. He would even anoint my head with sandalwood paste for 'no extra charge'.

'As part of this bargain, you will also get blessings from the god.' He beamed. 'That is for free. Then your wife will be in tiptop shape!'

I bought some offerings and took them up to the temple. At the entrance, as a foreigner, I had to pay a heavy bribe to be allowed inside. Taking the money, a Brahmin priest-cum-guide wearing flowing saffron robes instructed me to remove my shoes before he led me barefoot over the burning-hot tiles of the inner courtyard. Here, chickens and geese mingled with a wedding party waiting for their marriage ceremony to begin. The bride and bridesmaids were caked in make-up and decked out in psychedelic silk saris, elaborate nose rings and shimmering veils. As we passed by, doe-like eyes lined with kohl looked out at me and then shyly disappeared behind rippling gauze. Next to the temple's main entrance sat a line of beggars with their backs against a wall, the late afternoon sunlight reflecting off their tin mugs and begging bowls. Like a group of actors waiting to audition for a part in a horror film, each one showed off his injury or deformity to its best effect, moaning like so many Ghosts of Christmas Past.

'This is one of Hinduism's holiest sites,' began the priest, who spoke English well. 'It's the place where the genitalia of the goddess Shakti landed after Vishnu cut her into pieces and strewed her parts across India.'

Shakti, he told me, was just one of the many guises of the Mother Goddess. In the Hindu pantheon, she appears in a number of forms and reincarnations: as Durga, Uma, Devi and, most famously, as the bloodthirsty slayer Kali. When Shakti's body was cut up, the pieces are said to have landed in fifty-one places, sites in India known as *shakti pithas*. Kamakhya is considered to be the most sacred. For several centuries, it was a centre of Tantric Hinduism, a cult often steeped in bloody rites and black magic. Some experts believe Assam was the birthplace of this particular brand of the Hindu faith, thought to have its roots in the ancient rites of the primitive hill tribes who have long inhabited the region.

I followed the priest inside the temple and down a dark, dank passage that led into the innermost chamber. Burning incense-sticks and candles ate up what little oxygen was available and replaced it with suffocating, acrid smoke. Figures talking in reverent whispers moved about in the eerie atmosphere, their faces masked by shadows. The chanting of priests echoed and re-echoed all around us, the acoustics mysteriously amplifying voices that criss-crossed one another. Idols grimaced at me from the sooty walls. Their terrible images – tongues, fangs, serpents, horns – flickered in the dim candle-light and seemed to come to life.

The temple's innermost sanctum is home to a mound-shaped rock with a cleft in it, representing the goddess's *yoni*, or genitalia. The rock is kept moist by a natural spring which, during the monsoon, miraculously runs red with iron oxide and is drunk by devotees as 'symbolic menstrual blood' during the festival of Ambuvachi.

While I watched the priest begin the complex ceremony, it wasn't difficult to picture the horrific practices for which

Kamakhya was infamous in the past. Thousands of men were decapitated here amidst terrible rites designed to honour the goddess who, it was believed, relished human blood. Occasionally, there were even mass sacrifices – in 1565, 140 men died on one day alone.

Of those killed, many were volunteers known as *bhogis*. In return for their supreme sacrifice, these men were allowed to live in luxury for a year. During those twelve months, they could have as many women as they liked. They were pampered by servants around the clock, laden with presents and promised a place in paradise by Kamakhya's powerful priesthood. At the annual festival of Ambuvachi, the men would be taken to a sacrificial altar where their heads were cut off and placed on a golden platter before an image of Shakti. Later, their lungs were cooked and eaten, and their blood was drained and used to boil rice, which was consumed by those who had gathered to watch them die.

Today, the only offerings the goddess Shakti receives at Kamakhya are bananas, sugar balls and, if she's lucky, the occasional goat. Nonetheless, the *puja* was not without colour. Bells were rung, incense-sticks lit, yet more sandalwood was smeared on my forehead, mantras were spoken in reverent tones and the milk from my coconut was poured over the *yoni* rock.

Eventually we emerged into the dusk. At the gate, I paid the priest for his services and he thanked me gratefully, promising that my life would be filled with good fortune. As I made my way to meet Mr Choudhury, I could only hope that the priest was right.

Back at the hotel, Rishi the concierge told me that Mr Banerjee, the mysterious gentleman from the Ministry of Sports, had been and gone. It looked as if I was in the clear. But just to be on the safe side, as I waited in the foyer, I was careful to position myself in the shadow of a large potted plant where I kept my face partially hidden behind the collar of my coat.

Much to my relief, Mr Choudhury was on time. Shortly after eight, he strode through the hotel doors and spotted me in my hiding place.

'Everything's in order,' he said confidently, as we made our way outside. 'We leave immediately.'

Mr Choudhury had arrived with two vehicles: his battered 1953 Land Rover which had a long wheel base, a khaki green canvas roof, a winch at the front and extra jerry cans of petrol mounted on the back; and a white Hindustan Ambassador, India's answer to the Volkswagen Beetle. Modelled on the 1950s Morris Oxford and built like a tank, it is the only indigenous car tough enough to survive India's pot-holed national highways.

The hunter had brought along a small entourage that included two drivers and two guards on loan from the Forest Department who were armed with sub-machine guns for our protection against militants.

'We'll be driving all night. Let's take turns sleeping on the back seat of the Ambassador,' said Mr Choudhury as my bags were placed in the boot of the car. 'Tarquin, you sleep first. I'll go in the Land Rover and we'll swap in a few hours.'

The driver opened the back door of the car. I was about to get inside when I heard my name – or rather its Indian version – being called out hysterically.

'Mr Halls! Mr Halls!'

A man in a purple tracksuit was running towards the car.

'I am Banerjee,' he panted as he came to a stop.

I had guessed as much already. I turned to face him.

'Yes, Mr Banerjee? I'm in a bit of a rush. What can I do for you?'

He stood in front of me, his head bowed, his hands pushed together to form the traditional Hindu *namaste*, or greeting.

'Most terribly sorry for disturbing,' he apologized, wobbling his head and shuffling his feet. 'Are you really Mr Halls?'

I nodded my head nervously, expecting the worst.

'Well, I am most avid fan of British soccer. Please to be giving your autograph.'

He thrust a notepad and pen towards me, his brown eyes pleading to make his wish come true. My mind was reeling. Not for the first time in India I was completely baffled by the events taking place around me. Numbly, I reached for the biro and, steadying the pad, signed my name, making sure that it was illegible.

'Thanking you, thanking you very much, Mr Halls,' said Mr Banerjee, backing away from me. He bounced on his heels with excitement, his head bowed to the ground. I thought I noticed tears in his eyes.

'This is the greatest day of my life, Mr Halls! Thanking you! Thanking you!'

Mr Choudhury was standing next to his Land Rover, his eyebrows raised in astonishment. I caught his gaze and, as I did so, he tilted his head to one side.

'Who was that?' he asked.

I shrugged my shoulders.

'Oh, just one of my fans,' I replied.

Across Guwahati, the electricity had been cut off, throwing the city into darkness. Residents stood about in the streets like spectators watching an eclipse. While they waited expectantly for the power to be turned back on, children played in the moonlight and elderly people huddled around fires burning inside empty oil drums. Along the main road, lanterns hung outside shop fronts. On the pavements, the proprietors of the larger stores revved up their petrol generators, deafening passers-by.

Even the city's traffic lights had failed and the police were trying to direct the rush-hour traffic with torches. Vegetable stands were doing business by candlelight, dozens of flames twinkling in the gloom. Outside a cinema showing an Indian version of *Mrs Doubtfire* entitled *Aunty Number One*, angry customers, furious that the film had been interrupted, were demanding their money back. Down the road, a street-poster vendor who sold pin-ups of busty Bombay film actresses alongside garish paintings of Mother Teresa, Princess Diana, Jesus Christ and the usual Hindu deities, was doing a roaring trade by the light of his car headlights.

As we inched our way through the traffic, I caught glimpses of advertisements for everything from Tipsy Beer to East Wood Cigarettes. 'MOUNTAIN SPRING WATER. THE SWEAT TASTE', announced one poster. Next to it, a billboard promoted a certain brand of local soap as being the best 'FOR THOSE PRIVATE MOMENTS'.

Towards the edge of the city, we passed the Boogie Woogie Dance School where anyone with two hundred and fifty rupees to spare could learn to 'get down like Michael Jackson'. Next to it stood the Double Digest Restaurant. A mile on, I spotted the Good Luck Driving School which promised graduates a 'chance of survival'.

We passed out of the city limits and into the surrounding hills. A sign on the side of the road, erected by Assam's Department of Transport, warned: 'YOU ARE NOW ENTERING AN ACCIDENT PRONE ZONE.' The large number of chewed-up cars and squashed truck cabs that lay abandoned on the side of the road – perhaps left there as a warning to others – were proof that Highway 37 was indeed hazardous, if not a death-trap. More of Assam's dogs lay about on the tarmac in various stages of decomposition.

According to my driver Rudra, who described them as 'bad mens', it was generally the truck-drivers who were responsible for the inordinate number of accidents and deaths. Most of them were said to be on drugs, which they took to help them stay awake on long journeys. Only that morning, there had been a head-on collision. 'Both mens become like jams,' said Rudra.

Highway 37 wound its way through the hills and down into the Brahmaputra valley. Knowing that in India there is an accident every minute and a death on the roads every eight minutes, I sat back in my seat, making sure that I was unable to see the road ahead. If something was going to kill me, I preferred not to have to see it coming.

I had been looking forward to talking to Mr Choudhury and getting to know him better on the journey, and I was disappointed that I wasn't sitting next to him. Tired, I attempted to put such thoughts out of my head. Instead, I reached into my backpack and took out a collection of short stories and essays by George Orwell. I turned on the light and flicked through until I found his acclaimed piece, 'Shooting an Elephant'. With the car bouncing over pot-holes, keeping my eyes on the words wasn't easy. The story is set in Moulmein in Lower Burma where Orwell worked as a police officer. As a colonial, he was despised by the local population. One day while he was on duty, a trained elephant went beserk. Rather than lose face amongst the natives, Orwell decided to shoot it. But all he had available was a small-bore rifle, a weapon wholly inadequate for such a task. Despite this the first shot found its mark.

He looked suddenly stricken, shrunken, immensely old, as though the frightful impact of the bullet had paralysed him without knocking him down. At last, after what seemed like a long time – it might have been five seconds, I dare say – he sagged flabbily to his knees. His mouth slobbered. An enormous senility seemed to have settled upon him. One could have imagined him thousands of years old. I fired again into the same spot. At the second shot he did not collapse but climbed with desperate slowness to his feet and stood weakly upright, with legs sagging and head drooping. I fired a third time.

> That was the shot that did him. You could see the agony of it jolt his whole body and knock the last remnant of strength from his legs. But in falling he seemed for a moment to rise. For as his hind legs collapsed beneath him he seemed to tower upwards like a huge rock toppling, his trunk reaching skywards like a tree. He trumpeted, for the first and only time. And then down he came, his belly towards me, with a crash that seemed to shake the ground even where I lay.

Assuming I managed to talk Mr Choudhury into allowing me on the hunt I would see the same sad sight. I would see an elephant die.

A lump formed in my throat as Orwell's imagery flashed again and again across my mind and suddenly, feelings of revulsion and guilt swept over me. Surely elephants, animals we regard with awe, endangered the world over, should not be gunned down? Couldn't the rogue be captured, sedated and released elsewhere? But what of the people the rogue had killed? By all accounts, the victims' families were baying for his blood. Surely they deserved justice. No human being would be let off such crimes.

Even so, as I switched off the light and drifted into sleep, I pictured the tusker on his own in the darkness somewhere in northern Assam. And I found myself hoping that he would disappear deep into the jungle – far away, where Mr Choudhury would not be able to find him.

2

The Game Is Afoot

'If you roamed every continent for thousands of years, coming to consider the globe your own private football, and you were then confined to an open prison … you too might become unbalanced.'

Heathcote Williams, *Sacred Elephant*

RUDRA, THE DRIVER of the Hindustan Ambassador, had been chewing *paan* all night. He kept his stash in a stainless steel *dabba*, an Indian lunchbox, in the glove compartment and periodically would ask me to take it out and open it for him. Keeping one eye on the road, he would first extract a lump of lime paste with his index finger and smear it into the space between his teeth and his bottom lip. He would then pop one or two choice chunks of betel nut into his mouth. Finally, uttering a satisfied grunt, he would start to chew.

Rudra was clearly an addict. He had the desperate eyes of a junkie and had consumed so much *paan* over the years that his gums, tongue and lips were permanently stained a luminous red. His teeth had turned jet black at the roots, and when he grinned he looked like a prize-fighter who had just taken a beating in the ring.

Admittedly, his addiction was not as anti-social as some others I could think of, but having to watch him spit out of the window every other minute and wipe the drool from his chin with his shirtsleeve was something I would rather have done without, especially at four in the morning. Still, I took comfort from the fact that something in the betel nut seemed to be keeping him awake.

By Indian standards, Rudra was a good driver – that is to say, we only came close to death once during more than six hours on the road. But his vehicle's shock absorbers were defunct and many of the back seat's springs had come loose. As a result, I had managed only a few hours of continually interrupted sleep before midnight when Mr Choudhury turfed me off the back seat and put me in front with Rudra.

By now, I was in no mood for conversation. All I wanted to do was sleep. I tried conveying this to Rudra, but even when I closed my eyes and pretended to snore, he kept up his one-sided, tedious conversation. His main interest in life, apart from betel nut and playing chicken with oncoming heavy goods vehicles, was the vital statistics of Bombay's Hindi film actresses. The latest goddess to grace the Indian screen, Karisma Kapoor, had won a special place in his heart – and, no doubt, in his fantasies.

'She is the most beautiful pearl of our continent!' he boasted, pushing the Ambassador into fourth gear around a tight bend.

He slapped me hard on the thigh and guffawed, grunting and breathing through his nose and mouth simultaneously, a feat that would have been remarkable had it not been so revolting.

'You should see her dance! Her legs go *all* the way up! And as for her breasts – they are big! As big as mangoes!'

He sighed and for a moment his mind seemed to drift. Then he nudged me hard in the arm.

'Who is your favourite chick?' he asked conspiratorially.

'I don't have one, and I'm trying to sleep,' I replied grumpily.

However, Rudra would not take no for an answer and prodded me again. I knew that I had to name a name, otherwise he would never leave me alone.

'Madhuri Dixit,' I said, not daring to mention that it had once been my pleasure to interview this beautiful lady in Bombay.

'Madhuri! Yes, you are right. She is *good!*' He spat another mouthful of betel-nut juice out of the window and grinned mischievously, displaying his stained gums. Some of his saliva flew back in through the window, splattering his forehead. He wiped it away with his shirtsleeve, drew a deep breath and, with his smile broadening into a maniacal grin, added with finality: 'Madhuri Dixit is *very* good – very good for BAD purposes!'

While the Brahmaputra valley still lay under a cloak of darkness, the first rays of sunshine fell on the range of mountains to the north. Their snow-capped summits hovered above the viscous, milky haze, illuminated like so many shining cloud cities. Over the next hour, the morning light crept closer and the landscape below began to reveal itself, the sunlight dissolving the mist that swirled around us. Soon, I could make out dozens of paddy-fields stretching towards the horizon. Huts made of earthen walls, bamboo frames and straw roofs stood on little islands surrounded by floodwater. Farmers knee-deep in mud urged on their black water buffalo as they pulled wooden ploughs through the rich, sodden soil.

Near a roadside shrine that housed an effigy of the goddess Durga, women with lovely almond-shaped eyes and high cheekbones harvested rice by hand. If it hadn't been for the fact that they were wearing saris, I might have mistaken them for Vietnamese or Cambodians. Children on their way to school played with fighting kites. Their strings were coated with finely ground glass, the object of the game being to rub against your opponent's line in the hope of severing it. Fierce dog-fights were in progress, half a dozen red, yellow and green paper birds ducking and diving, attacking and retreating against a backdrop of pristine blue sky.

Ever since my arrival in India two years earlier, I had longed to visit this part of the country. Geographically, it is alluring, a misplaced piece of jigsaw puzzle. Assam is lodged between five nations: China, Bhutan and Tibet to the north, Bangladesh to the south and Myanmar, or Burma, to the east. And culturally, it is totally different from anything in the rest of the subcontinent. A land of diverse tribes, its peoples have more in common with those of South-East Asia and the Far East than with their Aryan or Dravidian cousins. The state is connected to the rest of the country by a slim corridor known as the Chicken's Neck; a legacy of colonial diplomacy, it runs between Bhutan and Bangladesh

Despite its staggering beauty and rich folklore, India's North-East is a part of the world avoided by even the most intrepid backpackers. As such there was little in my guide-book about Assam: it has been off-limits to tourists for many years. However it did say that the word Assam is derived from the Sanskrit *assama*, meaning 'peerless' or 'unequalled'. It was so named by Thai or Shan invaders called the Ahoms who conquered the valley in the thirteenth century and loved it so much that they never left. I was beginning to appreciate why. Wherever I looked, the landscape was lush and green. Rickety wooden bridges spanned streams and brooks whose surfaces were covered with sweet-smelling water-lily blossoms. Peepul trees, their branches straining under flocks of white birds that suddenly lifted into the air at the sound of our approach, lined the road. In the distance, hills bristling with jungle rose up above the fields, mist crawling across the foliage and pouring down into the valley like smoke brimming off a witch's cauldron.

We left Highway 37 and turned north, crossing the Brahmaputra on a high, mile-long bridge guarded by a legion of Indian soldiers armed with machine guns. The river, far below, was at least three times as wide as it had been at Guwahati. A dozen canoes bobbing on the surface of the water looked like miniature toys. Upstream, the Brahmaputra bulged northwards, the far bank lost in a haze of mist and bright sunshine, while downstream, thousands of water hyacinths lay beached on glistening sandbanks.

Just after six o'clock, a yawn from the back seat told me that the hunter was waking up. At last, I could talk to someone about something other than Bollywood bimbos.

'Good morning,' I said, trying to decide whether to call him by his first or last name. I settled on the latter. After all, he was old enough to be my father, and in India people still set store on courtesy.

Mr Choudhury stretched and glanced out of the window, quickly recognizing the area.

'I used to come here as a boy to watch wild elephants,' he said, rubbing his eyes. 'In those days, this was all jungle for miles and miles, as far as your eye could see. There were hardly any people. Now, there are millions of them.'

His voice had a bitter edge to it and he seemed sombre. Rolling down the window, he relaxed a little, breathing in the fresh air, relishing the smell of damp moss and pine.

'See over there,' he continued, pointing to a wide depression in the ground where sugarcane grew in abundance. 'That area used to be a lake. Entire herds of hundreds of elephants would come down from the hills and eat the aquatic weed. It's their favourite delicacy. I used to sit up in a tree and watch them down below me, all trumpeting, playing and splashing about in the water. It was wonderful.'

There was a glint in his eye as he reminisced. I sensed that he was in a talkative mood and I wanted to hear more.

Had he been much involved with elephants?

'Oh yes. I grew up surrounded by them,' he told me as we continued along back roads. 'We used them as transport. My father owned a huge estate, thousands of acres, and he always collected rent from our tenants on the back of Chamundi Prasad, his favourite tusker.'

In those days, elephants were the ultimate status symbol, as prestigious as the BMWs and Mercedes of today. No special occasion was complete without them. When Mr Choudhury's elder brother married, he arrived at the ceremony riding on an elephant in a silver lotus-flower *howdah*, or seat, and leading twenty other beasts, each decked out with bejewelled awnings and ornate headpieces decorated with gold braid and peacock feathers. Whenever a boy was born in the family, the child would be paraded around the estate on the back of a tusker. During religious festivals, the caparisoned animals were always the star attraction.

The Choudhurys employed more than a dozen mahouts, specialists who double as handler and rider, together with fifteen or so apprentices and several *phandis*, or professional catchers. It was the *phandis'* job to capture and train wild elephants. Every year, with a great deal of fanfare and pageantry, these men would head off into the jungle and on to the plains to hunt down promising calves. Using an age-old technique unique to Assam called *mela-shikar*, they would lasso the animals in much the same way as American cowboys catch cattle. The captured elephants were either kept for the stable or, once trained, were sold at the annual elephant *mela*, or fair, at Sonpur on the banks of the Gandak River in Bihar, to this day the largest elephant market in the world.

'All the mahouts and *phandis* lived in an encampment not far from the estate where I grew up,' continued Mr Choudhury. 'It was an incredibly busy place. Wherever you looked, elephants were being trained and taught to do tricks. It was like having my own private circus all to myself. From a young age, all I could think about was elephants.'

But Mr Choudhury's father did not approve of his son's fascination and affinity with the animals and sent him away to school in Shillong, the old British capital of Assam, a three-hour drive from Guwahati.

'He wanted me to become an engineer and planned to send

me to England to study at Rolls-Royce,' he said. 'I used to sneak back from school and spend time with the mahouts without my father's knowledge.'

Over the years, these men taught him all the tricks of the trade as well as some of their most closely guarded secrets. Eventually, however, thanks to land reforms introduced by India's socialist governments, the Choudhurys were forced to sell their estate. With it went the elephants and the men who had been the hunter's mentors.

'Throughout my life, I have continued to be involved with these animals, often working with them,' said Mr Choudhury. 'My first love is my family and my second is elephants.'

'How could you love elephants and still hunt them?' I blurted out, immediately regretting having showed my feelings.

'Believe me, there is nothing that saddens me more in the whole world,' he replied. 'It breaks my heart, truly it does. But sometimes it just has to be done. Sometimes I have to play executioner. Perhaps, as our journey continues, you will begin to understand more of my dilemma. It is all very painful.'

Something in his voice seemed to smack of insincerity. I couldn't quite put my finger on it, but I was sure he was hiding something.

'Why do you do it then, if it's so painful?' I asked.

'I am the only one in Assam who is qualified. I'm a trained marksman and an elephant expert,' he replied. 'Besides, when you have a rabid dog, you cannot allow it to run loose. It has to be killed. Is it not so?'

I could tell that he was growing more and more uneasy with the conversation, so I let the subject drop. But our chat left me as confused as ever about Mr Choudhury's intentions and motives.

The Forest Department headquarters, our destination, lay near the border with the mountainous state of Arunachal

Pradesh, Indian territory claimed by the Chinese. The compound was built on a low-lying hill that, during the monsoon, sat above the Brahmaputra floodwaters. Seven wooden bungalows with teak decks stood in a semicircle facing an enclosure several hundred yards across. Hundreds of tree-trunks, confiscated from timber smugglers, were stacked against a fence, each one spray-painted with a series of numbers and letters. Many had obviously been there for some time, no doubt held as evidence in ongoing prosecutions, and they were beginning to rot.

In the centre of the compound stood an ancient banyan tree, its trunk at least twenty feet in diameter, its base a mass of tangled roots that jutted out of the soil like flying buttresses. Characteristically, its branches had grown shoots that dangled down to the ground. Some had burrowed into the earth and developed into saplings.

'DO NOT TIE YOUR ELEPHANTS HERE!' read a sign attached to the veranda of the main office. A pile of buffalo skulls lay by the front door, while above these, hanging incongruously from a nail, was a pair of bright pink underpants.

While we unloaded our bags and equipment, the forest officers and guards emerged, still half-awake, from their bungalows. A dishevelled bunch, they greeted Mr Choudhury, whom they addressed as Shikari or Hunter, with fond smiles and hugs, as if he were some long-lost brother.

'I call these men the Dirty Dozen,' joked the hunter while I shook hands with them all. 'That's because they tell the dirtiest jokes.'

The senior officer was called Mole because as a child he used to squint through his glasses, which were as thick as the bottoms of milk bottles.

Mole was the most successful young officer in the department, having put a record number of timber smugglers behind bars and confiscated thousands of illegally felled trees in the process. Not surprisingly, as a result he had made many enemies, chiefly among the powerful timber-smuggling syndicate who were rumoured to enjoy the patronage of a number of local politicians. Mole was a man with a price on his head.

'The bounty stands at 25,000 rupees,' he joked. 'That's all my life is worth! Half as much as an elephant!'

Mole was uncouth, cocky and unpredictable. He also had the annoying habit of calling me 'man' every time he spoke to me – 'Hey, man', 'Good to see you, man', 'How are you, man?' – something he had picked up in the United States while studying environmental protection. But he was streetwise and knew how things worked in Assam.

'The local police are in on everything, man,' he told me once. 'So if I arrest someone, I keep him in custody until the court hearing so he can't escape. Then I make sure the judge gives me a conviction.'

When he wasn't arresting teak smugglers, Mole had to deal with the local wild elephant herds. As he explained over breakfast in the mess, there was very little rain forest left for the animals to live in.

'The elephants have lost their home and their traditional migratory routes, man. They're disoriented and angry.'

I asked him why the jungles and forests hadn't been protected.

'Corruption, man! The system is corrupt to the core. Mostly it's the Bangladeshis who have cut down all the trees. Hundreds of thousands of them have settled here. And guess who's allowed them in?'

I didn't have a clue.

'Our politicians, man! Our Assamese politicians!'

'Why would your leaders allow all these Bangladeshis to settle on your land?' I asked, confused.

'Vote banks!' cried the angry young man. He made it sound as if that was explanation enough.

'Vote banks? How do you mean?'

Mole smiled at my naïvety.

'They bring them over the border, teach them a few words of Assamese, give them ration-cards and assign them some land, usually a bit of forest,' he explained. 'When it comes to voting time, they show their ration-cards at the booth and they're eligible to vote. Each one marks a cross in the box of the politician who's patronized them. It's that easy, man.'

'Ingenious,' I commented, scribbling it all down in my notebook and eager for details. But our conversation was suddenly cut short by one of Mole's deputies who came running into the mess.

'The rogue ... the rogue. He killed again ... he killed again last night. In the middle ... of the night,' he stuttered. 'A m ... m ... man. He was dragged from his house. He was dragged and then trampled to death. Horribly trampled.'

Mr Choudhury, who was sitting next to me at the mess table, put down his mug.

'Where did it happen?' he asked slowly.

'Near Hathi Khal. Just a few miles from here.'

'I know the place,' said the hunter, standing up. He put on his Guwahati Rifle Association hat and made for the door.

'Let's go.'

Self-consciously, I followed everyone outside into the compound, hoping to be invited along. I felt like a dog anxious for a walk.

Mr Choudhury looked my way.

'Tarquin. Okay, yes, I suppose you can come for this.'

Eagerly grabbing my camera-bag, I jumped into the back of the Land Rover together with Mr Choudhury, Mole and two armed guards. We took a left out of the compound, Rudra at the wheel. He floored the accelerator, shooting along the dirt track at top speed. I bounced up and down on the seat like an india-rubber ball.

'I am Mister Grand Pree! Yes?' yelled Rudra. 'Just like Tom Crooooz!'

*

Our destination was an isolated hamlet surrounded by lush paddy and sugarcane fields. Along sandy lanes shaded by coconut trees stood rows of mock-Tudor cottages, a design introduced during the British Raj and still popular in Assam today. The white walls of each house were criss-crossed with black beams. Several homes had thatched or tiled roofs capped with chimneys. One or two even boasted porches over which crepe myrtle vines bloomed with brilliant scarlet flowers.

We parked the Land Rover in the middle of the village, leaving Rudra to keep an eye on it. A crowd had gathered near the scene of the disaster. We approached on foot and several of the villagers spotted us, whispering amongst themselves '*Firang, firang*. Foreigner, foreigner.'

Word of my arrival spread quickly and, one by one, with a nudge here and a wink there, the villagers turned to stare in amazement and curiosity.

The crowd parted and we made our way through a gate into a garden with a pathway leading up to a pretty cottage. It was a lovely place, the air filled with the perfume of jasmine bushes. Bottlebrush trees with red bushy flowers and weeping branches stood on either side of the path. White roses grew in carefully tended flowerbeds. Ostensibly, everything was peaceful.

We made our way around the cottage and into the back yard and suddenly I stopped short. On the ground just a few feet away, lying under a dirty, stained tartan blanket, was the crumpled, mangled body of the dead man.

Only a single foot jutted out from beneath the undignified shroud, the veins black against the deathly, bluish-grey skin. The ankle was twisted gratuitously, as were some of the toes. In places, slivers of bone jutted out from beneath the surface.

Nearby, the victim's grieving widow was slumped amidst rows of trampled cabbages, her expression empty, her eyes bloodshot, her cheeks stained with tears. She grabbed at her hair and moaned. The rest of the immediate family stood, traumatized, in tightly knit groups. One by one, we filed past them, offering our condolences and explaining our purpose for being there. Then, with the family's permission, Mr Choudhury, Mole and I approached the body.

The hunter kneeled down, peeling back the top half of the blanket. The forest officer stood back while I peered with trepidation over Mr Choudhury's shoulder. What I saw was to haunt my dreams for months to come.

The man had been reduced to little more than a pulp, barely recognizable as a human being, his face frozen in a contorted, agonized expression which told of an unbearable death. I had seen dead bodies before in various war zones, but nothing as grotesque as this. Feelings of nausea overwhelmed me and my immediate instinct was to look away. But curiosity eventually got the better of me, and I braced myself to take a closer look at the bruised, blood-encrusted body, grimacing at the sight of the head, crushed as if by a steamroller.

Gingerly, Mr Choudhury pulled the blanket back still further, revealing the man's arms. These had been wrenched from their sockets and were now hanging by a thin thread of skin.

The hunter let the blanket fall.

'This is just how we found the other bodies,' whispered Mole, his voice edged with fear. 'This elephant is evil. He has the devil in him, I'm telling you. He rips off the arms and legs, and crushes the body. He's a monster.'

'Are you sure there's only one elephant?' asked Mr Choudhury.

Mole nodded energetically.

'Yes. All the eye-witnesses have seen only one. They describe him as a giant. Some say his tusks are fifty feet long. They're terrified.'

Mr Choudhury looked interested but curiously unimpressed by these details.

'Look, you know that's not true. Come now, let us find out exactly what happened here.'

He rose and turned to the family, asking whether anyone had seen what had happened. An old man leaning heavily on his cane shyly volunteered to relate the story.

'The elephant came while we were eating,' he began, his voice croaking. 'We heard it trumpeting and then it crashed through the fence and came towards the hut.'

He pointed at a mud and straw structure in the right-hand corner of the compound.

'We felt the ground trembling as he came nearer. Stomp, stomp, stomp.'

The old man beat against his shrivelled thighs with clenched fists, making elephant sound-effects to add to the drama of his storytelling.

'He pushed against our hut. It shook as if there was an earthquake. There were seven of us inside. We were all terrified. None of us could even move. We did not make a sound. I was certain that any moment the elephant would kill us all. But he turned and attacked the other hut.'

The old man watched through a window as the animal tore down the other structure.

'He grabbed the roof and wrenched it off, tossing it on to the ground,' he continued. 'He tore down the wall as if it was paper. My son was inside. He was down on his knees, praying. The beast grabbed him with his trunk. He lifted him up high in the air.

'My son called out, "Help, Father, the elephant is killing me! The elephant is killing me!" Then it smashed him down on the ground. My son begged for mercy. Again, the animal threw him down. All the time, my son was screaming. I could do nothing.'

The father clutched at his face, the tears rolling through the gaps in his fingers. His shoulders rose and fell. Mr Choudhury put his arm around him and whispered a few kind words, while other members of the family stepped forward to console him. It took the old man some time to regain his composure.

'The elephant swung him against that tree until there was hardly anything left,' he continued, his voice now barely audible. 'Finally, it dropped him on the ground …' The old man paused for a moment to hold back his tears and then continued. 'The animal raised one foot and brought it down on my son's head.'

A sudden silence fell over the place, broken intermittently by sobs. I kept my eyes fixed on the ground, uneasily digesting this story, trying to reconcile the image of the mad, murdering rogue with my own mental picture of elephants gently grazing and splashing in watering-holes.

Save for a few details, the old man's story was very similar to that told by Monimoy in Das's Guwahati office. It seemed the farmer had been telling the truth.

Mr Choudhury was once again kneeling on the ground, examining the footprints in the soil.

'The rogue escaped that way,' he said to me, pointing to the north. 'See where the fence is broken again over there. He stayed here for some time before leaving. His tracks move over here.'

He followed the footprints around the compound like Sherlock Holmes on the trail of a promising clue. Mole and I tagged along behind him like a couple of confused and ignorant Watsons. At length, he stopped in front of an overturned plastic barrel lying by a fence.

'Well, what do we have here? Hmm, let's look at this.' He gestured for us to come closer.

I helped him lift the barrel and place it the right way up. Near its base, we could see that the thick plastic was punctured by a large round hole.

'Yes, just as I thought,' said the hunter. 'There's no doubt about it. This shows that this elephant is an alcoholic tusker.'

'An alcoholic? What on earth do you mean?' I asked.

Mr Choudhury paused and his face broke into a smile. Patiently, he explained that the villagers had been making bootleg liquor.

'That's what was in the barrel. Look at the hole. He's pierced it with his tusk.'

Mole and I examined the container again more carefully.

'This elephant is a heavy drinker, amongst other things,' concluded Mr Choudhury. 'Elephants love alcohol, particularly the rice wine these people make. They can smell it from miles away and they often break down houses to steal it.'

I learned later that such raids are extremely common. Every year across the subcontinent marauding elephants regularly go out for a night on the razzle, consuming hundreds of gallons of home-made booze. In Bengal, a wild herd recently invaded a military base, tearing down electric fences to get at the soldiers' supply of rum. As the distraught troops looked on, the elephants broke off the tops of dozens of bottles and guzzled the contents. While in southern India, a wild elephant attacked an off-licence, and was seen heading into the jungle with a case of whisky tucked under his trunk.

As with humans, drink seems to influence the animals in a variety of ways, depending on their character. Some turn rowdy, most simply stagger around belching, and many have been seen nursing hangovers. The experts cannot tell whether elephants drink for the taste or for the effect. But bootleg liquor, which is often laced with methyl alcohol, does the animals little good, causing severe damage to their internal organs.

Mr Choudhury was now back on the trail, reconstructing the crime and muttering to himself as he scanned the ground for signs and clues.

'He got hold of the barrel, punctured it with a tusk and drank its contents. This is a very clever and dangerous elephant. But why kill the man? There has to be something more.'

Before I could say anything, he was off again, walking briskly along the elephant's trail. He climbed over the broken fence and into the paddy-field beyond, surveying the ground. Mole and I followed. After a mile or so, he suddenly stopped.

'Yes, look at his tracks. Do you see?'

The earth was soft and the huge round footprints were clearly defined.

'Sure, we see them,' said Mole.

'No, look very closely,' said Mr Choudhury. 'Usually an elephant's back feet fall where the front feet have already walked. See his prints. His back foot falls off to the side.'

'So he's lame,' guessed Mole.

'Perhaps,' concluded the hunter. 'Most probably, he has been wounded, maybe by an arrow. That helps explain why he's so angry.'

'You can tell all that by just looking at some footprints?' I asked.

Mole looked equally impressed by his colleague's deductive powers. But the hunter didn't acknowledge my question. Instead he muttered, 'I have to check one more thing,' and knelt down on the ground in front of one of the deepest foot-prints. Taking a measuring tape from his jacket, he laid it around the circumference of the impression.

'You can calculate an elephant's height by doubling the circumference of its foot, man,' explained Mole, pleased to show off some of his knowledge.

Mr Choudhury read from the tape. It was four and a half feet long which made the animal about nine foot tall. He took the proclamation order printed with the elephant's descrip-tion from his shirt pocket. A quick glance confirmed that the height matched that of the wanted rogue.

'That seems proof enough that this is our man, or rather our elephant,' he said as he cast his eye along the tracks that led over the fields to distant green jungle. 'And I believe I have a very good idea where we are likely to find him.'

With that, he turned and headed back towards the scene of the crime, deep in thought. I hurried after him.

'What kind of elephant is this?' I asked. 'Why has he done all these terrible things?'

'He's definitely dangerous. There's no question about it. But we must find out whether he's a genuine rogue or not,' said Mr Choudhury. 'Some of the elephants sanctioned for execution by the government are just bad-tempered, sick or injured animals. If you give them time, they'll eventually calm down and go back into the jungle.'

The hunter explained that elephants periodically suffer from a strange and little-understood condition called *musth*, a period of psychological disturbance associated with sexual maturity and desire. During this time, they excrete a sticky substance from their temporal glands which runs down their cheeks.

'Many elephants turn dangerous and disobedient,' said Mr Choudhury. 'It lasts about three months. Then they calm down and become quite placid again.'

According to the hunter, a genuine rogue was an elephant turned man-killer. Although rare, the Assamese have a name for such an animal – *goonda*.

'Once in a while, a real *goonda* comes along,' he said. 'If we are dealing with such an elephant, then nothing can be done for him.'

'Surely, he could be put in a zoo or a wildlife sanctuary,' I said.

'No, I'm afraid not,' said the hunter. 'It would be too dangerous for the general public. Killing him would be the only humane thing to do.'

Preparations were soon underway for the funeral of the crushed victim. The body was carried into the cottage where it was washed and prepared for cremation. An hour or so later, wrapped in a white cotton cloth, it was placed on a stretcher constructed from bamboo and carried into the front garden where the rituals began.

In front of the cottage, I stood by the gate, watching a Hindu *pandit*, or priest, recite holy mantras while the family scattered rose petals over the shrouded body. Six male relatives then picked up the stretcher, lifted it up on to their shoulders and carried it into the lane. With the priest in the lead, the solemn procession wound its way through the village past kindly neighbours who lined the route, offering their condolences to the bereaved family.

It took just half an hour to reach the cremation site, positioned on the edge of a stream, down-wind from the village and its thatched roofs. Here, the stretcher was placed on a pile of wood five or six feet high that had been coated in ghee. Nearly a hundred people gathered in a semicircle around this edifice and, as the priest recited more prayers and the family wept more tears, the eldest son, carrying a flaming torch, circled the pyramid. Then he stooped down and, holding out the torch with one trembling hand, lit the kindling at the base of his father's funeral pyre.

Smoke rose up around the body, encircling it in a ghostly haze as flames licked their way up the branches, the clarified butter hissing and spitting like a pit full of snakes. The bamboo stretcher turned black, the flower blossoms shrivelled into nothing, and soon the shroud was alight. Sparks shot up into the air, flames reaching towards the sky, and while the rogue's latest victim was consumed in a blistering conflagration, his widow sobbed and wailed, the sounds of her grief barely audible above the roaring blaze.

As a final act, the eldest son took a wooden club in both hands and, raising it above his head, brought it down on his father's skull. There was a decisive crack and then, and only then, was the man's spirit finally released.

*

47

Back at the Forest Department headquarters, I caught up on some sleep in the guesthouse bungalow while Mr Choudhury and Mole went into town to stock up on supplies.

An hour or so later, I was woken by a strange noise coming from outside my door. It sounded like a young boy learning to play the trumpet. The notes, which were mostly spit and wind, were out of tune. Still half asleep, I pulled on my trousers and opened the door. Walking cautiously out on to the grass and rubbing the sleep from my eyes, I took a step forward and bumped straight into the backside of an elephant.

After everything I had seen and heard in the past twenty-four hours, my first instinct was to race back inside the bungalow, slam the door, fasten the latch and hide in the bathroom. I was certain that at any moment the animal would smash down the wall and tear me limb from limb. Several minutes passed. Nothing happened. Even the trumpeting stopped. I crept out of the bathroom and over to the window and very slowly pulled back the curtains to see if the coast was clear.

The elephant was still standing near my door. Now that I had got over my initial shock, I could see that she meant me no harm. Indeed, she was holding a pathetic-looking deflated football in her trunk and I got the distinct impression that she was looking for a playmate.

She was a beautiful, graceful, well-proportioned creature and there was no doubt that when she walked through the jungle, male elephants would look her way. She had lustrous brown eyes and long black eyelashes which she fluttered like a catwalk model. Her forehead and ears were speckled with pink freckles. Nature had also endowed her with a petite tail that swished flirtatiously, perfect ears the shape of India, and a little tuft of coquettish curly hair on the top of her sculpted forehead.

As this was the first elephant I had ever met, I was naturally nervous. My new acquaintance, however, was not lacking in confidence. Spotting me emerging from the bungalow, she strode straight over to the door and, without a moment's hesitation, extended her trunk in my direction as if she was offering to shake my hand. The end of her trunk hung before me, its spongy nostrils twitching. The proboscis then moved down over my chest, stomach and thigh. I felt it brush against my leg and, before I knew it, she had reached inside my pocket and pulled out a packet of strawberry-flavoured Fruitella sweets that I had been saving for later. As quick as a flash, she threw the whole lot, wrappers and all, into her mouth and began to chew, squinting at me and making satisfied gurgling noises.

'I see you've met Jasmine,' said Mr Choudhury, approaching us from the other side of the compound, having just arrived back from the shopping trip.

I chuckled.

'Yes, she just robbed me and ate the evidence!'

Mr Choudhury ran his hands down Jasmine's trunk. She stomped her feet lightly, apparently pleased to see him. The hunter patted her cheeks and she drooped her trunk over his shoulder affectionately, giving him a hug. Digging into his pockets, the hunter produced a handful of peanuts which Jasmine picked up with the end of her trunk and dropped into her mouth.

'Sometimes she's a very naughty elephant, especially when she meets someone new and she knows she can take advantage,' said Mr Choudhury.

'Is she trained?'

'Yes, she's a *kunki*, a domesticated elephant.'

'Domesticated?' He made it sound as if Jasmine was qualified to do the housework and eat with a knife and fork.

'She was caught in the wild when she was a calf,' he explained, patting her forehead. 'Now she's employed by the Forest Department.'

Jasmine belched quietly to herself as her digestive juices got to work on my Fruitellas and the peanuts.

'Go ahead and touch her,' said Mr Choudhury. 'Don't worry, she won't bite.'

I reached out with my right hand and, like one of the blind men in the story of the Elephant in the Dark, ran my palm over her trunk. I had expected the skin to be smooth but it was coarse and covered in prickly black hairs. Jasmine seemed to enjoy human contact and made a satisfied rumbling noise deep inside her chest that sounded like a cat purring.

'She's a new member of my elephant squad,' said the hunter. 'Come and meet the others. They've just got back from gathering fodder. They're over there.'

He pointed towards the banyan tree where one or two figures were busy cooking over a log fire.

'Who are the elephant squad?'

'They're the SAS of the elephant world.'

'The SAS?'

'My specially trained team. We work together during the winter when the herds come down from the hills looking for food.'

The elephant squad, he explained, was employed by the Forest Department to patrol the district and prevent wild elephants from straying into the fields and destroying the farmers' crops.

'The herds come every year and we have to drive them back,' he said. 'There's not enough food left for them up in the hills and the jungle. Down here, there's a lot on offer. For the elephants, it's like going to the supermarket – only the food is all free.'

Mr Choudhury took hold of one of Jasmine's ears and led her over to where the elephant squad was camped near the banyan tree. As I followed, watching Jasmine's sagging bottom bob up and down, another elephant strode through the compound's main entrance carrying a load of freshly cut banana trees. He was a gigantic animal, almost twice the size of Jasmine, with a great arching spine and a gigantic cranium crowned by two prominent frontal lobes. His ears, which flapped and beat continuously against his sides, were frayed and torn around the edges like pieces of worn leather. His tail, which was covered in porcupine-like hairs, swung from side to side as rhythmically as the pendulum of a clock.

'That's Raja,' said Mr Choudhury.

I stared at him transfixed, suddenly feeling incredibly small.

'He's what we call a *makhna*, a tuskless male. Isn't he magnificent?'

A mahout sat astride Raja's thick neck, gently rocking back and forth in time with the elephant's stride. The mahout's back was erect and his feet were lodged behind the animal's ears. He was a short man with rock-hard calf muscles. Chunky blue veins ran across the length of his arms like the roots of a well-nourished plant. With an apricot complexion, slanting eyes and a wispy beard, he could easily have been mistaken for a Turkoman from Central Asia. His clothes – a rough tunic, old shirt and fatigues – were scruffy and marked with dirt and grease stains. He went barefoot and his toes were like bits of gnarled ginger. His hands were filthy and the palms had the texture of sandpaper. And yet, despite his slovenly appearance, his face exuded character. Like a piece of antique furniture, it had a worn, mellow finish, the grain and lines of his skin adding depth and substance.

Raja approached the banyan tree and the mahout barked out an order. The elephant stopped dead in his tracks. The rider called out again and this time the animal sank to his knees, allowing his master to slide down his bulky side on to the ground.

While we watched the two at work, Mr Choudhury told me something about mahouts.

'They are revered by many people because they have power over the elephants,' he said. 'Some believe they use *jadoo*, magic. But this is nonsense. They just know and understand the elephants and have a special affinity with them.'

Mahouts, he said, were inseparable from their *kunkis* and they spent every waking moment together.

'There have been many cases in the past when an elephant has died and soon after the mahout has died from a broken heart, and vice versa,' said Mr Choudhury.

'Do you ever get female mahouts?' I asked.

'I have only ever heard of one,' he said. 'The mahouts believe that elephants do not like women riding them because they menstruate. But I'm sure that's just a way of keeping their wives at home.'

The head mahout walked over to where we were standing and clamped my hand in a vice-like grip.

'Tarquin, this is Churchill,' said Mr Choudhury before leaving us together.

'Churchill? Well, that's an interesting name.'

The mahout grinned, the creases around his mouth spreading from one side of his face to the other.

'Yes. I am christened Churchill Nongrang,' he replied. 'We're given different names in my tribe, no? My niece is "Dolly", like "Dolly Parton". My cousin is "Elvis", like Elvis Presley. My younger brother, he is "Nasser".'

'Like the Egyptian president?'

'No, no. Like NASA. American space peoples.'

I tried to disguise my amusement.

'You said you were christened. Are you a Christian then?' I asked.

'Yes, Presbyterian, all the way,' replied the mahout. 'I was teached by Welsh missionaries, no?'

He explained that many of the hill tribes of the North-East Frontier, including the infamous Nagas, were never converted to Hinduism by the Aryans, sticking instead to their own animistic religions. When European missionaries of various denominations flooded into the area during the nineteenth century, offering education as well as the concept of one god, many converted. Churchill's tribe, the Khasis, who live in a range of hills in Meghalaya, another Indian state bordering Bangladesh, are a mix of Roman Catholics, Anglicans, Methodists and Presbyterians. And yet much of their culture remains intact, including a matrilineal system which ensures that all property and land remain in the hands of the tribe's women. It is a tradition that is resented by many Khasi men, Churchill included.

'We men, we have nothing. We can be throwed from the home!' he complained. 'Women. They in charge. Women nightmare. That why I become mahout. I am free man!' Once again, his face broadened into an infectious smile.

'What you do here?' he asked, curious.

I explained that I had come to write a book about the rogue and Mr Choudhury.

'What you want with book? Book boring, no?'

'Maybe.'

'You learn about *hathi!*'

'*Hathi?*'

'It mean eley-phant in my language,' he explained. 'You stay here. Learn many thing.' He shook me playfully by the shoulder. 'Make you mahout. Okay?'

'Sure.'

He showed his excitement by doing a little jig.

'Come, meet eley-phant squad. They never seen *firang*. What kind of *firang* you? You not white. You red. Why so red?'

It was true that I had caught a little too much sun during the funeral.

'I'm British.'

In most parts of the world, this would have sufficed as an explanation. Churchill needed more persuading.

'Britishers not red.'

'Some of us are, if we stay in the sun too long.'

'Yes, yes. Your country weather very bad. Worse than Himalayas, no?'

I had to agree.

The rest of the squad were a rough-looking bunch, unshaven, dirty and as thuggish as a group of escaped convicts. Chander, the 'number two mahout', had a deep scar running across his right cheek and neck, which he claimed to have been given during a tumble with a wild bear. Bodo, the senior apprentice, had a broken nose that jutted out at a sharp angle. And the other two apprentices, Prat and Sanjay, who were covered in tattoos, looked as if they might come in handy in a bar brawl.

When we were introduced, the four of them gawked at me, shaking my hand cautiously. Amazingly, none of them had ever seen a white man before, even if he was, well, red. What's more, none of them, with the exception of Churchill, had ever travelled to Guwahati, let alone New Delhi, and between them they had seen very little of the world, even on television.

We crouched around the campfire and they served me 'ready-made tea', the leaves and milk boiled together in a spitting steel kettle. There was an awkward silence followed by much whispering amongst the men who were, no doubt, puzzling over my presence in their midst.

Eventually, Chander plucked up the courage to ask me where I was from and, before too long, all of them were firing random questions at me in rapid succession.

How old was I? Where was my country? Was it near America? Was it true that we ate cows? What did I think of Punjabis? Did we have elephants in Britain? How did I like India? Did I have children? How did British people drink tea? Had I ever met Princess Diana? Had I seen the ocean?

Eventually Churchill broke in.

'I have been London,' he said proudly. 'I have seen the Big Ben and the Bucking-ham Palace. Also, the zoo. Many *hathis* there, no?'

I was surprised to learn that Churchill was an extremely well-travelled man who had worked in zoos around the world.

'How many country you visit?' he asked, his eyes shining with anticipation.

'About twenty-five or so,' I replied.

The mahout cried out with joy. He obviously had me trumped.

'Me, thirty country – yes,' he said. 'I have been all Asia, all Europes – all places.'

For several years, Churchill had worked in a zoo in Malaysia and had used his savings to travel all over the Far East. In the 1970s, when India donated an elephant to Iraq, he was recruited to accompany the animal to Baghdad.

'I wash *hathi* in Euphrates River. Iraqi peoples, they come to watch. Very nice peoples. One day, Saddam he come give me sword. I make many friend, no?'

After travelling on to Europe, eking out a living as a manual labourer, Churchill returned to his beloved Assam and joined the Forest Department.

'Now I'm here, no? This is my belonging.'

By the time the mahout had finished telling me his life story, it was feeding time.

'Come,' said Churchill. 'To be mahout, you learn many thing.'

Draining their glasses, Chander, Bodo, Prat and Sanjay then offloaded the banana trees from Raja's back and started cutting the curly outer bark into squares roughly one foot across. These they folded in half, making pouches, or 'rolls' as they called them, which they filled with uncooked rice and tied up like packages using lengths of vine. Once we had prepared about forty, they were split into two uneven piles.

'Now watch,' instructed Churchill.

Turning his back on the *kunkis*, he extracted a container from one of his trouser pockets and took out an antibiotic pill.

This he crushed between his fingers, adding the powder to one of the rolls.

'Medicine. Let's see if Jasmine is eating,' he said, putting it back amongst the others.

Prat laid the pouches in front of the animals. Raja and Jasmine's trunks slithered about, pulling, touching, feeling and smelling, like Kipling's Elephant Child with its 'satiable curiosity. One by one, they picked up the pouches, popping them into their mouths, their powerful molars making short work of the crunchy banana flesh.

Soon, all the pouches had been devoured, all, that is, except the one loaded with antibiotics which Jasmine treated with suspicion and pushed to one side.

'How did she know?' I asked Churchill.

'She was smelling,' he said, clearly frustrated. 'I am trying to trick her for days, but no, she is too clever for old mahout.'

The squad kept me busy for the rest of the day. As a new recruit, I was assigned all the menial tasks. There were pots and pans to clean, clothes to wash, tents to sweep out and firewood to collect. It was hard work but it was more physically satisfying than anything I had done for months. More importantly, it was the perfect way to get to know the elephant squad and gain their confidence. Prat and Sanjay were delighted to have a helper, and in spite of the language barrier, we soon hit it off.

At dusk, we led the *kunkis* to the edge of the compound near the main gate where they were provided with cakes of rough wheat, or *ragi*, which was mixed with *jaggery*, a kind of molasses distilled from sugarcane juice. Chains were attached to their legs, which in turn were secured to two trees. As the sun dipped down behind the hills, leaving subtle hues in the sky, Prat showed me how to brush down the elephants with a coarse broom. Afterwards, he applied some cream to an open sore on Raja's back to prevent any infection.

Our chores done, we sat on some logs watching the scene unfold around us. The *kunkis* were stripping the banana trees and shoving pieces into their mouths. Periodically, Raja tilted back his head and roared like a lion, showing us his gums. Jasmine replied with a little squeal, blowing air down her trunk and making a noise like water going down a hose-pipe.

Flashes of bright light burst across the compound from inside the garage where a forest guard was busy welding together two pieces of metal. At the entrance, an armed guard paced languidly back and forth, a cloud of insects circling above his head. Laughter spilled out from the main office where Mole and his deputy were sharing a drink.

At eight o'clock, the clanging of the dinner gong resounded across the compound. Churchill rubbed his hands. 'Let's go get some grubs,' said the mahout.

'Actually, Churchill, the word is grub, not grubs,' I said.

'Are you sure? I was taught grubs.'

'Absolutely certain,' I said, as diplomatically as possible. 'Grubs are insects and you wouldn't want to eat them.'

Churchill screwed up his upper lip.

'That odd thing. A Britisher teach-ed me this word. Twenty years ago he teach-ed me,' said the mahout. 'I am using it since.'

As we walked into the mess-room and washed our hands, I said nothing further on the subject. But privately I smiled to myself, certain that Churchill had been the victim of a practical joke.

Mr Choudhury had spent the afternoon making preparations for a night-time operation. After dinner, he called everyone together for a meeting. We gathered round a map of the

Sonitpur district which he spread out on the table in the mess-room and listened as he outlined his plan.

According to 'local intelligence', the hunter told us, the rogue had visited the same village every night for the past week, killing three men. The chances were therefore high that he would visit the village again. But there was one serious complication. A wild herd had moved into the vicinity and they would first have to be driven back into the rain forest and hills to the north. Mr Choudhury, Rudra, Mole and the guards were to go on ahead and set up look-out posts, while the elephant squad followed. It would take the *kunkis* roughly two hours to cover the distance.

That took care of everyone except me. My agreement, struck with Mr Choudhury, was that I would stay in the camp out of harm's way. However, given the chance, I was sure that I could persuade him to allow me to tag along. In the event, I was wrong.

'I am afraid you have to stay here,' said the hunter. 'This may get very rough. At night, there are many insurgents in the area. Besides, there is a killer elephant on the loose.'

He placed his rifle and ammunition in the back of the Land Rover and climbed inside with Mole and the guards. With that, Rudra revved the engine, slipped into gear and they all sped out of the compound. I was left behind with the elephant squad in the twilight, bristling with disappointment.

3

The Elephant Wars

'For that which befalleth the sons of men befalleth beasts; even one thing that befalleth them; as the one dieth, so dieth the other; yea, they have all one breath; so that a man hath no pre-eminence above a beast, for all is vanity.'

Ecclesiastes 3:19

As he knelt in front of the compound's shrine and began to intone his prayers, flickers of mellow orange light darted across Churchill's face. In his right hand, he held a green coconut; in the other, a fistful of marigold petals. These he placed on the ground in the centre of a semicircle of burning candles, taking care not to singe his hand. Stooping piously, the mahout lit several incense-sticks, pushing the ends down into the soft earth. He stared reverently at the deity before him, pressing the palms of his hands together in front of his chest. Sweet-smelling smoke wafted up into the cold night air. The rest of the elephant squad knelt behind him, lowered their heads in obeisance and began to say the prayers traditionally recited at the beginning of a journey.

I stood just a few feet away, eager to watch their act of worship, yet at the same time anxious not to disturb them. The shrine was positioned at the base of a towering oak tree not far from the front gate of the compound. By the light of the candles, I caught a glimpse of the clay idol, housed in a shallow alcove fashioned like a seashell. It was Ganesha, the elephant-headed god, one of India's most popular deities.

Painted in gaudy pinks and purples reminiscent of a Las Vegas casino, he lounged atop the black rat Vahana, his traditional servant and vehicle. A garland of flowers hung from the god's neck and a golden crown perched on his head. His trunk curled above his characteristic pot-belly, while in his four hands he held a shell, a discus, a club and a *modaka*, a sweetened rice ball, his favourite food.

One by one, Churchill and the others made their offerings. Whispering invocations, they poured coconut milk over the statue. The liquid dribbled down the god's body, dripping off his belly and forming a pool at his feet.

'King of all beings, the Eternal,' they mumbled, 'blood red of hue, whose forehead is illuminated by the new moon, Remover of all Difficulties ...'

The sound of their devotions mingled with the chirping of an orchestra of crickets and the urgent croaking of toads – as if all of them, animals and humans, were paying homage to the elephant-headed god together. A breeze rustled in the oak tree, its branches creaking in a gentle, hypnotic rhythm. Up above, a million stars sparkled in the darkness like jewels in a vast celestial treasure-trove. A satellite passed across this canopy in a wide arc above the earth, an insignificant speck amidst the countless galaxies.

I began to daydream and thought back to the time, some years earlier, when I had attended Ganesha's annual birthday celebrations in Bombay. Under a similar sky, an elderly guru had told me the legend of the elephant-headed god.

Originally, Ganesha, son of the goddess Parvati, was a perfectly normal little boy. But one day, as a result of a misunderstanding, his father Shiva cut off his head. Ganesha's mother, who was naturally distraught, called upon the other gods to bring her son back to life. To do this, the deities required a new head, so they set off around the world in search of one.

The first living being whom they met along the way happened to be an Asian male tusker elephant. The unfortunate animal was quickly relieved of his head by the gods and it was duly placed on the boy's shoulders. In a flash he was miraculously resurrected as Ganesha, the corpulent and often mischievous deity.

Until the seventh century, Ganesha was feared as a god who brought nothing but catastrophe. In about AD 650, however, a powerful sect sprang up called the Ganapatyas who looked upon the elephant-headed god as the supreme deity and built countless temples dedicated to his worship alone. Because the cult did not recognize any caste distinctions, it grew in popularity, and over the next three hundred years, the pot-bellied deity underwent a complete transformation. Today, Ganesha is worshipped by Hindus as the god of wisdom and the remover of obstacles. Businessmen always make an offering to Ganapati, as he is also known, at the start of a new venture, and before embarking on a journey Hindus invoke his name. It is also believed that whoever recites his twelve sacred titles every morning will enjoy good fortune.

The prayers came to an end and the elephant squad rose from where they were kneeling. Bodo, the apprentice with the broken nose, lit a kerosene camping lantern. At first, it hissed and spluttered and sent flames shooting four feet into the air, but soon the silk wick began to burn with dazzling intensity, lighting up half the compound and casting evil-looking shadows behind the twisted branches of the banyan tree. The devotees gathered their offerings from the foot of the idol. According to Hindu custom, these were now considered blessed and, as *prasad* or sanctified food, must be shared and eaten.

Churchill handed me a chunk of coconut and dropped two yellow sugar balls called *ladoos* into my cupped hands. Although I'm not particularly partial to dry Indian sweets, I knew that it would be bad etiquette to refuse them, and to throw any away might be construed as an insult, so I ate everything.

The *kunkis* were also given their share of the *puja* spoils. Jasmine took just a few seconds to cram most of the bananas into her greedy little mouth and gulp them down in one go, and no sooner had she swallowed these than her trunk, acting like a guided missile, went in search of more treats. She homed in on a bowl of sugar balls and, before anyone could stop her, had vacuumed up the lot in her trunk, quickly blowing them into her mouth. Apparently pleased with herself, despite the mahouts' protestations, she waggled her bottom from side to side and squawked excitedly.

Bodo and Sanjay produced a plastic bag full of rust-coloured sandalwood paste which they proceeded to rub on to the elephants' foreheads, creating two marks or spots.

'These things, they called *tilaks*,' explained Churchill as I admired the apprentices' handiwork. 'It is for good luck, no?'

I knew that Hindus traditionally place a dot or symbol in the middle of the forehead to mark the spot where the spiritual centre of a human being is believed to reside. The *tilak* also serves as a mark distinguishing caste or sect, although in twentieth-century India it is worn by many young urban women as a mere fashion accessory. However, this was the first time I had seen an animal sporting one. What's more, I was confused as to why Churchill, a self-professed Presbyterian, was participating in such rituals and even praying before a Hindu deity. Surely for a Christian such behaviour was sacrilegious?

'Better to be safer than sorrier, no?' he said when I asked him about it.

'How do you mean?'

Churchill pulled me aside out of earshot of the others.

'One or two prayers, some *puja*, it not hurt,' he whispered. 'Anyway, worship *hathi* not Hindu thing only. Tribal people, they pray to *hathi*. Going long, long back in past.'

I read later in my trusty *Elephant Gold* that long before the Aryans arrived in India and the elephant-headed god became an established part of the Hindu pantheon, India's aboriginals worshipped pachyderm deities and totems. To this day, most Indian villagers believe that living elephants are manifestations of the god.

'Ganesha is like father. We ask for safety from him. Protection also,' continued Churchill. 'We ask it's okay to kill rogue, otherwise Ganesha be angry. Then big problem for mahout.'

'Really? Do you believe any of this, being a Christian? Isn't it just superstition?'

As he considered my question, the mahout said nothing but picked up a leaf from the ground. He let it fall back to earth.

'I am believing.'

He raised a finger in caution and suddenly his usual jovial tone and benign expression vanished. He became deadly serious.

'You don't believe. Okay, but be careful. *Hathi* all-knowing aneemal. He look into man's mind and read like book. He hear, see all thing. Rogue *hathi*, he know we come. He know.'

'If that's true, won't that mean that he'll simply run away and you won't be able to find him?'

Churchill was still chewing on a slice of coconut. He bit off a piece and spat it out. Behind him Raja stood staring at me and winking knowingly.

'If rogue *hathi* run, that is fate. If he killed, that is fate. If we killed, that is fate,' answered the mahout sagely. 'Everything is fate, no?'

The fire in the elephant squad's camp was extinguished. Tents were taken down, rolled up and squeezed into their polythene pouches. Bedrolls were tied up with lengths of twine. Pots and pans, ladles and spoons were packed into potato sacks, together with cans of cooking oil and tins of salt and mango pickle. All this was loaded into the back of a jeep which was due to meet the squad later at a prearranged rendezvous point.

Next, the apprentices prepared the *kunkis* for the journey. Bodo and Sanjay gave them numerous buckets of water to drink. Chander and Prat draped potato sacking over the animals' backs which they secured with ropes drawn around the *kunkis*' necks and under their bellies and tails, creating crude saddles. Finally, wicker baskets packed with essentials such as tea, sugar and tin mugs were loaded on to the *kunkis* together with two kerosene lamps, four torches and half a dozen boxes of spare batteries. Once loaded, the beasts looked like Hannibal's elephants setting out for their epic journey across the Alps.

By the time the squad was ready to depart, it was past eleven o'clock and it had turned bitterly cold. To keep warm, Chander and the others wrapped themselves in blankets which they tied around their chests with rope. Churchill put on a Border Security Force jacket trimmed with fur which he claimed to have been given by an officer whose life he had saved some years earlier. He unlocked the chain around Raja's foot and prepared to mount him.

'Ganapati protect us,' he called out to his squad, quickly adding, half under his breath, 'and our Lord Jesus Christ.'

Standing to the side of his elephant, he called out a single word in Assamese. Responding immediately, the *kunki* thrust out his trunk. Churchill stepped up on the extended proboscis, took hold of the ears and pulled himself up, quickly taking his position astride Raja's neck. The mahout shouted out another order and the pachyderm, with the dexterity and grace of a ballet dancer, turned 180 degrees. Behind him I watched as Chander mounted Jasmine in much the same way. The younger mahout then rode the female elephant around the compound, turning periodically and checking her steering.

'*Baith! Baith!*' bawled Churchill. '*Baith!*'

Again, without any hesitation or sign of reluctance, Raja responded to his master's voice, sinking to his knees, tucking his back legs underneath his enormous frame, and sweeping his trunk across the ground like an anaconda.

Meanwhile, I sat under the banyan tree, watching the squad and sulking. Although I had toyed with the idea of disobeying Mr Choudhury's orders and following on foot, it seemed too risky. I didn't know the terrain, didn't speak any of the local languages and had no guide. There were probably dangerous insurgents in the area who would be only too happy to kidnap me and hold me for ransom. And there was the rogue to consider. The last thing I wanted to do was run into him in the dark.

I had little choice but to stay in the compound, but that didn't mean I was happy about it. In fact, I was livid. Mr Choudhury might well track down the elephant in the middle of the night and shoot the poor creature, and then I would have lost the whole story. I slumped back against the tree, cursing my fate and wondering whether I hadn't wasted my time.

In the event, I needn't have worried.

'Tar-win,' bawled Churchill, 'you come. Come, get on Raja.'

I scrambled up from the base of the tree. Had I heard the mahout correctly? Was he inviting me along? Hadn't he heard Mr Choudhury tell me to remain in the camp?

'I was told to stay here,' I said, playing it safe.

The mahout shook his head.

'No, no. You part of eley-phant squad. We look after you. Come. You must.'

'But Mr Choudhury will be angry. He wants me to stay here,' I said, nervous that I might jeopardize our agreement and find myself packed off back to Guwahati.

'No worry. I talk with Shikari. Make all okay, no?' he

continued. 'I look after you, Tar-win. No problem. Yes, yes. Come.'

The mahout motioned for me to climb on to the *kunki*. I dithered for all of a second and then made up my mind. If Mr Choudhury got angry, Churchill and the others would back me up. And even if they didn't ... well, it was worth the risk. I ran into the bungalow, grabbed my bags, put them in the back of the jeep and prepared to mount the elephant.

I had ridden broncos in Texas, *buz-kashi* stallions in Afghanistan, camels in northern Kenya and one or two donkeys in Wales. I had even been on the back of a few cows at an Arizona rodeo. But I had never ridden an elephant. Now the moment of truth had finally arrived, I faltered. Raja was a giant. Even when he crouched on his knees, he towered above me. His stomach alone was ten times my size. How on earth was I meant to mount this thing? There weren't any stirrups, there wasn't even a ladder. I looked up at Churchill despairingly.

'Er, how do I do this?'

'You come up side. Put one foot on leg, grab rope, pull,' instructed Churchill.

I stepped up on Raja's thigh. The flesh wobbled underneath my boots like jelly. I grabbed hold of one of the ropes with both hands and prepared to climb up on to the elephant's back. But just then, Raja suddenly decided to stand up. In one surprisingly quick and agile movement, he rose to his feet. The rope snapped tight against my fingers, the support beneath me jerked away, and I found myself hanging from the elephant's side like a stranded mountain climber. Desperately, I tried to free my trapped hands as the elephant's abrasive skin rubbed against my knuckles like coarse sandpaper. Whimpering with pain, I kicked out helplessly. It felt as if my fingers were being wrenched from their sockets.

'*Baith! Baith!*' shouted Churchill, reaching back and slapping his mount hard on his side. 'Down! Down!'

Grudgingly, Raja sank to his knees, trumpeting an irritated staccato note. The rope slackened, my fingers came loose and I jumped to the ground, hopping around in little circles and nursing my injured fingers. The apprentices laughed so hard the tears began to roll down their faces.

'*Firang!* Get up on *hathi!*' scolded Churchill. 'Raja not like this. I don't like! Hurry!'

'What about my hands?'

'You like old woman! No complains!'

Not wanting to be left behind, I tried again, stepping up on to Raja's leg and taking hold of the rope. This time, with a helping hand from Prat who had to give me a push from behind, I managed to reach the summit, albeit with my dignity in tatters. I had just enough time to grip the elephant's sides with my legs and take hold of the 'saddle' when Raja surged upwards, his powerful muscles moving like great pistons beneath me.

'*Hathi* play. He joke,' laughed Prat and Bodo, who were now sitting behind me. '*Hathi* joke.'

'Yes, very funny,' I said, nursing my bleeding knuckles.

One of my little fingers was throbbing terribly and looked as if it had been put through a mangle. But Churchill was quick to dismiss my injuries.

'Not bad. Worse to come. Mahout need strong skin, no?'

With this, he swung Raja around and made for the main gate. Jasmine followed behind, carrying Chander and Sanjay. Two armed forest guards marched beside us, machine guns slung prominently over their shoulders.

Exhilarating as it was to be on my first elephant, it was also extremely uncomfortable. Apart from the sacking, there was no seat or cushion, and the animal's enormous shoulder blades jostled to and fro, giving me the sensation of being at sea. The rough sacking scoured my backside like wire wool, and Raja's prickly hairs and Jurassic-like hide rubbed against my calf muscles and ankles, soon shaving away my hairs as well as some of my skin. To make matters worse, the *kunki* smelt of dung and the stench quickly rubbed off on my clothes, leaving me reeking of manure.

'Don't you have a howdah?' I asked.

My godfather Charles had always ridden on a howdah. It said so in his letters. But Churchill scoffed at the very idea. Howdahs, in his view, were for wimps.

'No seat. No pillow. This is best way. You must be relaxed,' advised Churchill. 'Don't make legs tight, no?'

'Right.'

I looked to see how he was sitting. His back was perpendicular, his legs were hanging down either side of Raja's neck, and his hands rested on top of the animal's head.

'So, how do you drive this thing?' I asked.

'*Hathi* is best trained aneemal,' said the mahout proudly. 'He never forget.'

'Is it really true that elephants never forget?' I asked.

'*Hathi* never forget. If I go today, return ten years, he remember.'

We moved off the sandy lane and took a short-cut through waterlogged rice-fields. Jasmine followed behind, her feet making slurping noises as she splashed through thick mud. In her trunk, she clutched a clump of grass which she bashed against her front legs to shake off the dirt and then shoved into her mouth. Somewhere off in the darkness there was a sudden squawking and screeching. Bodo switched on a torch and turned it on some bushes to our right. Jackals glared at us from beneath thickets, rows of fluorescent eyes catching the light like mini bicycle reflectors. Insects chirped in the grass. Fireflies blinked as they zigzagged past like microscopic space ships.

I leaned over to watch Raja's legs. The skin hung down in sagging folds, like baggy grey trousers. As they plodded along, never missing a step despite their clumsy appearance, his trunk swung from side to side, occasionally reaching out and pulling up a clump of grass. From the rope around his neck hung a metal object. It was an ominous-looking weapon, essentially a metal rod with a sharp point at one end and a hook welded to the other, the kind of object a gladiator might have used to carve up his opponents in a Roman arena. Churchill called it an *ankush*, a tool that has been carried by Indian mahouts for thousands of years.

'This for emergency only. Many mahout, they use all the times. Not right, no? These mens not good,' scoffed Churchill.

He demonstrated how, nowadays, many elephant drivers jab the metal spike into a sensitive spot on the top of the head in order to enforce a command. They also use the hook behind the ears to bring the elephant to an abrupt halt. This causes the animal considerable pain and explains why elephants are increasingly turning on their mahouts and frequently killing them.

'*Hathi* like camel,' continued my self-appointed guru. 'If you treat bad, he run away. One thing different. *Hathi* will kill mahout. Camel not doing this.'

Mr Choudhury told me later that, until relatively recently, communities of mahouts were to be found across India wherever there were elephants. Even states like Rajasthan, which has been reduced to desert, once had their own elephant populations. Yet with the rapid depletion of the forests and jungles, seventy per cent of the country's elephants have been wiped out. With them have vanished the mahouts and much of their expertise and experience. Today's apprentices often learn shoddy habits from their trainers, and India's domesticated elephants are too often badly treated and abused.

'No need for *ankush*. *Hathi* intelligent animal,' said Churchill, petting his mount's ears. 'He is knowing many thing.'

Raja had been caught as a calf not far from Guwahati. His captors intended to sell him to the timber trade and he might have spent a lifetime lifting and dragging felled trees. But the *makhna* proved too intelligent for such mundane work and he was sold to Assam's Forest Department.

He responded to more than forty-three words, all of them derived from Sanskrit and traditionally used by mahouts throughout India, except for distant Kerala and the Western Ghats. In this vocabulary to stand was '*mile*', to go forward '*ageit*', and to lie down '*terre*'. He could be instructed to pick up something and hold it in his trunk. And there was even a command to get the animal to suck up water and blow it over his back.

Usually, Raja obeyed these commands to the letter. On the rare occasions when he turned stubborn, Churchill applied pressure to certain points on the backs of the *kunki's* ears to bring him into line. Only in an emergency, if he required the elephant to charge or to come to an abrupt stop, would the mahout use the *ankush*, and then with much reluctance.

While we continued through the night, I asked Churchill how he rated Mr Choudhury as an elephant man.

'He is number one,' said the mahout without hesitation. 'He know all thing about *hathi*. All thing.'

This was high praise indeed, for the mahouts were often scathing of other half-baked 'experts' who they had to work with from time to time.

'He is having special power,' continued Churchill. 'He is having extra sense, no? He is knowing *hathi's* mind. Rogue *hathi* is very scared of Shikari.'

The mahout believed that in a past life, Mr Choudhury had been an elephant. At any rate, that was how he explained his affinity with the animals.

I asked the mahout what form he himself had taken in his past life.

'I was movie star. Very famous, no? All women, they liked me too much!'

*

We had been travelling for nearly two hours when Churchill called a halt next to a stream where the elephants drank. The apprentices set up a camping-stove and boiled a pot of water for tea, while I climbed down from Raja and nursed my sore legs. Bodo and Prat cut some banana trees with their machetes for the *kunkis* to eat. The others adjusted the 'saddles' and checked the pads of the animals' feet for any cuts or sores.

Churchill and I stood in front of the camping-stove as the mahout continued my initiation. Elephants, he said, are different to most animals in that their brains expand during their lifetime, usually by sixty-five per cent. This renders them curious and gives them a natural ability to learn.

'*Hathi* is doing so many tricks, no? Like play piano, use calculator, juggle ball, all things,' he elaborated.

According to the experts, these are but crude examples of a deeper, hidden elephantine intelligence. Stories abound of extraordinary, 'almost human', feats demonstrated by these animals. Many elephants held in captivity respond to whole sentences and not just key command words. An Asian elephant called Ruby who resides in the Phoenix Zoo, Arizona, paints on canvas and can differentiate between colours. Another in Assam stands by the roadside blocking traffic and extorts food from passing drivers. Researchers at Cornell University have discovered that herds communicate over distances of up to twelve miles using low-frequency calls inaudible to the human ear.

During my time in Assam, I was to hear dozens of stories illustrating just how smart and intuitive – as well as vengeful – elephants can be. Churchill's favourite story, which he told me more than once, was about a tusker wounded by poachers in 1996.

'He was intelli-gent *hathi*,' began the mahout. 'He was escape from hunters. They want tusks. So he hide in courtyard of house of one old lady. *Hathi* knows she is good lady.'

The woman awoke in the morning to find the elephant lying in the courtyard of her house. He was bleeding badly from a wound to the leg. Cautiously, the woman approached the animal and, much to her surprise, found that the tusker allowed her to tend to his wound, which she cleaned and bandaged. Several days passed during which she nursed the animal back to health. Then, one night, the elephant rose and, finding that he could walk, limped off into the forest.

'So what happened to him?' I asked as we prepared to set off once again.

'The lady not see *hathi* again,' replied Churchill. 'The poacher mens, they were both kill-ed.'

'Who did it?'

Churchill's eyes bulged.

'Both mens were killed by one wild *hathi*,' he said, his voice suddenly mysterious. 'One man from village, he saw *hathi*. Said strange thing. Said *hathi* had big bandage wrapped around leg!'

Silence reigned over the Brahmaputra valley as the *kunkis* plodded on through the night. We crept through sleepy hamlets where the farm animals were dozing, through fields where water buffalo lay snoring, and past brick factories where the kiln fires had long died out and bonded labourers slept on charpoys, huddled in threadbare blankets.

Only the jackals watched our progress as we continued over fallow fields and down deserted lanes, passing under rows of betel-nut and mango trees. Churchill had grown quiet, and behind me the apprentices had fallen asleep, their heads bobbing up and down in time with Raja's gait. I too was beginning to feel drowsy and, despite the constant chafing against my legs, sleep threatened to overtake me as I listened to the hypnotic padding of Raja's feet.

Then suddenly, somewhere off in the darkness, the silence

was rent by a deafening explosion and a great flash of light. Raja reared up in alarm, trumpeting fiercely, his ears spread wide and alert. I leapt up in fright, my heart pumping so hard that it felt as if it might burst. The apprentices awoke with a start. Prat only just prevented himself from falling off. Up in the trees, birds took to the air amidst a great flapping of wings.

'What the hell was that?' I cried.

But before anyone could answer, another thunderous noise crashed through the valley, echoing off the hills to the north. In the distance, flashes pierced the night, accompanied by bursts of what sounded like machine-gun fire. Then, absolute silence. The *kunkis* came to a complete stop. Their trunks probed the air nervously. Their chests rumbled and their ears flapped like enormous butterfly wings. I could feel Raja's heart pounding beneath me. He blew down his trunk, making a sound like a didgeridoo. Jasmine, who stood just a few yards behind us, squealed in fright.

Churchill sat upright and alert, staring with anticipation into the darkness. Behind me, Prat switched on his torch, but the beam was feeble and shone for only a few yards, revealing nothing of interest except a bunch of feathers under a hedgerow where some creature had evidently met its fate. A couple of minutes passed. Nothing stirred. Even so, I readied myself for further explosions, gripping the sacking beneath me tightly. When the next bang came, it was even louder and I felt myself flinch involuntarily.

'What's going on?' I whispered to Churchill. 'It sounds like fighting. Where is Mr Choudhury?'

The mahout held up a hand to silence me as a succession of thuds, not unlike anti-aircraft fire, pierced the night. Next came the tremendous whooshing noise of two rockets streaking across the sky, trailing clouds of brilliant purple stars in their wake as they shot into a forest and exploded amidst the tree-tops. Bursts of incandescent greens and reds erupted into the air, showering the earth with white-hot sparks that fizzled out harmlessly. A flare shot upwards. It hung above us by its parachute, spitting and twisting back to earth, its brilliance illuminating patches of the land below with a heavenly light. In nearby fields, I spotted figures running helter-skelter. Men shouted to one another in panicked voices. Firecrackers danced at their feet.

'The farming mens, they shoot fireworks,' explained Churchill at last. 'Come. We must go, no?'

The mahout urged Raja towards the battle zone. Rockets and Indian bangers, appropriately known as 'bombs', continued to explode in the fields about half a mile ahead and to our left. As we drew closer, some of the farmers lit flaming torches which they waved like members of the Ku Klux Klan at a cross burning; others blew whistles and beat on drums. A bugle trumpeted a series of jarring notes.

We were just nearing the centre of the action when a powerful beam of light streaked across the fields like a prison searchlight. It illuminated trees, faces, huts, bushes and thick clumps of towering bamboo. Clouds of firework smoke hung in the air. At length, the beam settled on two dozen or so grey lumps clustered together in a trampled sugarcane field. In the darkness, frightened little silvery eyes reflected back the light.

'There! Over there! You see?' shouted Churchill, pointing to where the elephants stood together pulling up sugarcane. 'Wild *hathis*. Crop raiders. Look. There is thirty at least, no?'

The beam jerked up and down, and I caught glimpses of trunks, tails and ears. One or two babies cowered in between their mothers' legs. A defiant matriarch stood guard before them, paying only scant attention to the farmers' assault, while nearby rockets were exploding. Behind her, a pair of tusks glinted in the torchlight. I wondered if they belonged to the rogue.

Churchill reached for his walkie-talkie and, turning a couple of knobs, talked into the receiver. Mr Choudhury's voice came back, interrupted by the pops, whoops and whizzes of static. The mahout listened carefully, signed off and gave fresh instructions to the rest of his squad.

'What's going on? Has Mr Choudhury seen the rogue?'

'No. Rogue not here. Farming mens drinking and throwing rockets.'

'Why? What are they trying to accomplish?'

'*Hathi* eat crops. Farmer mens, they try to save crops but all too drunken and stupid. *Hathi* fight war.'

During harvest-time, battles between Assam's wild elephants and farmers rage nearly every night. The herds sneak on to the farmland under the cover of darkness and, given half a chance, will eat and eat until dawn. Often, the crafty elephants also break into the farmers' storehouses, tearing open gunny bags and smashing clay pots to get at harvested crops. All this can mean catastrophe for the locals. A wild elephant can eat up to eight hundred pounds per day. One or two elephants can wipe out a farmer in a single night; a herd can bankrupt an entire village within a matter of days.

But as Mole had pointed out back at the compound, the animals are hardly to blame. Their habitat – the forests and jungles – has been hacked down; their traditional migratory routes, which they have followed for millennia, have been blocked or destroyed by countless new houses, factories, drainage ditches, roads, railway lines and a thousand other human infringements upon the landscape. Assam's dwindling pachyderm population is confused, disorientated and angry. But most of all, they are just plain hungry.

The animals are especially clever and, over the years, have come to ignore the farmers' firecrackers and burning torches. If a ditch is dug to prevent them from entering a particular area, they topple trees, thereby creating their own bridges. If a farmer erects an electric fence, it is simply short-circuited by the elephants squirting water on the wires. However, superstition prevents Assam's farmers from killing elephants. Only occasionally will they take pot-shots in order to drive the animals away.

'Many people think that if they kill an elephant, they'll be cursed,' Mole told me later. 'They're very superstitious, man.'

Also, as Hindus, they believe in *ahimsa*, non-violence or compassion, towards animals.

'That's what's saved the elephant in India so far,' he said. 'No one wants the blood of an animal on their hands.'

Another ten minutes passed before we reached the Land Rover. It was parked on the far side of the village where the rogue had made his last kill. Mr Choudhury and Mole were standing nearby, surrounded by a group of angry locals, some of whom I recognized from the funeral. To a man, they were drunk, all shouting, raising their fists and pointing their fingers accusingly at our two friends. Apparently the local men felt that the Forest Department had not done enough to prevent the wild elephants from entering their fields and were demanding to know what action Mole planned to take.

The forest officer was trying to explain the situation, his hands held up before him in a vain effort to calm the crowd. But his voice was lost amidst the uproar, and he was being forced to take quick steps backwards.

The farmers inched their way towards him. Mr Choudhury and Mole looked frightened. In the past, mobs like these had lynched officials. But with the arrival of the squad, the farmers backed off, muttering uneasily to one another.

'You arrived just in time,' said Mr Choudhury to Churchill as he walked up to Raja.

He took hold of the elephant's right ear and then spotted me and frowned.

'What are you doing here?' he asked sternly. 'I told you to stay in the camp.'

I opened my mouth to explain, but before I could say a

word Churchill took over, talking rapidly in Assamese. Mr Choudhury shook his head.

'Well, I suppose you had better stay for now,' he said. 'The rogue is not here so there is no apparent danger, but I will talk to you later.'

I didn't like the sound of that, but Churchill gave me a reassuring wink.

'No worry, Tar-win. All okay, no?'

Mole, Mr Choudhury and Churchill huddled together to plan how best to tackle the herd, while I popped behind a bush for a pee. In the darkness, I nearly bumped into Rudra.

'No chicks here,' he said, disappointed. 'Village girls ugly. You want betel-nut?' he continued, dipping into his tin and taking out a chunk.

'Uh, no thanks,' I replied. 'Maybe later.'

'Yes, later. Come to Land Rover. I have picture of Raveena Tandon. Very big mangoes!'

As I returned to the squad, one of the farmers walked up to Raja, gaping up at him like a curious child at the zoo. Timidly, the other locals gathered in a semicircle behind him. Then, to my amazement, they all knelt before the *kunki* and began to pray, imploring the elephant to stop the wild herd from eating their crops.

The elephant watched his devotees disdainfully, like some haughty monarch. As they chanted in unison, he lifted his trunk in salute, making a noise that started off as a squeal and ended as a roar. I was told later that this was how Raja behaved when he was annoyed or scared. However, the farmers took his action as a favourable sign and prayed even harder. Two or three of them prostrated themselves on the ground; several of them began to cry, raising their hands to heaven; while one madman shouted hysterically and pulled at his hair, his eyeballs rolling back in their sockets.

The farmers carried on like this for nearly ten minutes until Churchill, who was beginning to grow thoroughly irritated, ordered them to leave his elephant alone. Reluctantly, they picked themselves up off the ground and backed away, gathering in a group nearby to knock back bottles of rice wine and smoke cheroots.

'These men are not very intelligent,' said Mr Choudhury with masterful understatement.

It was time for the elephant squad to go into action. Churchill and I got on board Raja, and Chander mounted Jasmine, while Mr Choudhury, Mole, the apprentices and the forest guards remained on foot. The aim of Operation *Hathi*, as Mr Choudhury called it, was to drive the herd into the rain forest at the foot of the hills to the north-west. We set off from the east, making sure the wind was behind us.

'The wild ones are afraid of *kunkis* because they're used to capture wild calves. The herds have come to recognize the *kunkis*' smell. They know it is a threat,' explained Mr Choudhury, as he walked beside Raja. 'It usually drives them away.'

Skirting the edge of the fields to avoid trampling any crops, we soon covered the distance that separated the farmers' village from the area where the wild elephants had last been spotted. With military precision, the squad fanned out in a line stretching two hundred yards across. The *kunkis* remained in the middle, while Mr Choudhury walked a few yards ahead of us.

All of us remained quiet. Lamps were extinguished and torches switched off. In the darkness, I caught glimpses of figures walking on either side of me, their faces impossible to make out. A twig snapped to my right; keys jingled nearby; to my left, someone tripped, stumbled and cursed. My eyes strained, trying to make out several shapes up ahead. There was something directly in front of us that looked as if it might be an elephant. It was large, grey and seemed to have a trunk.

Perhaps it was the rogue, I thought for one dreadful moment. As we drew closer, I could see that it was a pump-house. What I had mistaken for a proboscis was in fact a thick hose-pipe.

Just then, without any warning, Mr Choudhury called out a single word in Assamese. Hearing it, Raja came to an abrupt halt; to my left, Jasmine did the same. Waiting with anticipation, the elephant squad stood stock still. No one made a sound. I sat up straight, alert as a guard dog. Dead ahead, something was moving in the fields.

Mr Choudhury let out a loud bark. This was the prearranged signal for everyone to make as much noise as they could. All at once, the apprentices began to blow hard on plastic whistles; Mr Choudhury rang a hand-bell with a resonating clang; the guards beat on cooking pots, clashing them together like cymbals. Churchill blew on a kazoo, Mole rattled a tambourine and I squeezed on a bicycle horn. Prat shook a rotating rattle made of tin cans with pebbles inside. And everyone shrieked and hollered, sounding like a bunch of football fans urging on their team.

Mr Choudhury barked a second time, signalling us to switch on our torches. A dozen or so beams criss-crossed the terrain, bobbing up and down as they searched for the herd. At the same time, we moved forward, crossing fields where sugarcane lay trampled underfoot, the earth pitted with elephantine footprints. We passed broken dykes, splintered bamboo fences and an uprooted telegraph pole that hung half suspended in the air.

Soon, we spotted the herd. They were about a hundred and fifty yards away, huddled together in front of a wall of sugarcane, dazzled and frightened, their trunks raised like periscopes as they tested the air for foreign scents. In their midst stood a tusker with magnificent incisors crossed over one another like out-of-shape scissors. His head was covered in a mass of bushy hair. Enraged, he paced up and down, picking up clods of earth with his trunk and tossing them over his shoulder. Behind him, I spotted a scrawny female with a scarred trunk. Frightened calves clung to their mothers' legs, hiding behind the grey pillars. Those elephants still holding lengths of sugarcane in their trunks now dropped them to the ground like children caught stealing from a sweet-shop. Nervous eyes blinked in the light. Ears bristled. Tails swished.

The matriarch strode out in front of the herd to confront us. She was not the largest animal amongst them, but it was easy to see why she was the dominant female. Strong and determined, she was, judging by her defiant stance and the scars on her trunk, also tremendously brave. For a moment, she seemed prepared to take on Raja and Jasmine. But as we drew closer – still making a clamour to rival a school playground during break-time – the matriarch's trunk shot out erect and she sounded the elephantine equivalent of the retreat.

All at once, the herd turned and stampeded in the opposite direction, fleeing blindly towards the rain forest. Tails and hind legs, backsides and flapping ears disappeared in a cloud of dust. Sugarcane was trampled underfoot as panicked trumpeting filled the air. Calves ran as fast as their short legs could carry them, trying desperately to keep up with their mothers. Powerful feet thundered through the farmers' livelihood, clearing a path twenty feet wide.

'Charge! Charge!' yelled Churchill, working the back of Raja's ears with his feet to make the *kunki* move faster.

'Make sure they don't double back!' shouted Mr Choudhury.

The elephant squad broke into a run, the forest guards uttering manic screams as if they were going into battle. Torch beams flew about like lasers in a discotheque. Raja's shoulder blades pumped up and down, tossing me from side to side. Sugarcane smacked into me and I had to grip hard with my legs and hold on tight to the saddle to stop myself from being swept off the elephant.

Raja soon outpaced the rest of the squad, leaving them far

behind. We emerged from the fields, crashed through a fence, crossed a lane and found ourselves by a wide, shallow stream. There, Churchill reined in his elephant, halting by the water's edge. The mahout turned on his torch and directed it at the fast-flowing water.

It wasn't difficult to locate the place where the elephants had crossed, for the stream was still murky with sediment. The torch beam followed their path, soon finding the far bank where the rain forest began. I could make out the elephants' footprints in the mud on the other side.

Of the herd, there was not a sign. They had disappeared inside the fortress of trees and foliage that rose up before us. Here, in one of the last remaining stretches of forest or jungle in Assam, they would be left unmolested, at least for the time being.

But as we got down from Raja to stretch our legs, I wondered how long this last bastion would remain intact before the farmers invaded it with their axes, saws and ploughs, leaving the elephants with nowhere else to run.

The same locals, who just an hour earlier had been threatening to lynch Mole and Mr Choudhury, soon came running up behind us, whooping with excitement. With cheers of joy, they lit more firecrackers and congratulated the elephant squad, whom they treated like conquering heroes. Bottles of home-made booze were produced and the farmers did a jig in front of Raja and Jasmine, trying to persuade the mahouts and their assistants to join in. But despite their apparent 'victory', the elephant squad were not in a celebratory mood. If anything, they seemed subdued.

'We're not here to help these people,' said Mr Choudhury. 'They're causing these problems by cutting down the jungle. We try to keep the elephants out of the fields for their own protection. That is all.'

Rather than join in the villagers' celebrations, we headed back to the village where we set up camp for the night, pitching our tents around a blazing log fire. The apprentices and forest guards took turns to keep watch in case the rogue should suddenly appear. However, the night passed without incident. It was only the next morning, at around seven, that we learned that an elephant had raided another settlement several miles to the east. No one had been killed, although the description of the culprit matched that of the wanted elephant.

Shortly after hearing this news, we packed up our gear and set off once again, hoping to pick up his trail. According to a local informant, the rogue had been spotted in a tea estate only a few hours earlier. There was every chance of our catching him – if only we could reach the place quickly enough.

4

Bruiser Harry

'To the elephant, our scrap of consciousness may seem as inconsequential as a space-invader blip.'

Heathcote Williams, *Sacred Elephant*

'A BUGGER OF an elephant once broke into the medical centre, donchya-know,' Harry Baker told me, as we sat on the veranda of his sprawling bungalow. 'Rather an unruly chap. Pulled down the building before he got at what he was after – or at least what he thought he was after ...'

My host was the last British tea-planter left in Assam as well as the manager of the tea estate where the rogue had been spotted. Mr Choudhury and I had gone to his office that morning to seek his permission to pursue the elephant across his land. Harry had been happy to oblige and allowed us to set up camp on the edge of his gardens. He had also invited me up to the house for lunch, so, with Mr Choudhury's permission, I had slipped away for an hour or so.

Harry, or 'Bruiser' as he was known, had a handlebar moustache and a lazy eye. Periodically, with a flourish like a magician on stage, he would pull a polka-dot handkerchief from his trouser pocket and blow into it until his bulbous nose turned red. His complexion was ruddy, his hair a dignified silver, and his chins and round tummy betrayed a weakness for sherry trifle.

It was obvious that this old Harrovian was someone who

enjoyed centre stage. He was also a mine of stories about life on the North-East Frontier. I felt as if I had struck a rich vein, even if Harry's anecdotes were punctuated by numerous red herrings.

'You see elephants love salt,' he continued. 'And this old boy, a large tusker as I remember, got a whiff of some inside the medical centre – only the funny thing was that it wasn't salt at all. It was a bag of … whatcher-ma-call-it.'

He looked at me quizzically as if I might know what he was talking about.

'Whatcher-ma-call-it?' I asked.

Harry puckered up his lips and nursed his chin.

'Damn memory's gone,' he lamented. 'Never been the same since I fell off Gregory.'

'Gregory?'

'Ma horse. Used to ride him around the estate every day. Can't now, though, you know. Arthritis. Damn shame.'

He called out to his wife who had gone inside to fish out the family albums.

'Marj,' he bellowed, 'what the deuce do you call that stuff you take when you're all bunged up?'

'All bunged up, dear?'

'Yes, you know, when you can't *go*.'

'Can't *go*?'

'When you're stopped up like a bottle of bubbly.'

'Are you referring to laxatives, dear?' answered Marj cheerily.

'Yes, that's the ticket,' concluded Harry. 'Laxatives. The fella ate the lot – a large sackful.'

'So what happened to him?'

'Well, that twit of a doctor chappy was absolutely convinced the tusker would die. What was his name, now? Adams or Arkwright, or was it Williams … ? Anyway, where was I?'

'The elephant,' I prompted.

'Oh yes. Well, of course, all this did the beast the world of good. Cleaned out his stomach in a jiffy. Only problem was, he emptied it all over ma tea bushes. It was like having one of those mechanical fertilizers walking around. Damn shame.'

Harry rang a hand-bell that lay on the table and, in the twinkling of an eye, a servant wearing a gleaming white uniform appeared at the far end of the veranda. The soles of his shoes clipped their way across the flagstone floor as he approached the antique cane furniture in which we sat. Like a soldier on drill, he came to attention, his chin as rigid as his starched collar and cuffs. My host looked down at his watch which he kept on 'garden time', an hour behind Indian Standard Time.

'Time for my elevenses, Ravi. One whisky and soda if you please.'

It was Sunday which, Harry pointed out as his 'man' marched off to fetch the sahib's drink, was the one day of the week when my host had a 'tipple' before lunch.

'Haven't spent a day sick in bed in forty years, apart from the odd bout of malaria, of course. Whisky's the answer to a healthy life, if you ask me.'

The servant soon returned carrying a crystal tumbler on a silver tray, together with a soda siphon.

Harry fixed himself a drink.

'Sure you won't join me?'

'I can't,' I explained. 'I made a promise to Mr Choudhury to keep off the sauce.'

'Pity. Last of the foreign stuff.'

Harry raised his glass.

'Well, cheers.'

Half a century after India gained independence, there was something surreal about running into a British couple carrying on as if the Raj was still alive and well. I knew that some colonials had stayed behind after 1947, but I had never imagined that, fifty years on, any of them would be left, especially in such a remote part of the country. However, Harry had been born in Assam and, although he spent his formative years at Harrow, he regarded the North-East Frontier as his home. His polo-playing chums might be long gone, but he was determined to live out his years in his adopted land.

'Love the place and the people. Could never leave,' he told me. 'Besides, what the deuce would one do in Blighty? Sit in some two-up-two-down? Not me!'

True to character, Harry still lived in the manner to which he had always been accustomed. His bungalow was set amidst a sea of perfect lawns interspersed with rose beds, a croquet lawn and an aviary full of green parrots. He also maintained a rifle range where he shot clay pigeons every morning, and there was a summerhouse complete with teak deck-chairs and an overhead wicker fan which used to be operated by a *punkah-wallah*.

A few hundred yards down the pebbled driveway lay the estate's private club which boasted its own golf-course, squash court and library. In its heyday, the white families living in the district had frequented it.

'We used to have grand parties. Dinner-jackets, ball-gowns – the works. Even had our own track where we raced ponies. Had a few winners m'self,' reminisced Harry fondly.

Harry's wife of forty years, Marjorie, emerged from the bungalow carrying a tower of photo albums frayed with age. She had spent most of her life in the tropics but was still as pale as the day she had left her native Hastings in 1936. Nevertheless, behind the fragility there lay a tremendous amount of strength and resolution. Marjorie had survived malaria more times than she could remember, had defied the Chinese when they invaded Assam in 1961 by remaining in her home, and had escaped from kidnappers when they seized her in 1988.

She had been brought to Assam as a child and had only left a few times to visit Europe.

'In the twilight of the Empire, we lived charmed lives,' she explained. 'It was a lovely, lovely life, especially for a young girl like me. There was no shortage of romance as there were lots of young men to choose from and we got the pick of the crop.'

Planters and their families enjoyed busy social lives and plenty of sport and, despite living in one of the most isolated patches of the Empire, they never wanted for luxuries. Every month, a flight from Calcutta would arrive at the estate's private airstrip laden with goods imported from the best shops in Knightsbridge and Piccadilly.

'You name it, we could get it,' Marjorie said as she showed me a catalogue dated 1938 which advertised everything from pith helmets and gramophones to pewter beer tankards, 'anti-obesity preparations', anchors, top hats, Knights Templar outfits, and ladies' promenade shoes – not to mention Union Jacks and galvanized steel boats, the latter described as 'SPLENDID FOR DUCK SHOOTING'. There was even a taxidermist's advertisement that listed prices for the stuffing of elephants, rhinos and tigers.

When the planters went on leave, they travelled on luxurious ocean-liners and stayed in five-star hotels. Their children were educated at the best private schools England had to offer. And upon retirement, managers and their wives could look forward to the security of a generous pension.

'Wasn't always like that, of course,' interjected Harry as he helped himself to his second whisky and soda. 'Not for the original fellas.'

Harry's great-grandfather was amongst the first British pioneers to travel to Assam. He did so in the 1850s, shortly after wild tea was discovered growing in the valley, when the British administration encouraged adventurers to establish plantations in this obscure stretch of rain forest inhabited by hostile tribes.* In what amounted to a 'Tea Rush', thousands of young men set off for the new frontier, many of them with only a few pounds in their pockets, determined to make their fortunes.

It took these pioneers ten weeks to travel from Calcutta by paddle-steamer up the Brahmaputra, a notoriously difficult river to navigate thanks to its shifting sandbanks and raging monsoon floodwaters. During the journey, there was little to do but shoot crocodiles on the banks of the river. Upon their arrival in the promised land, they found conditions hostile and dangerous. The valley was infested with ferocious animals, most of the land was flooded for three months of the year, clean water was scarce and disease rife. And since there was little stone available for building, the planters had to live in flimsy bamboo huts while they worked to cultivate their precious tea from dawn to dusk.

Planters were isolated for months and sometimes years on end. Visits from other Europeans – even fellow-planters – were rare and, in their loneliness, many turned to drink and some to suicide.

'Quite a number topped themselves,' said Harry, as Marjorie headed back into the bungalow to check on lunch. 'It was the isolation that did it, of course. That and the lack of fillies. In those days, a white woman was as scarce as a white elephant.'

Nevertheless, like Harry's great-grandfather some did survive and they gradually pushed back the rain forest and drained the swamps. Over the years, they turned Assam into the largest tea-producing region in the world.

'Nowadays the life of a manager is comfortable, of course,'

---

* Tea was discovered in Assam in 1823 by C. A. Bruce. Various histories give the impression that it was not used by the local tribes because they never cultivated it. In fact, many of them had used tea for centuries, primarily as a medicine for treating colds and fevers.

said Harry. 'But it's still a hard grind. Can't take your eye off the ball, not for a moment.'

Harry, who was sixty-eight, spoke fluent Assamese and Bengali. He still rose at five and worked at least ten hours a day, six days a week. Much of his time was spent managing the five thousand employees who lived in various villages on the estate. His main interest, however, was the tea itself. He prided himself on its quality and, with the aid of his highly sensitized taste-buds, he kept a careful check on each new batch. Every few hours, he would prepare a brew from the various strains of leaves growing in his gardens. Much like a wine taster, he would suck the liquid into his mouth, swill it around and then spit it into a spittoon.

'Won a few awards in my time,' he said proudly, before we went in for lunch. 'Tea's my life. Always has been. Imagine I'll be buried in the gardens. Nothing fancy.'

The bungalow, which boasted seven bedrooms, was decorated like a cosy Sussex cottage and oozed British gentility and an old-world tranquillity. The lavender-coloured curtains matched the furniture, which was upholstered in Warner fabrics brought from Chelsea. Porcelain figures of Peter Rabbit and friends stood on the mantelpiece above the wide fireplace. On the far wall hung a portrait of Harry's great-grandfather who had started out life as a lowly foot soldier in the Indian Army and who eventually made his fortune in the tea business.

The only reminders that we were in India were the geckos on the walls, the fans whirring above our heads, the smell of spices emanating from the kitchen and the sound of a Hindi news programme coming from a television playing some-where in the bungalow.

'Did you know that bungalow's a Hindi word,' said Harry, as we moved into the dining-room. 'In fact, there are dozens

of Indian words in English. Been a bit of a hobby of mine collecting 'em. Kedgeree's another one. And Blighty, of course,
is a corruption of *bilayati*, which means foreign or European.
British troops during the Great War started using it, and soon
it came to be known as England. Caught on after that.'

We ate at a polished mahogany table laid with silver. A
number of mounted leopard and bear heads stared down at us
from the walls. Servants bearing platters served various north
Indian curries followed by a selection of British desserts.

'I had the cook trained in Calcutta at the Oberoi Hotel,'
said my host when I praised the food. 'They soon whipped
him into shape.'

Harry's last cook had been involved in Marjorie's kidnapping and was currently serving ten years in a prison not far
from Guwahati. He had acted as the inside man for a group
of Naga dacoits, whom he informed about the comings and
goings of the household.

'They abducted me one Thursday when Bruiser was out
for his bridge night,' said Marjorie. 'It wasn't very nice being
tied up and shoved into the back of a jeep.'

'What did they do with you?' I asked.

'Oh, they took me up into the hills. Fortunately, they didn't
hurt me. They were just young bullies. All they wanted was
some money from Bruiser. They're always kidnapping people.
These so-called freedom-fighters hold the whole tea industry
to ransom.'

I read later that all the big-name tea companies have paid
tens of millions of pounds in protection money to the various
insurgency groups such as ULFA, who are estimated to hold
large fortunes in Bangladeshi bank accounts. The militants are
a ruthless bunch, armed with machine guns and bombs, and
tea-estate managers are, on the whole, powerless to protect
themselves. Those who have tried standing up to them have
been dealt with harshly.

'You see, Bruiser refused to pay his dues, so that's why they took me,' continued Marjorie, as the servants cleared the table and laid it for tea. 'In the end, he had to raise thousands of pounds and hand them over. Poor old Bruiser. What he didn't know at the time was that I had already escaped.'

'How did you do that?'

'When the guards were asleep, I slipped my ropes off and got away. After that, I walked down from the hills and was back at home in time for breakfast,' said Marjorie.

Just then, a pot of tea was carried in and Harry helped me to a cup. I took a sip. It tasted smooth and mellow, without a hint of acidity.

Harry took his without milk.

'Don't need it. Not like the rubbish you get off the shelf in Blighty, all mixed in with old and inferior leaves,' scoffed Harry. 'This is the real thing.'

Harry claimed to have developed the secret of producing the perfect cuppa. When and how you added boiling water was academic, he insisted. It was all a question of blending together just the right selection of leaves. Those picked from his garden's southern, steeper slopes produced a mellow flavour, while leaves from the north-facing slopes lent a tangy taste, which he added for zing.

'The riff-raff say Darjeeling's the best, but that's poppy-cock.'

He took a sip and swilled it around in his mouth before swallowing.

'Golly,' he exclaimed, reaching for his third plateful of sherry trifle, 'that really is a damn nice cup of tea, donchya-know.'

With his riding days over and Gregory put out to pasture, Harry relied on India's version of the Jeep, the Maruti Gypsy, to move around his gardens. As he drove at a leisurely pace, giving me the grand tour of his estate, we passed through thousands of acres of tea bushes, a regimented ocean of emerald green. Dark-skinned women wearing conical straw hats and dressed in bright reds, pinks and yellows, stood picking the new flush, singing as they worked.

In the middle of the gardens stood the factory. Harry was critical of many production methods and had not updated his plant for nearly thirty years. Inside, the machinery was archaic, the air full of the chug of bolts and pistons and the hiss of bellows and pumps. Harry claimed his old techniques, taught to him by his father, still produced the best flavours and he was one of the few to continue packing his product in wooden tea-chests.

From the factory, Harry drove to the other side of the estate, where the bushes stretched towards the foothills to the north. All the while, we kept an eye out for the rogue elephant who was thought to be hiding somewhere on the estate. Harry turned down a lane and pulled up next to a footpath.

'Want to show you something,' he said.

He opened the door and his Dalmatian, Roger, raced off along the footpath. We followed, my host waddling like a goose, cane in hand. Another group of women workers filed along the path, their baskets brimming with leaves. They all averted their eyes as we approached and giggled shyly amongst themselves.

'Dainty things but damn hard workers,' commented Harry. 'Don't know what one would do without 'em.'

Half a mile on, he led me in amongst the tea bushes and came to a halt next to an old grave marked only by a flat granite stone.

'Thought this might interest you. Bit of a story behind it.'

I searched for a name but was unable to find one. Who did it belong to?

'I call it "The Grave of the Unknown Planter",' said Harry. 'Father told me the resident was a British fella who died after eating a wild duck. Must have been a bit off.'

Harry took off his panama hat and wiped the sweat from his brow.

'Story goes he wasn't discovered for at least a week after he'd kicked the bucket. No one knew who the devil he was, so they buried him where he dropped. Rotten luck.'

We stood there for a few moments in silence. I wondered about the occupant of the grave. More than likely, he had been my age and had travelled all the way from England and endured untold hardships and dangers only to die alone and forgotten.

'Poor bugger,' I said out loud.

'Yes, quite,' agreed Harry. 'Suppose we should say a prayer for him, really. Us being fellow-countrymen and all that.'

'Yes, I suppose we should,' I said.

Harry placed his hat over his heart and lowered his head, clearing his throat.

'Um. Yes, well. Lord, we humbly beseech you to care for the soul of this fella. Hum. Now and for ever more. The power and the glory. Um ... Aaa-men.'

'Amen,' I echoed.

Harry put his hat back on.

'Never been very religious. Couldn't think of anything else to say,' he explained.

'It's the thought that counts,' I said.

'Yes, quite,' replied Harry.

And we turned and headed back to the Maruti Gypsy, Roger leading the way.

It was early afternoon by the time Harry dropped me back at the camp.

'Better get home,' he said, although he was obviously tempted to stay. 'Otherwise the wife'll give me a bollocking.'

Wishing me 'God speed', the old boy turned the vehicle and headed off towards his home, waving his panama hat out of the window. I watched him for a while until he disappeared from view.

The elephant squad was camped on the bank of a river near the edge of the tea gardens. Raja and Jasmine, who stood face to face, their trunks curled around one another like a courting couple, were chained to a tree. The apprentices were playing cards near a smouldering log fire. Churchill sat on the ground in the lotus position, carving a piece of wood with his knife and listening to the BBC World Service on his short-wave radio. 'Tarwin, you take long time, no? Waiting for you,' he scolded, jumping up.

'Sorry. I was having lunch with a tea planter.'

'Yes, I know. You're eating good grub?' he asked.

Noticing the pot of sticky black dhal spluttering like crude oil on top of the fire, which had, no doubt, been the mahout's lunch, I thought it tactful to make my meal sound as unappetizing as possible.

'Terrible English food,' I spat. 'Disgusting.'

'Ah yes,' replied Churchill. 'English peoples eat very bad grub, no? Junk food. Same as Naga peoples. They eat all things. Dogs, cats, even snakes.'

'That's not junk food,' I protested. 'And besides, we don't eat cats or dogs. Anyway,' I added, trying to change the subject, 'what news of the elephant?'

'No news. Shikari and Mole searching,' explained the mahout. Apparently the rogue had been spotted entering the tea gardens that morning but had since disappeared.

'How does an elephant simply vanish?' I asked.

The mahout shrugged his shoulders. 'Clever *hathi*' was his explanation.

For now, it seemed, there was nothing to do but wait for the others to return. When they did, I would have to face Mr Choudhury, who had yet to deal with my disobedience the night before. I was worried that he might confine me to Mole's headquarters.

'Now time for wash,' announced Churchill suddenly.

'But I've already had a shower,' I protested, explaining that I had made use of Harry and Marjorie's bathroom after lunch.

'Not you. Washing *hathi*, no?'

'Where?' I asked.

'In river. Come.'

The mahout clapped his hands and the rest of the squad dropped their cards and set to work, quickly unfastening the *kunkis*' chains and leading the animals down to the water's edge. Jasmine trumpeted with glee as she waded in and keeled over on her side, half-disappearing into the murky eddies and sending a tidal wave surging towards the far bank. Raja lumbered in after her, slowly easing himself down into the water until his belly formed an island mid-stream, the current churning against the arch of his great spine.

As Churchill explained, elephants are at their most vulnerable when they are lying down and it was a testimony to the unreserved trust that Raja and Jasmine placed in their human keepers that they so willingly presented themselves for their ablutions. For the mahouts, and especially the apprentices, washing the animals was the most important part of their routine. It was when they and the animals were at their most intimate, a daily ritual that helped strengthen the bond between them. But it was also just good plain fun for humans and elephants alike.

'Roll up jeans,' instructed Churchill, who was busy pulling up handfuls of dry grass from the bank which he twisted into something resembling a loofah. This he soaked in water and then he scrubbed Raja's side, rubbing the rough folds of skin and getting into every nook and cranny.

'Insects, they living on *hathi*. Cause problems, no?'

'Don't you use soap?' I asked. 'It would make them smell nicer.'

'No soap. *Hathi* not like. Here, you try.'

The mahout handed me the grass and I started on one of

Raja's hind legs. When I had finished, Churchill barked an order and the *kunki* raised his limb, enabling me to scrub underneath. The elephant's ears floated on the surface like two giant water-lilies, his trunk coiling and slithering through the water, the tip blowing bubbles and making gurgling noises like a drain.

Next, Raja was ordered to sit up and squat on his knees so we could get at his toenails. These we scoured with handfuls of pebbles to get rid of parasites and general muck. Soon, the *kunki* had been washed from top to toe, his dark skin glistening in the late afternoon sun.

'Now my turn,' said Churchill.

Stripping down to his underwear, the mahout dipped into the water and then proceeded to lather himself in suds. When he'd finished, he ordered Raja to suck up trunkfuls of water which the *kunki* sprayed over the mahout, rinsing off the soap in short, sharp bursts.

'Like shower, no?' shouted the mahout as Raja rinsed his hair for him. '*Hathi* is best aneemal!'

I ran back to the camp to fetch my camera. Along the way, I passed a stranger heading towards the river. He looked Nepalese or perhaps Tibetan and was wearing black army boots and fatigues. By the time I returned, the others were gathering round him, each of them taking turns to give him a hug.

'Tarwin, meet my best, best, *best* friend. This is CP. He is Gurkha. Very danger man, no?' joked Churchill.

CP, who had smooth yellow skin and high cheekbones, looked like a harmless, five-foot-tall version of a native American minus the war paint. I offered him my hand.

'Hello. Pleased to meet you. Do you speak English?' I asked.

''Course I do,' he said, 'what d'ya fink I am?'

I blinked, not sure whether I could believe my ears.

'Where are you from?' I asked incredulously.

'Darjeeling's 'ome,' he replied.

'But your accent. It's …'

'… British Army. Twenty-two years. Plus I lived in the UK for six years,' he said, shaking my hand. 'This lot call me CP, but I prefer Badger, my nickname in the forces.'

Badger had been recruited as a teenager and trained in the UK. He was an expert in jungle warfare and had served in the Falklands, the Gulf and later in Hong Kong, where he patrolled the border with China, preventing illegal immigrants from crossing into the former colony. Sadly, during the hand-over of the colony to China, the Gurkha was 'retired' along with most of his comrades. For six months afterwards, he worked as a bodyguard for a Chinese 'businessman' who ran various dubious enterprises. But thanks to his short stature and innocent appearance, no one took the Gurkha seriously.

'Whenever there was trouble, everyone would try to take me on,' explained Badger, who was a black belt in aikido and had trained with the Japanese riot police. 'A bodyguard is supposed to stop fights from 'appenin', not encourage 'em, so it didn't work out – even though I put a few people in 'ospital.'

After that, the veteran returned to the UK, but he found the going hard and, only recently, had returned to Darjeeling armed with just his *kukri*, the traditional curved knife carried by all Gurkha men, and his British pension.

'The pension's worth bugger all,' said Badger as we sat around the campfire, drying off.

The Gurkhas, he claimed, were the most effective and loyal foot soldiers in the world and had won a record number of Victoria Crosses. Yet despite this, they weren't treated as equals.

'We take their bullets and this is 'ow they repay us,' complained Badger bitterly.

Now, the former soldier was trying to start a new life and had come to see Churchill, a childhood friend, to ask for help and advice.

'I don't know about nothin' more than fightin',' he said. 'I've 'ad plenty of offers to join terrorist groups, but I don't want nothin' to do with 'em.'

As we had tea, Churchill told him about the rogue. Could he help track the elephant?

'If 'e's 'ere, I'll find 'im,' said the Gurkha, as he sharpened his *kukri*. 'He can't 'ave gone too far, now can 'e?'

We spent the rest of the afternoon trying to pick up the rogue's trail, but our best efforts were hampered by what Badger called 'local unintelligence'. Each time we stopped to ask someone whether they had seen the elephant, we were given conflicting information. Some people claimed to have seen him heading south, others north. A good few swore they had seen him leaving the gardens altogether, while one travelling *sadhu*, or holy man, tried to convince us that the elephant had the power to render himself invisible. The solution, he said, was to buy one of his charms which would enable us to see the enchanted animal.

By nightfall, neither our party nor Mr Choudhury's had come across his tracks and, when we all met back at the camp soon after seven, it was a dejected group that sat around the campfire eating their mandatory plates of rice, dhal and raw onions. Even Mole seemed downcast.

'What am I going to tell the local people?' he asked me. 'If the rogue kills again, it's going to be on my head. We've got to find him and we've got to find him fast, man.'

Only Mr Choudhury was still confident of success. Indeed, for someone who had spent the day chasing shadows, he seemed remarkably positive and upbeat. After returning to the camp, he had washed in the stream and put on a clean shirt and a pair of worn jeans. For the first time since I had met him, he had taken off his glasses. Without them, he squinted which made him appear less stern.

'He will come out in the open soon, it's only a question of time,' he said.

Rather than wait until dawn to recommence our search, however, Mr Choudhury proposed setting up posts at several strategic spots along routes the elephant had used during recent raids. To do this, he divided up the squad and the forest guards into four teams, each equipped with torches and a walkie-talkie. Soon after ten o'clock they were sent off in various directions. Clearly still angry with me for having ignored his orders the night before, the hunter also gave me a severe reprimand. For a moment, I thought I would be confined to camp, but he was obviously in a forgiving mood.

'You can come with me, Tarquin. I want to keep a close eye on you. You're not to sneak off with Churchill again.'

Privately, I was delighted. Spending time with the hunter was exactly what I wanted. Only then would I gain his confidence and only then would I be sure of being on hand when he confronted the elephant.

Mr Choudhury, Mole, Rudra and I set off in the Land Rover. Three miles to the north, Rudra cut across fallow fields before stopping below a *masang*, a wooden platform built twenty feet up in a tree. This rickety structure was used as a lookout post by farmers anxious to keep elephants away from their crops. Mr Choudhury had chosen this particular *masang* because it enjoyed a commanding position over the land that lay between the rain forest up ahead and the village behind. It was also equipped with a bell, which could be rung to alert the villagers.

Only a week earlier, the *masang*'s owner, a young Bangladeshi farmer called Latif, had had cause to ring the bell for all he was worth when he spotted the rogue coming across the fields. Hearing the alarm, all the families fled to the safety of a brick building. Only one person was caught out in the open, the local drunk, who was too far gone to register the impending danger.

Latif, who appeared still to be suffering from shock, had watched from his *masang* as the elephant trampled the drunkard to death. As the farmer described what had happened, Mr Choudhury and Mole listened with expressions of disgust and sheer disbelief.

'What did he say?' I asked, prodding the forest officer in the arm.

Mole ignored me and proceeded to cross-examine Latif. I pestered him again. 'What did he say?'

'Impossible!' said the forest officer.

'What's impossible?'

'No elephant does that, man.'

'No elephant does what?'

Mr Choudhury explained: 'This man says he saw the elephant tear out the man's intestines with his tusks and then eat them.'

It was my turn to grimace.

'That's disgusting!' I said.

'That's what I've been saying. But he swears he saw it happen,' said Mole. 'He swears it, man!'

I asked Mr Choudhury what he thought.

'I've heard tales of elephants doing this kind of thing before,' he replied. 'It's strange that this elephant always seems to attack drunken men. But most probably this man's imagination has got the better of him.'

Frowning, Mr Choudhury put his hands in his pockets and turned away.

It was a bitterly cold, dark night. The only light for miles around came from the blinking beacon of a television tower high up on the faraway hills. Giant bats swooped all around us, flapping their elastic wings as we sat on the edge of the *masang*. Ahead, the landscape was a patchwork of faint shadows cast by billowing clouds as they passed in front of the moon. Off in the distance, I could hear the eerie chanting of mantras coming from a Hindu temple.

Soon after midnight, the wind changed direction and began to blow from behind us. This was exactly what Mr Choudhury had hoped for. Before climbing up on to the *masang*, he had placed a barrel of locally made rice wine at the bottom of the tree in the hope that the wind would carry the smell into the rain forest and draw out his quarry.

Should this bait prove effective, Mr Choudhury was ready. His Magnum rifle, which was loaded, lay across his lap. Rudra sat in the Land Rover, ready to flick on the headlights and two specially mounted searchlights screwed on to the bonnet at a moment's notice. I didn't envy him his exposed position.

'Shooting an elephant is a difficult undertaking at the best of times, but at night it is practically suicidal,' explained Mr Choudhury. 'To kill an elephant you must be close. You have to bring him down in one shot. So you need an extremely powerful rifle and you must aim for the heart or for the brain. That is the only way to stop him.'

Any mistake might cause the tusker to stampede into the neighbouring village where he would cause havoc.

'He could kill many people and I would be blamed,' he added.

There was also the hunter's own safety to consider. In order to shoot the elephant, he would have to be standing or kneeling on the ground and, as a result, risked being trampled. *Elephant Gold* and Charles's diaries were full of tales of hunters who had only managed to wound charging elephants and who had died as a result. Mr Choudhury had no intention of becoming another fatal statistic.

'Unless I can get a clear shot, I will not shoot at him. I will fire over his head to frighten him away. Then I will track him until first light,' said the hunter. 'This will also go down better with the farmers. They believe bad elephants come back as ghosts. If I shoot the rogue here, they will say that he is haunting their fields and homes, and they will want compensation. Some of them might even lynch us.'

While we waited, I asked to see the hunter's rifle. I had always imagined that a Magnum was a handgun, like the one used by Dirty Harry which he claimed would 'blow your head clean off your shoulders'.

'A Magnum is a type of handgun and rifle,' explained Mr Choudhury. 'Mine is made by Winchester. It's a .458, one of the most powerful rifles available.'

'What about bullets? Do you use dum-dums?' I asked, remembering that they had been invented by the British in Calcutta.

He shook his head. 'Don't be ridiculous. They're banned by the Geneva Convention. I use Remington high-speed bullets with a 500 grain full metal jacket.'

He showed me one. It was three and half inches long and made of brass. When fired, it would travel at a velocity of 2,130 feet per second.

Next he told me about the sights.

'I don't use telescopics for shooting elephants because you have to get up close and they're too powerful. I rely on the mounted sights on the rifle. They've never failed me.'

The conversation drifted away from elephants and I began to ask Mr Choudhury about his personal life. Did he have a family?

'I've been married nearly twenty years,' he whispered, pausing to listen for any movement up ahead. 'It was an arranged marriage, but from the start I loved my wife and she loved me. An arranged marriage can be a wonderful thing.'

Indeed, as I discovered, Mr Choudhury was fairly conservative, although ready to bend with the times. Two of his three children were approaching their twenties and, once they were of marriageable age, he hoped to find them partners.

'If they meet someone independently, then so be it,' he said. 'But you must appreciate that we are more traditional here than in London. The family is our most sacred treasure and we must protect it, is it not so?'

Mr Choudhury also strove to protect his way of life from modern influence and was determined never to own a fridge. Instead, he bought fresh produce from the market every day. He also grew his own rice, which he stored in a bamboo hut in his back garden. But he did have a weakness for one Western appliance.

'Television is wonderful,' whispered the hunter, who had recently bought his first set. 'We have cable and my favourite is the Discovery Channel. They have excellent documentaries, even some on elephants.'

Each time I looked down at my watch, hoping the hours had slipped past, it seemed as if the minute hand had hardly advanced at all. I pulled my jacket tight around me and shivered, burying my hands in my armpits and pushing my chin down on to my chest. After five hours on the *masang*, I could hardly tolerate sitting on the hard boards a moment longer.

To my relief, shortly after four o'clock Mr Choudhury decided to call it a night. None of the other teams had reported any sightings, and the likelihood of the elephant venturing into the village so close to dawn was remote.

We climbed down, all aches and pains, and Mr Choudhury and I made our way on foot towards the village where Latif the farmer had promised us a cup of tea. We had gone only a few yards when the hunter suddenly stopped dead in his tracks and grabbed me by the arm, hard.

'What is it?' I asked.

He didn't answer but stared intently ahead. In the darkness, all I could make out was the faint outline of a few bushes and a tree.

'There's nothing there,' I whispered.

Yet one look at Mr Choudhury told me I was wrong. The

muscles in his face were rigid, as if he were gritting his teeth, and his eyebrows were raised in alarm.

Cautiously, still holding on to my arm, he drew me backwards, whispering to Mole who was now just behind us. The forest officer quickly switched on his torch and the beam shot along the ground and up into the bushes. Soon, it settled on a large, motionless, grey lump camouflaged in shadows. I might have mistaken it for a boulder. But from the moment I laid eyes on it, I knew it could only be one thing.

It was the rogue tusker.

Releasing his hold on my arm, the hunter motioned for me to step behind him. He slipped his rifle off his shoulder. As he did so, the animal moved through the bushes and half-emerged into the open. Dry brushwood snapped beneath his feet. I felt the hairs rise on the back of my neck.

The elephant was a menacing sight, with two long, curved tusks that glinted in the torchlight, and a powerful trunk, which he swung from side to side like a bullwhip. Compared to Raja, he was large, his ears spread wide, exaggerating his overall size. He kicked at the ground with his front feet, sending clods of earth flying through the air.

Seized with terror, I tried to decide whether to run for it or stay put. The *masang* was only a hundred yards away. With a quick sprint, I might just make it ...

I backed away, while Mr Choudhury, who was standing no more than thirty feet from the elephant, held his ground. Here was his opportunity to end it all.

He slipped the safety catch off, raised the rifle butt to his shoulder and took aim.

My heart and stomach quivered. 'Any second now,' I thought to myself, braced for the sound of the powerful Magnum rifle.

Mr Choudhury's finger curled round the trigger. He was just about to fire when the rogue stopped kicking the ground and raised his trunk, as if in salute. Then he bowed his head, shaking it from side to side, and disappeared into the night, dragging his bad foot behind him.

Mr Choudhury lowered his rifle, turned and walked past me. Still shaking, I raised my hands, stupefied.

Why hadn't he fired?

5

The Horse Might Talk

'Till now man has been up against Nature, from now on he will be
up against his own nature.'

Dennis Gabor, *Inventing the Future*

BACK AT THE camp on the edge of Bruiser Harry's tea
garden, Dinesh Choudhury fiddled with his good-luck
charm, a solid silver rupee coin dated 1802, cast with the coat-
of-arms of the East India Company. It had been given to him
by his grandfather, a memento from the days when his family
were influential Assamese land-owners and collected thousands of such coins from their tenants every month.

The hunter turned the piece round and round in his
fingers, caressing the worn image of George III with his
thumb as he contemplated the events of that morning.

'The rogue was waiting for us,' he said ominously.
'Somehow he knew we were in the *masang*.'

'Why didn't you kill him? Wasn't there enough light?'

'No, no. There was plenty of light from Mole's torch,'
replied Mr Choudhury. 'I could see his head very clearly.'

'So *why* didn't you shoot?'

The hunter slipped the silver medallion back into his
pocket and smiled at me wryly.

'I wanted to give him a warning,' he said.

'A warning?' I spluttered. 'What kind of warning?'

'I have thrown down the gauntlet. Now the rogue will

either mend his ways or I will deal with him. Last night, he didn't charge because he knew it would be suicide. Let us hope he continues to be so wise.'

Mr Choudhury was beginning to sound like Churchill. Indeed, as I was about to discover, when it came to dealing with elephants, he had a sixth sense.

'Sometimes when I arrive in an area to shoot a rogue, he runs away,' he continued. 'The elephants know when I am coming for them.'

A year earlier, he had been dispatched to shoot another killer tusker in the southern part of Assam. On the day he arrived in the neighbourhood, the animal disappeared and has not been seen or heard of since.

'If a human kills, he is given a fair trial before sentencing is carried out. Therefore, I always give each elephant a chance to redeem himself. I say to him, "If you stay, you will die. If you go, you will live."'

As well as elephantine ESP, Mr Choudhury believed in fate. In his opinion, providence and providence alone dictated when a bullet should be used.

'But you're a hunter,' I pointed out, still puzzled. 'Don't you get a thrill from hunting?'

He shook his head vehemently.

'Not for elephants. I've told you before, I love them. Traditionally, we Assamese have never hunted elephants. We have only ever captured and trained them. They are our friends.'

He patted Raja on his flank and the animal nodded his head as if in agreement. Churchill, who sat in front of me, was uncharacteristically quiet, although I could tell he was listening to every word of our conversation.

'So why do you agree to shoot them?' I asked, still trying to come to terms with his real motives.

'If I hadn't taken this assignment, then another hunter would have come in my place,' he said. 'Any other hunter would be only too happy to shoot the animal and collect the reward. At least with me in charge, the elephant has a chance.'

I sat quietly mulling over these new revelations. It seemed that I had misjudged Mr Choudhury.

'Why didn't you explain all this to me before?' I asked.

'I knew you wouldn't believe me,' he said. 'You had already decided certain things about me. The only way to show you the truth was to bring you here. Also, I did not know whether I could trust you. You might have been some crusading environmentalist out to portray me in a bad light.

'I could not have kept you from travelling here. But you would have got in the way and might even have ended up dead. So I allowed you along this far to keep an eye on you.'

'So where does that leave us?' I asked, chagrined.

'Nothing has changed. We still have to deal with the rogue and I think you will find that you still have lots to write about.'

That didn't mean, however, that I shared his superstitions. There had to be a plausible explanation for the rogue's behaviour that morning. Surely he had been waiting in the bushes because he wanted to stick his trunk in that barrel of homemade booze. And as for the idea that he could somehow recognize Mr Choudhury as his Angel of Death ... well, the very idea seemed, at best, fanciful.

In my opinion, Mr Choudhury's approach ran the risk of getting more people killed. Certainly, Mole was not altogether pleased with the hunter's strategy. The tusker had proved himself dangerous and the officer was only prepared to go so far to put the animal's life before those of the local population.

After the tusker's sudden appearance, Mr Choudhury had sent two forest guards armed with one sub-machine gun and a walkie-talkie to follow the rogue, who had gone into the rain forest. Now, having met up with the *kunkis* at the camp, we packed our gear and set off once again on elephant-back.

Entering the rain forest felt like walking into one of the hot-houses at Kew. The atmosphere was damp and sultry, the hissing sound of the sprinklers mimicked by legions of bugs and insects. We picked our way through dense vegetation as the midday sun pierced the canopy of leaves. Overhead, monkeys swung from creepers, their chattering mixing with the incessant screeching of hidden parrots. Raja and Jasmine brushed aside tall elephant grass and meandered through groves of bamboo whose gigantic poles arched thirty feet or more above us, some of them as thick as tree-trunks.

Until relatively recently, the whole of Assam had been covered in a rain forest that stretched on through Myanmar, or Burma, and into South-East Asia. According to local legend, the elephants maintained their own secret route through this immensity of jungle, a highway or tunnel that allowed the animals to pass unseen by man from as far away as Malaya. It was said by the Assamese that once every hundred years, thousands of wild herds travelled along this route to a hidden meeting-place in Upper Assam. There, a council headed by the mythical white elephant, the four-tusked Airavata, would hold celebrations, settle disputes and appoint new matriarchs.

Sadly, however, the tea companies and the burgeoning population had eaten away at the rain forest to such an extent that it was now just a few miles wide – barely enough to sustain the few thousand remaining elephants, let alone a mythical highway. Indeed, in patches, the flora petered out altogether and only tree stumps and scorched earth were left in its place.

As we headed east, marching deeper into the rain forest, Mole tried calling the guards assigned to the rogue on his walkie-talkie, but for some reason they didn't respond. With no way of knowing their position, we could not decide which direction to take. So it was left to Badger to find the way by deciphering the guards' footprints from the dozens of others in the soft sand.

'Blimey. There's more bloomin' tracks 'ere than if an army 'ad marched through,' said Badger, as he set to work. 'Not to worry, though. I could track a turd through a sewer.'

The Gurkha wasn't boasting. It took him less than half an hour to find the right footprints.

'They went that way,' he said, pointing east. 'The rogue's tracks lead in the same direction. Judging by 'is prints, 'e's shifting it.'

We set off with the former soldier leading the way and humming an old Gurkha folk-song.

Lack of sleep had left the rest of the squad exhausted. The apprentices, who were following on foot, were beginning to lag behind. Mole, who was riding Jasmine, was yawning repeatedly. The two forest guards accompanying us appeared to be sleepwalking. I could barely keep my eyes open.

'This place full of insurgent mens. Very bad, no?' said Churchill.

'Which group?' I asked.

There were dozens of rebel outfits in North-East India. The TNVF, the ATTF, the PREPAK, the ULVA, the ULMA, the BSF. The list read like alphabet soup.

'They are ULFA. Big danger. Mahout no like these mens.'

I asked Mr Choudhury whether he sympathized with the insurgents' cause, but it was the one subject he refused to discuss. Fortunately, I could count on Mole to give me the 'low-down', as he put it.

'These guys are wasters, the lot of them,' he said in his inimitable fashion. 'I went to school with many of them. They're just out-of-work kids making easy money, man.'

'But what are they fighting for? Don't they want independence?'

Not for the first time, Mole chuckled at my ignorance.

'Does Bill Clinton tell the truth? Give me a break,' he said. 'That independence stuff is just talk. Everyone knows Assam will never split away from India. No chance. They're just in it for the money. They kidnap people, blackmail them. They're scum.'

'So they're dangerous?'

'Oh yeah, they're dangerous all right,' he replied. 'We'd better hope we don't bump into any of them in here.'

I asked him what had happened to Sanjay Ghoshe, an aid-worker whom they had kidnapped and allegedly killed.

'He messed with them,' said Mole. 'From what I heard, they put a bullet in him and dumped the body in the Brahmaputra.'

Not long after Mole had finished talking, we heard something coming through the undergrowth.

Churchill and Chander reined in the *kunkis*. Mr Choudhury pulled back the bolt on his rifle with a clunk-click. The guards raised their sub-machine guns. The rest of us froze.

Dead ahead, we spotted two men running blindly towards us. As they came closer, I recognized them as the two forest guards.

Quickly we dismounted and rushed towards them as they both collapsed on the ground, gasping for breath and babbling incoherently.

'Give them some room,' said Mole, urging us to step away as we crowded round. 'I'll handle this.'

We stepped back to a respectable distance as the officer plied the guards with water from a hip-flask. Had they been attacked by insurgents? Or had the elephant turned on them? Where was their walkie-talkie?

It took a full ten minutes before we got our answers. It was Rajesh, the older guard, who spoke first.

'We were a mile or so behind the elephant,' he began. 'He was moving at a steady pace, I could tell from his tracks. After an hour or so, we spotted a local farmer illegally felling a tree, so we arrested him. We planned to take him with us and charge him later back at HQ.'

The guards, with the farmer now in tow, continued along the main path. Several miles on, the ground became harder and it was increasingly difficult to make out the elephant's tracks. Then, just as they emerged from a particularly thick area of bamboo, the rogue stepped out on the path directly in front of them. Rajesh, who was carrying the sub-machine gun, raised his weapon to fire, but it jammed.

'We turned and sprinted as fast as we could with the elephant right behind us,' said Rajesh, who, in the confusion, dropped the walkie-talkie.

The three men ran for their lives. But after a couple of hundred yards, the farmer suddenly broke rank and turned left, sprinting down another pathway.

'The elephant ignored us and charged after him,' said Ashok, the younger guard. 'We didn't see what happened. The elephant caught up with him quickly. We heard him screaming. But he must have been killed instantly.'

I looked to see how Mr Choudhury was reacting to this story. Had it occurred to him that if he had killed the rogue the night before, none of this would have happened? Did he feel guilty, I wondered. If he did, it didn't show.

'What happened next?' the hunter asked Rajesh.

'We climbed up a tree and waited,' continued the guard. 'When the elephant had finished with the farmer, he came after us.'

For nearly twenty minutes, the tusker rampaged through the undergrowth, trumpeting and tearing up saplings with his trunk as he tried to locate the guards. At one point, he unwittingly smashed into their tree, almost shaking them from the branches.

'I thought I was going to fall out,' said Ashok, 'but eventually he gave up. We waited for some time and then came down. Just then we thought we heard him again, so we ran.'

That had been about an hour earlier and the two men hadn't stopped running since.

It took us roughly half an hour to reach the scene of the rogue's latest attack. We found Rajesh's walkie-talkie lying undamaged on the path, hissing static. Further on, behind a clump of bamboo, Mr Choudhury discovered the tusker's footprints, clearly defined in a patch of mud.

'This is where the rogue waited,' concluded the hunter. 'See. He was here for some time.'

'You make it sound like an ambush,' I said, as sceptical as ever.

'That's precisely what it was,' he replied. 'He knew he was being followed. The guards had the wind behind them. It gave them away.'

Badger soon located the farmer's remains, several hundred yards off the main path.

'You don't wanna see that, mate,' he said to me. 'He's been done over good and proper. Never seen anything like it – except in *Silence of the Lambs* or somethin'. This elephant's like a serial killer.'

Mysteriously, the body was partially covered with earth and branches torn from a nearby tree – as if some thoughtful passer-by had attempted to hide the corpse from wild animals before going for help. That, at least, was the only possible explanation I could think of.

However, as usual Mr Choudhury saw things differently and slipped into his detective routine, studying the crime scene for seemingly invisible clues. His attention was particularly drawn to a row of gouges in the earth near the farmer's feet and, after emitting two or three 'Hmmms' and a decisive 'A-ha', he stood up and announced: 'The rogue covered him.'

'You must be joking,' I said, exasperated.

I could just about believe that an elephant might spring an

ambush. I could even come to terms with the concept of elephantine ESP. But an elephant burying the dead?

'Let me guess,' I said, unable to prevent myself from sounding sarcastic. 'The elephant came back here to hide the evidence and then slipped into a cunning disguise before fleeing the country.'

Mr Choudhury smiled, raising his hands defensively.

'I know, I know. It sounds fantastic. But it's true,' he told me, pointing to the gouges in the earth. 'See here. He dug up the soil with his tusks. Elephants often bury bodies,' said the hunter, as Churchill and the others covered the farmer with a sheet. 'Their attitude towards death is very similar to that of humans.'

Over the years, Mr Choudhury had often come across the carcasses of wild elephants killed by poachers and subsequently 'buried' by their herd, behaviour verified by experts in Asia and Africa who believe elephants recognize death and mourn their lost ones. Indeed, when wild elephants discover the body of a fallen comrade they treat it with what can only be described as reverence, touching and feeling it with their trunks.

'I once had to shoot a tusker known locally as the Gravedigger who always buried his victims,' said Mr Choudhury. 'He would sometimes carry them for up to a mile, and if you moved the body, he would come looking for it.'

Rajesh and Ashok were assigned the task of taking the farmer's body to Mole's headquarters while the rest of us went after the rogue. It was mid-afternoon and the shadows in the forest were growing longer. The latest murder had left the elephant squad tense and jittery, and we proceeded with caution. Every bamboo grove now appeared as a potential hiding-place, every blind corner a possible trap. Sudden sounds startled us – a deer jumping out from behind a thicket, a crow's caw, a ripened mango falling from a tree. Only Mr Choudhury seemed unconcerned as he walked ahead of the *kunkis*, his Magnum rifle held tightly across his chest.

What was the hunter thinking now, I wondered. Did he value the life of an elephant above that of a human being? How many more lives was he prepared to sacrifice before doing the Forest Department's bidding?

As I considered his motives we came to a clearing where the elephant's tracks turned south. At first, the squad imagined that the rogue had taken a detour. However, after a mile or so, it became clear that, rather than heading north into the sanctuary of Arunachal Pradesh as Mr Choudhury had hoped, the elephant was making for the edge of the rain forest.

Clearly disappointed, the hunter called a halt, kneeling down on the earth and running the palm of his hand over an impression of one of the elephant's footprints. For a few minutes, he seemed lost in thought, his eyes closed as if he were making a wish. By now, it must have dawned on him that beyond the forest to the south lay more villages and homes. Once the rogue reached the area, he would wreak death and destruction – unless, of course, he could be stopped.

The hunter opened his eyes and straightened up. I could see the anguish on his face as he stared ahead. He sighed deeply. Then, at last, he appeared to make up his mind on his course of action. Standing up, he turned and faced the elephant squad.

'I have given him a chance and he has shown that he is a truly bad elephant. Therefore, I have no choice but to award him capital punishment,' he announced, the resolve sounding in his voice. 'We must catch up with him – and quickly.'

Surprisingly, I was beginning to agree. Just three days earlier, the thought of killing this elephant had filled me with regret; I had felt nothing but pity for him. Now it was clear that he was out of control and would go on killing more and more people. I had become more comfortable with the idea of Mr Choudhury completing his contract.

However, the hunter still had misgivings about shooting the rogue and hoped providence would intervene.

'Do you know the story about the man who tried to teach a horse to talk?' he asked, as we set off once again.

I shook my head.

'Well, there was once a man who was sentenced to death. But as he was about to have his head cut off, he pleaded with the King to be given one more chance. "Give me a year and I will teach a horse to talk."

'The King was intrigued by this idea and granted his wish. Afterwards, a friend said to this man: "You're mad. You'll never teach a horse to talk and you'll be killed."

'But the man replied: "Don't be so sure. A lot can happen in a year. The King might die. I might die. The kingdom may be invaded. Or the horse might actually learn to talk."'

'So, what's the moral?' I asked.

'No moral. I just hope something intervenes,' replied the hunter. 'The elephant might still disappear, we might find a way of helping him – or, if it is his time ... well, then, it is his time. Only God knows.'

He sighed, looking pensive, and for the first time I began to feel sorry for him.

The squad tried to make up for lost time. Churchill and Chander urged the *kunkis* to move faster, driving them on with harsh, uncompromising commands, and we began to make good progress. But by the time we reached the edge of the forest, we still lagged behind the rogue whose tracks disappeared into a river from which they did not emerge.

Mole, who was growing frantic, ordered everyone to fan out along the banks and search for tracks. But it was now dusk, and as hard and as long as we looked, we found no clues to

1. The Brahmaputra is revered by the Assamese as a life-giver. But it is also a life-taker. Every year, it floods the valley, sweeping away homes, livestock and wild animals, and drowning dozens of people

2. Sunset over the Karbi Anglong hills on the edge of the Kaziranga National Park, home to the largest population of one-horned rhinos in the world

3. On the trail of the rogue elephant: Dinesh Choudhury *(centre)* on the back of Jasmine. The hunter started riding elephants when he was a young boy, and was considered by the mahouts to be a skilful and knowledgeable elephant man

4. Churchill, mahout and head of the elephant squad. His tribe, the Khasis, are thought to have originated in Vietnam

5. Collecting fodder in Kaziranga National Park. This mahout ordered his elephant, a *makhna* or tuskless male, to salute me with his trunk simply by calling out a command. The same elephant had also been taught to stand on his head and to play a drum

6. Chander, Churchill's assistant. A dedicated mahout, he was inseparable from his *kunki*. 'Being a mahout is like being married,' he joked. 'But elephants are easier to manage than women.'

7. Mahouts wash their elephants at least once a day – a time the *kunkis* relish – in order to remove parasites and prevent infection. Some elephants take care of themselves and have been seen working out the bits of dirt from between their toes with sticks

8. This farmer lost a year's supply of rice when wild elephants pulled down part of his home, tore open his gunny sacks and helped themselves to the contents. 'Wherever we hide our food, the elephants find it,' he said. 'They know our thoughts.'

9. Mr Choudhury measuring one of the rogue's footprints. By doubling the impression's circumference, he was able to calculate the elephant's height

10. A forest guard. Several were assigned to the elephant squad as protection against Assamese insurgency groups who regularly kidnap civilians and hold them to ransom

11. Kaziranga's guards stand over the bodies of three poachers who have been shot dead inside the sanctuary.

12. At the elephant's grave: the pit took nearly two days to dig. When the elephant was finally pushed into it, his back protruded, leaving a mound to mark his last resting-place

indicate the direction the elephant had taken. Clearly, he had walked along the river-bed, thereby masking his trail.

'This elephant is really beginning to piss me off!' shouted Mole. 'The son of a bitch is going to kill someone again! I'm calling in more guards.'

He got on the walkie-talkie and ordered his remaining men back at headquarters to meet us in the nearest village. From there, he planned to send search parties into the surrounding area.

'He's bound to show himself soon,' said Mole.

Churchill agreed.

'This *hathi* just like Mrs Mahout,' he joked, endeavouring to raise everyone's spirits as we plodded towards the village. 'Like her he is very angry and has big stomach. Soon he will need food, no? He will be crop raiding.'

'You have a wife?' I replied, somewhat surprised by this news.

'Yes. She like female *hathi*. After children making, she push male away. Then male live in forest. Like me.'

'Is that what the matriarch elephants do? Push the male out?'

'Yes. But it is good. I prefer. Life of elephant and mahout is same. Is free, no?'

'How many children do you have?' I asked.

'Five, six, seven, maybe. I not remember. Too many.'

The light was fading fast, and as the sun set over the valley, farmers hurried home, driving their lazy water buffalo before them. Goatherds skipped along pathways running between the paddy-fields, the sound of their laughter and the bleating of their animals carrying for miles in the still air. In the distance, smoke from brick kilns drifted horizontally across the sky like broken spider webs. Heat rising from their ovens distorted the horizon, creating a mirage in which trees bent and rippled, and houses appeared to melt.

As we approached the small settlement, smells of baking

chapatis and roasting kebabs wafted out to greet us, and pi-dogs barked and growled in protest at our presence. One brave hound ran snarling towards us but backed off quickly as soon as he saw the *kunkis*.

Fortunately, the villagers, who were tea labourers, were more welcoming. Dozens gathered along the way, watching our slow but steady progress with expressions of awe and interest. Many showered the way with flowers, small coins and fruit in the hope of receiving a blessing from Ganesha, the ele-phant-headed god.

'I feel like Jesus entering Jerusalem,' I said to Churchill, as a banana landed in my lap.

'Jesus, he no ride *hathi*,' replied the mahout. 'He ride donkey, no?'

'Yes, I know. But … oh never mind,' I said, too tired to explain.

On the edge of the village, we passed a fish market, the stalls spread out in the shadow of two banyan trees. Vendors crouched on squares of plastic sheeting, selling their catches by the light of dozens of candles. Amidst patches of mellow light, which shimmered on the ground like reflections of the moon on water, I caught glimpses of carp flipping about in shallow basins, their tails beating in desperation. A freedom-loving turtle tried to make a break for it, but he was soon caught and placed on the chopping-block where he paid the ultimate price for his lack of speed.

Plump, silvery *hilsa* fish were pulled from buckets and held up by their tails for closer inspection by discerning house-wives. Freshwater shrimps were peeled by nimble fingers and then packed in boxes with lumps of ice. Tiny fish no larger than paper clips were weighed on scales and sold by the pound for use in *tenga mass*, a stew made with tomatoes.

Outside the village meeting-house, a circle of men watched a cockfight, all urging the birds on with shouts as they swilled down bottles of home-made booze. We stopped to watch as a fierce-looking red cockerel clawed his scrawny white opponent, who was trying desperately to escape from the ring. As feathers flew and sharp beaks drew blood, money changed hands amidst much raucous cheering.

With all the commotion, we went virtually unnoticed as we made our way into the centre of the village, until we stopped near a temple where men with less than perfect pitch were chanting mantras through a loudspeaker. We dismounted, and a crowd gathered round us, all staring at me.

Being stared at in public was one aspect of travelling in India I found hard to cope with. As a child, I had always been told that it was rude to stare. So when ten people stood just a foot from my face, looking straight at me with numb expressions, I had to remind myself that they meant no offence. Like moths drawn to light, they were attracted to anything out of the ordinary – and a strange white man riding on an elephant was about as out-of-the-ordinary as you could get in northern Assam.

Mole and Mr Choudhury went to talk with the head of the village to ask for help in recruiting messengers. Rudra was called by walkie-talkie and told to bring the Land Rover to the village. Meanwhile, the rest of us unloaded the *kunkis*, watched by an ever-increasing crowd whom the mahout apprentices tried, in vain, to shoo away. Fortunately, a local man soon came to our rescue, dispersing the spectators with an appeal for them to respect our privacy.

Our saviour was called Shankar, a mild-mannered Assamese in his late twenties. He had studied engineering at Guwahati University and spoke English with a heavy accent. 'It's impossible to get a good job these days,' he complained, as we stood at a cigarette-stand, drinking tea out of disposable clay cups and eating stale Nice biscuits. 'Now I work as a lifeguard at the public swimming-pool in Guwahati. It's the only work I can find – apart from joining ULFA.'

Shankar, who was visiting his brother, a local doctor, hailed from Majuli, the largest river island in the world which lies in the Brahmaputra in Upper Assam. The island, hundreds of square miles in size, can only be reached by ferry and is virtually cut off from the outside world.

'You must come and visit. You will be my guest,' he said. 'Every year, most of the island floods, so no one lives in a permanent home because you never know when you'll have to pack it up and move.'

We took a stroll along the main street. Passers-by stopped to greet Shankar.

'You seem to be popular,' I commented.

'Yes, I'm famous,' beamed the lifeguard. 'Everyone knows me. I am the man who swam the Brahmaputra River. I was even on TV.'

'Did you swim across it or down it?'

'Across it? That's nothing. I swam down it, all the way from the very top of Assam, near the Burmese border, to the bottom, where it meets Bangladesh. It took more than a month. No one had ever done it before.'

Indeed, as Shankar explained, most Assamese, even the local fishermen, dare not dip so much as a toe in the water as they believe the Brahmaputra is infested with crocodiles, monsters, evil mermaids and giant whirlpools.

'No one thought I would survive. But I don't believe in these things.'

'Why not?'

'It is bullshit only.'

'How do you mean?'

'These things do not exist. Monsters, mermaids – it's rubbish. Only these ignorant uneducated people believe in all that.'

I told him some of Mr Choudhury's superstitious beliefs about elephants. Did he think there was anything to them?

He dismissed them out of hand.

'Superstition is the source of all evil,' he said.

I didn't agree. Much of it struck me as fascinating.

'No. It keeps people blind, makes them scared.'

I changed the subject. Were his river-swimming days over?

'I want to do the Mississippi and the Amazon. But it is difficult to get sponsorship. No one in India wants to give money for swimming rivers. What to do?'

By the time I checked in with the others, Mole and Mr Choudhury had dispatched a dozen messengers and seven teams of guards to search for the rogue. The moment they reported anything, the squad would move out.

'In the meantime, chill out,' advised Mole.

On our way into the village, I had noticed a temple that housed an effigy of Kali, the goddess of destruction. I asked Shankar if he would take me to see the place and we strolled over to the cone-shaped building, positioned across the way from an off-licence that stocked only Knock Out Beer.

Inside the temple stood a giant statue of Kali. Black-faced, with bared teeth and a protruding scarlet tongue, she held, in her four hands, a severed head, a sword, a shield and a garotte. Her naked body was smeared with blood and around her neck hung a garland of skulls.

However, it was the congregation and not the statue that really interested me. Unlike the other villagers, these people were very short, with coal-black skin. I asked Shankar where they were from.

'They are Biharis,' he answered.

Bihar is a state in eastern India notorious for its lawlessness, caste wars and dacoits, who regularly hold up trains at gunpoint. So what were a group of Biharis doing in the middle of Assam?

'You Britishers brought them here to pick tea,' he said.

I wanted to know more, so, after making inquiries, we went to meet the local schoolteacher, Mr Yadhav. He was a spindly character, only five foot tall and with great welts on his chin.

He showed us into his humble shack where we sat on two cracked plastic garden chairs, the only other furniture being a stained mattress on the floor, which constituted his bed, and a table made from a tea-chest. A single light-bulb lit the room. Yet despite Mr Yadhav's evident poverty, he was not lacking in hospitality and insisted on fetching us tea and rice-cakes.

His family, like thousands of others in the area, had originally lived in northern Bihar, he told me. They were Harijans, or Untouchables, Gandhi's so-called Children of God. Thanks to the age-old Hindu system that has at its core the belief that people born into the lower castes have sinned in their past lives, they were considered to be unclean, or untouchable, and laboured all their lives as rat-catchers.

Then, one day, they were visited by an *arcuttie*, a professional recruiter, who was hiring labourers for the recently established tea estates on the North-East Frontier.

'He promised my family lots of money, good conditions and cattle if they came to work in the gardens. He promised to make them rich.'

The British, he said, badly needed tea labourers, as the Assamese had refused to work in the new gardens, preferring to remain independent. Thousands of *arcutties* were sent into impoverished, drought-ridden states such as Bihar and Orissa, where they persuaded tens of thousands of peasants to sign on as coolies.

'It is said that the water of Assam, a land of tea leaves, is very sweet,' went a song the British lackeys circulated at the time. 'Friends, let us go to Assam! There, we shall pluck leaves and pass away our time in pleasure and in happiness.'

When the coolies arrived in Assam, however, they were anything but happy. Health care, sanitation and housing were non-existent. Of almost 85,000 men and women transported between 1 May 1863 and 1 May 1866, more than 30,000 perished.

'Our people became slaves,' continued Mr Yadhav. 'We

were bought and sold by different estates and we were unable to leave. Those who tried were dealt with harshly and sometimes killed by the "coolie catcher".'

Today, conditions have vastly improved. Companies are required to supply proper health facilities and schools. Yet the tea-workers, or *adivasis* as they are known, remain underprivileged. Ninety-five per cent of the tea-garden population is illiterate, and very few have aspired to much more than farming or plucking tea leaves.

'None of my family has ever returned to Bihar,' said Mr Yadhav. 'In over a hundred and fifty years, none of us have been able to afford the 300-rupee train fare to Patna.'

So did they now consider themselves to be Assamese?

'That is a good question. But the answer is difficult,' he said, as we went for a walk outside. 'The sahibs kept us isolated from the local population and we never integrated with them. Even today, we live in our own communities and have no contact with the local Assamese.'

This isolation, Mr Yadhav explained, had created a unique tea-garden culture in which representatives of hundreds of different Indian tribes and castes had been thrust together, thereby mixing and corrupting ancient traditions and practices. Each group had forgotten their original language – some did not even know where their ancestors came from – and a new *lingua franca* had evolved called Sadani, a mix of Hindi, Bengali, Bihari and Ariya, with a smattering of Assamese.

'Do you know what is really strange, though?' asked Mr Yadhav, as we sat outside the Kali temple, watching devotees filing in and out. 'We *adivasis* make up half the population of Assam. But we are not considered to be Assamese, we have not been assimilated into the local population, and most of us don't vote.'

It was as if the Blacks in America still lived on cotton plantations, segregated from the rest of society and speaking only bastardized West African dialects.

I wondered whether the original natives were concerned that eventually, when the tea labour population grew too large for the estate, they would go looking for more land and come into conflict with the original inhabitants.

'Maybe it will happen. But my people are timid,' said Mr Yadhav, as we thanked him for his time. 'They have lived on an island all their lives and are too scared to leave.'

The elephant squad had set up a temporary control-room in a grubby eatery called the AꓐBA Restaurant. It was owned by a fan of the Swedish pop sensation and the walls were plastered with faded posters of the four Scandinavian performers decked out in glittery Seventies disco outfits. From the cobweb-covered speakers up on the wall boomed the song 'Super Trooper', followed by 'Money, Money, Money'. The young waiter sang along with the lyrics, except he had the words wrong and, as he moved from table to table, sang instead 'Bunny, Bunny, Bunny'.

Unfortunately, Assam's first stab at a theme restaurant did not serve genuine Swedish food – not that I am a particular fan of pickled herring and schnapps. But anything would have been better than the slop the cook was serving, which consisted of greasy samosas fried in rancid oil, barbecued fish heads and various sickly looking yellow substances which he ladled out on to moulded plastic plates rather like the ones used in prisons. Each ladleful hit its assigned compartment with such force that the food splattered in all directions, covering the cook's already food-encrusted T-shirt with fresh splotches.

The 'restaurant' was furnished with a row of trestle tables and wooden benches. Four shifty-looking men were huddled together in one corner, talking in low whispers as if they were plotting a murder. The village idiot crouched next to the cash register, chortling harmlessly to himself.

Mr Choudhury was sitting with Churchill in the middle of the room, talking into his walkie-talkie and drawing red lines and blue arrows across a Survey of India map. Red indicated possible routes the rogue might have taken, blue showed where the forest officer had dispatched his guards. Mole, Badger and the others were off helping with the search.

I sat down and the waiter brought me a plate of dhal and naan. Usually, I would never have eaten in such a place. Experience had taught me that South Asia's roadside food comes with extra helpings of bacteria. Ever since a bout of amoebic dysentery in Afghanistan, I had been careful. On this occasion, however, I was famished and succumbed.

Almost instantly, I knew I would regret the decision, though not that I would regret it quite so quickly. The effect of the ABBA Restaurant's house speciality on my insides was almost immediate. Within minutes of swallowing the last disgusting spoonful, my stomach began to churn like a washing-machine on full spin. A giant gas bubble grew inside me, threatening to burst out of both ends at once. My face went cold and clammy, and soon I found myself bent double out in the street.

It was in the middle of a particularly violent retch that Mr Choudhury and Churchill ran out of the restaurant.

'It's the *hathi*,' shouted the hunter, as I stood over a ditch. 'He's been spotted a few miles from here.'

I had just enough time to grab a bottle of water from the restaurant, say a hurried goodbye to Shankar, and climb into the Land Rover, my stomach still reeling. Rudra shifted gears and the car jerked forward. We took off along the road leading south out of the *adivasi* village. He shifted gears again and thrust his container of betel nut under my nose.

'Eat. Very good,' he said, spitting red juice out of the window. 'Make you into man like me!'

6

Shoot to Kill

'If a man decides to indulge in this dangerous sport [elephant hunting], he should also be prepared to accept all the dangers that go with it as part of the game, otherwise he is no sportsman.'

Patrick Hanley, *Tiger Trails in Assam*

A THICK FOG had descended across the valley. Visibility was down to zero, the Land Rover's headlights rendered useless by the bank of swirling mist that was closing in all around us. Even the powerful searchlights mounted on the bonnet were no match for its sheer density.

Looking out of the window, it was easy to imagine that we were flying through cloud cover at ten thousand feet. The landscape seemed to have been erased and a wall of whiteness left in its place. If the gods were on the side of the rogue elephant, then this was a last-ditch attempt to help him escape the .458 bullet that lay waiting, even now, in the barrel of the hunter's Magnum rifle. For the tusker was close at hand, perhaps only a few hundred yards up ahead – and we were gaining on him.

During the night, I had slept on the back seat, too exhausted to keep my eyes open any longer. Fortunately, I had missed little of interest. Churchill, Mr Choudhury, Rudra and Badger had spent hours driving from village to village, chasing alleged elephant sightings, all of them bogus.

Then, shortly before the fog had set in, they had come

across a distraught mullah. While he was in the middle of his ablutions at a water tank, the animal had launched an unprovoked attack and had chased him up his minaret.

Later on, a few miles down a back lane, Churchill spotted a night-shift worker clinging to the top of a tree like a koala bear. He too had been chased by an angry tusker that had taken a dislike to the man's bicycle and had smashed it to pieces.

That incident had taken place only a few minutes earlier. Now, with dawn fast approaching, we inched our way through the chilling fog, Mr Choudhury sitting on the bonnet of the vehicle, keeping his eyes peeled for a glimpse of tusk or trunk.

'He could be anywhere,' I whispered to Churchill as the mahout, Badger and I got out of the Land Rover and walked alongside the moving vehicle, searching for fresh tracks on the sandy lane. 'He could be three feet ahead of us. He could even be behind us.'

I began to feel scared again. At any moment, the rogue might come charging out of the fog, and I shuddered to think what he might do to me if I came within the clutches of his powerful trunk.

'No worry, Tarwin,' said Churchill over the bonnet. 'If elephant come, you run. He not finding. In fog difficult, no? He not see. Odds even now, yes?'

A mile or so down the road, Badger noticed a break in the hedge and investigated. The elephant, it appeared, had smashed through into the fields beyond and was heading cross-country.

'He's not far ahead, maybe only a few minutes,' said Mr Choudhury, examining the footprints. 'If we hurry, we'll catch him.'

The hunter took off his jacket and shoes and rolled up his jeans. Methodically, he wiped the mist from the lenses of his glasses with the tail of his shirt. Then he cracked his knuckles and took deep, heavy breaths.

'You two stay here,' he said to Churchill and me. 'We'll handle this.'

Before I could even open my mouth to protest, he and Badger slipped through the opening in the hedge and disappeared into the fog like two commandos off on some covert mission.

I kicked at the earth, furious at being left behind.

'Oh, damn this!' I shouted. 'I haven't come all this way to wait here.'

I thought of Sydney Schanberg, the journalist in *The Killing Fields* who never allowed any obstacle to get in the way of a good story. Sydney would have gone after Mr Choudhury, I thought to myself. He wouldn't have waited here, twiddling his thumbs.

'Churchill, let's go,' I said. 'We could be standing here for hours. We'll miss everything.'

'Shikari, he said stay,' said the mahout firmly.

This was no time for niceties.

'Fine, do what you like. I'll go alone,' I said. 'I'm not missing this.'

I made for the hedge, expecting Churchill to run after me.

'Are you coming?' I called out.

The mahout did not reply. Furious, I marched off into the fields. Mr Choudhury's footprints were clearly defined in the mud. It would be easy to follow them. I didn't need the mahout.

But after only a few yards, it dawned on me that I might run into the elephant. I stopped. Standing there in the fog on my own, I cursed my luck. Then, sheepishly, I returned to the Land Rover. Churchill was sitting on the bonnet with Rudra, chewing *paan*.

'Hello,' he said cheerily. 'You going after *hathi*, no?'

The driver joined in the joke, grinning like an infantile monkey. I sat down next to them, sulking.

'I want to go. Please.'

Churchill slid off the bonnet.

'Please. Yes, magic word. Now you say "please," we go. Come, we follow Shikari, no?'

The mahout took off his shoes and rolled up his trousers, urging me to do the same. I was beginning to realize that Churchill liked breaking the rules and could be counted on to do so, provided one remembered to say please.

'Now follow. And if *hathi* come, run for hell, no?' he advised, as we started off after the others.

We crossed the paddy-fields, our feet squelching through gooey mud which clung to my soles and heels like sculptor's clay. Following in the hunter's tracks, now superimposed over those of the elephant, we slipped and slid and occasionally crawled, stopping only momentarily to catch our breath. To the east, the rising sun was a faint, white blur – as dull as I imagine it will be on Doomsday, in the hours before it implodes.

As we crossed ditches, swamp and earthworks, the fog cleared momentarily, affording us a brief view of the terrain up ahead. For a split second, we caught sight of Mr Choudhury and Badger, two hundred yards away. But as quickly as the fog had parted, it closed again, like stage curtains coming down on a final act.

Anxious not to distract Mr Choudhury, we stopped in a ditch and stayed low. By now, we were covered in mud.

'Do you think the rogue is close?' I asked Churchill as we waited, catching our breath, the condensation mingling with the fog.

'Very close. Look at footprint,' he replied.

'How can you tell?'

'Easy.'

Churchill pointed out that water had not yet seeped into the elephant's footprints. That meant they had been made recently.

'Perhaps only a few minutes.'

The rogue was only a few hundred yards away. He would be in sight, I reflected, if it hadn't been for the fog.

'Shikari shoot soon. *Hathi* die today.'

We stood up again and suddenly the fog cleared. This time, we were given a longer view of the fields ahead. The elephant was less than a mile away. His pursuers were catching up with him, bounding through the fields like jack-rabbits.

Then, for some inexplicable reason, Mr Choudhury and Badger stopped just two hundred yards behind the elephant. Churchill and I ducked down, afraid they would turn and see us.

'What's he doing?' I asked the mahout. 'Why's he stopped?'

We peeked over the edge of the ditch. As if replying to my question, the hunter and the Gurkha started hollering at the top of their voices and clapping their hands together in an effort to attract the rogue's attention. Yet despite their efforts, the elephant did not stop or turn around.

Again they shouted, but to no effect. The rogue kept going, soon disappearing into what appeared to be a deep depression in the ground. Mr Choudhury and Mole broke into a run, chasing after him. In a few minutes they too vanished from sight. Then the fog closed in again, effectively blinding us.

Desperate not to miss the finale, Churchill and I charged across the fields. But as we reached the spot where the elephant and the two men had vanished, we found ourselves standing on the edge of a high bank, looking out over the Brahmaputra River. The rogue's tracks went down the bank and disappeared into the choppy waters.

Mr Choudhury stood by the water's edge, looking out over the swirling rapids with an expression of utter bemusement.

'Where's he gone?' I asked, trying to catch my breath.

'He's gone for a swim,' replied the hunter, who wasn't the least bit surprised to see Churchill and me.

'I don't believe it,' I said.

'Clever *hathi*,' said Churchill.

We all stood on the bank, scanning the surface for a glimpse of the elephant, but found nothing. For two or three minutes not a word passed between us. Then, for the first time since I had met him, Mr Choudhury began to laugh. It was the laugh of a man who has been relieved of some great burden, deep and sustained. But it was not infectious.

'Won't he drown?' I asked.

'No, *hathi* strong swimmer,' volunteered Churchill, as the hunter continued to chuckle to himself, sitting down on the bank, his rifle at his side. 'He swim like dog, no?'

'Yes, he can stay under water and use his trunk like a snorkel,' added Mr Choudhury. 'Elephants often swim across the Brahmaputra. In fact, years ago, there used to be an annual elephant swimming race in Guwahati.'

There were no boats near by to ferry us across the river in pursuit of the rogue. The nearest bridge was at Tezpur, three miles away, so for the time being we waited by the water's edge to see if the elephant would appear on the other side.

Downstream, a barge carrying an enormous turbine, no doubt destined for a power-station or factory, appeared through the mist, blowing its horn as it chugged against the current. Sails on fishing boats sliced through the fog like shark-fins. Further down the bank, a clutch of women were washing clothes by thrashing them against flat rocks just as their mothers and grandmothers had done – only without the aid of Nirma, a popular Indian detergent.

I sat on a beached log, puzzling over what had prompted the elephant to head for the river. Had Mr Choudhury been right, after all? Was the tusker trying to escape? Did he realize the hunter was after him? Who was to say that elephants couldn't read human minds?

We waited for ten minutes before Churchill, who was watching the river through Mr Choudhury's binoculars, let out an excited yelp.

'*Hathi*, there he is! There, no? See!'

On the far bank, half a mile downstream, the elephant staggered ashore. Ropes of water rolled down his back and sides as his feet negotiated the sandy bank. He walked up the beach and, without a backward glance, disappeared into dense undergrowth.

Mr Choudhury turned and started back towards the Land Rover, smiling to himself. He was clearly impressed.

'Now you really have seen something,' he said to me. 'He is a truly amazing elephant, is it not so?'

'Yes, but are you going to the other side? Are you still going after him?' I asked impatiently.

He gave me his hand, helping me up the slippery bank.

'Yes, of course we're going there,' he replied, as we headed back across the brush. 'But that is Kaziranga, a reserve. They will not allow us to shoot him inside. For the time being, the elephant is safe.'

He chuckled to himself and looked up to heaven, as if praising providence.

'The horse has talked,' he said.

Half a dozen guards stood chatting in the sunlight outside the ranger's office on the edge of Kaziranga National Park. A scruffy bunch, their uniforms sewn with patches, their caps ragged and worn, they looked like convicts on the run. Few of them had shaved, their hair was unkempt and, judging by the dark bags under their eyes, they hadn't had much sleep. Some wore only plastic sandals, others old shoes through which toe-nails poked. Buttons were missing and trousers were held up with lengths of twine. Even their weapons were old and out-dated, mostly archaic Lee-Enfield .303 rifles better suited to the days when British redcoats patrolled the Khyber Pass.

Men of all ages, ranging from their early twenties to mid-fifties, they earned a mere twenty or thirty dollars a month, barely enough to keep their families fed. Often, they went without pay for months at a time, a consequence of Assam's crippling corruption. Yet, these were the men I had read about in India's national press, the guardians of the world's largest population of one-horned rhinos. Dedicated individuals, they had vowed to die protecting the 1,200 magnificent animals in their care – even if the government was unwilling to provide them with adequate footwear.

Their leader, a man named Amu, who had been making his early-morning rounds of the park, screeched to a halt in his jeep outside the office bungalow where we all stood waiting for him. He was a short man with a baby face, neither his demeanour nor his stature measuring up to his fierce reputation. Decorated by India's President and honoured by the United Nations as a fearless champion of the environment, he had a simple approach to dealing with poachers: 'If you kill one of my rhinos, I will kill three of you.'

Amu had the determined bearing of a man with a mission, the resolution written clearly in his shining eyes and in the purposeful, upright manner in which he walked. As he greeted his troops, it was plain to see how genuinely they admired and respected him. After all, he, unlike his predecessors, had given them the satisfaction of saving an endangered species.

'We are on a war footing,' he told Mr Choudhury and me, as we followed him into his office. 'We are the soldiers. The poachers are the enemy. The rhinos are the cause.'

We sat down in front of his desk and Amu fished out his album of photographs, a gruesome testament to the war he has waged against the poachers. In black-and-white, Amu and his guards stood over the bodies of men caught attempting to snatch rhino horns. In one print, two Nagas lay on the ground, their heads twisted sharply to one side, their teeth bared in an expression of agony. A close-up showed another man splayed on the ground, a bullet-hole drilled through his forehead. In the past four years, the ranger and his men had shot dead more than twenty poachers. Eight guards had given their lives to the cause.

'I have 1,200 rhinos in my care. My men and I will do anything to protect them,' said Amu. 'The only way to deter poachers is to tell them: "Set foot in my park and you will have to face the consequences."'

The statistics showed that the policy was working. In the four years since he had taken over Kaziranga, the number of rhinos killed had fallen from hundreds to single figures.

'The government gives us nothing,' continued Amu, who complained that ministers were forever bringing their families to see the park and the rhinos but did little to help improve the facilities. 'They don't care about the animals, only about making money. We, as citizens of Assam, have a responsibility to look after our heritage, even if they won't do it for us.'

Amu also ran educational programmes in the local villages to teach people to respect the environment and protect the animals. And with funding from international aid groups, he built wells and schools.

'Help the people and they will help you,' said the ranger, who had developed a network of informers, many of them former poachers whom he had persuaded to change their ways. 'Education is the key. The people must be taught to appreciate the environment.'

His telephone rang. Amu picked up the receiver and grunted into the mouthpiece.

I glanced around the room. The Assam Forest Department's motto was emblazoned across the wall: 'YOU CAN TAKE A MAN OUT OF THE JUNGLE. BUT YOU CANNOT TAKE THE JUNGLE OUT OF A MAN.' Next to it hung a framed certificate presented by the UN for 'extraordinary dedication and service'. Behind us hung a wooden plaque with the names of Amu's predecessors going back to 1926, the year Kaziranga was founded.

Amu replaced the receiver and reached across his desk,

picking up a silver bell which he twisted around on its plastic base, thereby winding the spring inside. Then he released it and the bell rang.

I had come across similar contraptions before. They were standard government issue, the prized possession of India's bureaucrats, used to summon subordinates in thousands of offices across the land. Yet whenever I had seen them used they never seemed to have the desired effect. On this occasion, Amu gave the bell a couple of tries and then reverted to old-fashioned lung-power. That soon brought his assistant running.

'Sir!' bawled the lackey, standing to attention by the desk.

Amu gave him instructions in Assamese. The man turned and backed out of the door.

'That phone-call was from one of my informants,' said Amu. 'Some poachers have infiltrated the park. We are mounting an operation against them. We leave immediately.'

Outside there was a sudden commotion as the guards prepared to move out. Amu had only a few minutes to spare.

'What can I do for you?' he asked briskly.

Mr Choudhury showed him the warrant for the rogue's destruction and explained that the elephant had escaped into Kaziranga.

As the hunter had predicted, Amu would not allow anyone to hunt the elephant inside the sanctuary. All weapons, except those carried by the park's guards, were banned.

'Last week three jeep-loads of army people drove into the park illegally,' Amu told us, as he stood up and made for the door. 'They shot a whispering deer and tried to smuggle it out. Later, we arrested their commanding officer. His men came here last night and threatened us. They want us to drop the charges. But we do not take kindly to threats. I am talking to their superiors in Guwahati. I have many contacts. They will face many problems.'

We followed the ranger out of the office. His men were lined up outside the bungalow, ready for a briefing. Amu kept it short. Two poachers had entered the park to the east, he said. The guards were to lay an ambush along their projected route.

A senior officer handed out ammunition, four or five rounds for each man, a pitiful amount considering that the poachers, funded by rich smuggling syndicates, were armed with the latest automatic weapons, silencers and Russian night-vision equipment, readily available on the open market.

'Tomorrow, I will organize guards to take you into the park to find your tusker,' he promised, although he warned that it could take time to locate the animal. The park covers one hundred and sixty square miles of jungle and swampland, much of it inaccessible by road.

'Come and see me in the morning,' he said. 'By then I should have dealt with these poachers – one way or the other.'

The ranger jumped into the passenger seat of the lead jeep and sped off into the park, his guards following behind.

After the exertions of the elephant hunt, I was privately over-joyed when Kaziranga's administrators ruled that, as a for-eigner, I would not be allowed to sleep inside the park along with the elephant squad. Mr Choudhury and I checked into the Wild Grass Hotel nearby.

That afternoon I rediscovered the joys of a four-star estab-lishment – a comfortable bed, room service, a hot bath, fresh towels and a long and untroubled sleep.

Going downstairs in the evening, I found Mr Choudhury seated on a couch in the lounge, talking to an elderly Englishman with a rotund, smiling face and bushy eyebrows.

'Stewart Keegan. Me friends call me Stew,' he said, intro-ducing himself.

'Tarquin Hall,' I replied, somewhat surprised to meet another Brit so far from home.

'Tarquin!' he blurted out, spraying the table with a mouth-ful of Kingfisher lager. 'Bludy hell! You've got to be jokin'?'

I couldn't help smiling at his outburst. My name has been a source of amusement to people the world over.

'That's my nickname,' I joked. 'I'm really called Bob.'

Stew laughed even harder, blowing the froth off the top of his pint as he held it to his lips.

'Well, good to meet you. No hard feelings, like. Just never met a Tarquin before.'

'What brings you to Assam?' I asked.

'Oh, bit of a walk down memory lane, like. I was here during the war, I've come back for a look-round. You know, see what's happened to the old place.'

'Where did you fight?'

'At Kohima. Helped push back the Japs, didn't I?'

I sat up straight in my chair. Kohima was where my god-father Charles had fought. Had the two of them met, I asked with a sudden swell of anticipation.

'No, name don't ring a bell. Not like Tarquin. Now there's a name I won't forget in a hurry.' He collapsed into laughter again.

'So what was it like, Kohima? It's been described as one of the worst battles of the Second World War.'

'It was bad, all right. Never seen anything like it in me life. Bodies, there were, everywhere. Rats, too, thousands of 'em. See, the fighting was mostly hand-to-hand, like, with us dug in on the hills, desperate to hold on to our trenches, and the Japs not more than a breath away, the lot of them willing to fight to the death.'

The battle for Kohima in Nagaland had taken place in April 1944 when 12,000 men of the Japanese Fifteenth Army swept into India from Burma and tried to capture the eastern gateway to the subcontinent. Pitted against these ruthless jungle veterans was a force of no more than 1,200 British and Indians.

'It was do or die, really,' continued Stew. 'If those Japs had got through, well, there's no tellin' where they would have stopped. I was just a lad at the time and scared half out of me

wits. But the bravery of me fellow-soldiers and officers …
well, put it this way, they gave it all they had – and more.'

The old man's eyes clouded with tears as he took another
sip of beer and sat back in his chair. Fifty years on, he said, the
faces of his fallen friends still came to him in dreams. At night,
he sometimes woke up with the bitter taste of the battlefield
in his mouth.

'Some of the officers were right extraordinary,' he continued, clearly embarrassed about showing his emotions to two
complete strangers. 'There was one lad who was said to be
able to do the whole *Times* crossword puzzle in his head.
Apparently, he didn't write down a word till he'd solved the
whole thing. Another officer, he would sit in his trench with
shells and mortars goin' off all round 'im and he'd read classi-
cal Greek and the like.'

During research on Kohima some time later, I was to read
of the bravery of the handful of men who, cut off from the
rest of the British Fourteenth Army, held back an entire divi-
sion of the Japanese army for four weeks. In some of the most
savage and intense fighting of the war, they battled it out with
Bren guns, grenades and bayonets.

Yet the British and Indians, fighting side by side, refused to
yield. Their bravery became the stuff of legend: one officer
was awarded a VC after he took out several Japanese trenches
single-handed and got a bullet in the spine for his trouble. A
certain sergeant-major, injured by shrapnel in the head,
refused to leave his post and demanded that the signallers
bring some pliers to remove the pieces of metal from his skull.
Indeed, such was the spirit of defiance that one young private
is quoted as saying to his commanding officer: 'When we die,
sir, is that the end or do we go on?'

'There was next to no water', Stew went on, 'and not much
tiffin. We all had malaria, and just about everything else too,
come to think of it. Don't know how we carried on, really.
The stench of the bodies was bloomin' awful. The Japs blared

propaganda at us night and day, wanting us to surrender. As if we would have surrendered to the likes of them!

'I remember this one officer. One day, he sees this Jap charging towards him with a fixed bayonet. Pretty cool, like, he raises his tommy gun and fires. But the gun jams, doesn't it, and he gets the bayonet right here.'

Stew indicated where the blade had made contact just above the waistline.

'Luckily for him, he has one of them thick army belts on and that saves 'im. Then he gets up, unjams his tommy gun and empties all twenty-five rounds into the Jap – poor bastard.'

'So how did you all survive?' I asked.

'Well, by the time reinforcements knocked through, there was hardly any of us left,' said Stew. 'But we gave 'em a good hiding and eventually they turned and fled, like.'

The Japanese defeat at Kohima put an end to their attempts to invade India.

''Course we don't hold it against 'em now. The Japs, I mean. Just had to teach 'em a lesson, that's all.'

I asked Stew whether he had met any Nagas.

'Oh yes, plenty of 'em. Nice lot, the Nagas. All wear colourful shawls and the like, and plenty of jewellery,' replied Stew. ''Course a lot of 'em were head-hunters back then. I remember when a few Yanks crash-landed their plane into one of them backward tribal areas. Ended up with their heads on a stake, poor blokes.'

He smiled over the top of his glass.

In the annals of history, Kohima had been a small battle. Did his grandchildren remember the words on the memorial in Kohima that read:

WHEN YOU GO HOME
TELL OF US AND SAY
FOR YOUR TOMORROW
WE GAVE OUR TODAY

Had the sacrifice been worth it, I asked.

'Oh, don't know about sacrifice,' he replied, trying to make light of it. 'Did what we had to do, really. But of course it was worth it. Like I always say: every generation has its battles, like.'

Stew rose from his armchair, draining his glass. Behind him, Flo, his wife of more than thirty-five years, was ready by the door with their bags.

'Better be off then,' said Stew. 'We're going to Kohima. See the war graves and memorials and all that. Show the Missus where I gave the Japs what for.'

He winked at me, put his arm round his wife and turned for the door.

The squad's tents were pitched about a mile inside Kaziranga. It was here that the twenty or so mahouts employed by the Forest Department to look after the park's resident *kunkis* lived with their animals. The place was a sea of mud, a flat open area littered with piles of fodder, the ground pitted with elephant footprints of all sizes.

Wherever I looked, there were elephants – baby *makhnas* with fuzzy tufts of hair and delicate eyelashes, proud mothers with protective trunks, gigantic Ganeshas with enormous tusks, and a couple of old-timers with worn ears, greying hides and an air of wisdom.

Down in the river, a stone's throw from the squad's new camp, a playful female was having her tummy washed as she squirted water at a group of admiring children. On the far bank, a mahout was teaching a young male with pink freckles how to stand on his hind legs, while a young mother tramped towards us, her two calves clutching her tail with their trunks as they trotted behind.

In the middle of the camp stood Raja and Jasmine, happily munching on some banana trees, their chains attached to two posts driven into the ground. The squad's apprentices were chatting with their counterparts amongst the Kaziranga team, boasting of their adventures with rogues and wild herds.

We found Churchill, Badger and the others helping to tend a female elephant who had been attacked by a wild tusker. The wounded animal had deep gouges across her back where her assailant's tusks had done their work. The night before, she had been left in the jungle in the hope that a passing wild male would impregnate her. A suitor had appeared and made the usual elephantine advances. But the *kunki* had played hard to get and had infuriated the male, who was less than delicate during their subsequent coupling.

A wizened old mahout called Baba was preparing a herbal mixture for the wounded elephant in a pot over a charcoal fire. His back was hunched and where his right eye should have been was a patch of scaly skin. The hairs on his head had been dyed with henna, but the tufts that sprouted from his ears were grey. Unlike the other mahouts, he wore no shoes, revealing hideously deformed toes, six on one foot, four on the other. Nevertheless, he clearly commanded the respect of all the other mahouts.

While the tar-like concoction in the pot spat and bubbled, Baba gazed into the vessel, muttering strange and incomprehensible incantations.

'Very special thing, no?' said Churchill, warming his hands over the fire as the air temperature dropped by degrees. '*Hathi* medicine. He go to jungle and choose.'

I didn't quite follow but Mr Choudhury came to my rescue.

'When *kunkis* are sick,' he explained, 'the mahouts take them to the forest where the elephants pick the herbs or plants they need. Somehow, they're able to prescribe their own medicine. It is then up to the mahout to prepare them.'

Baba stirred the potion, inhaled its fumes and nodded to himself. At last, the peculiar mixture was ready. He ladled it out into a clay pot. As it continued to bubble like lava, he crushed a fistful of dried herbs in his hands and sprinkled them over the surface. The injured elephant was brought forward. She was clearly in considerable discomfort, but she allowed the mahout to climb up on her back, where he smeared the smoking substance on to the wounds.

Churchill stood watching Baba in awe.

'Legend mahout, no?' he said, when I asked him why he was so impressed. 'Very good, this man. Knowing all thing. He has no mother, father. Live in forest with *hathis* only. Knowing everything, no?'

Mr Choudhury, too, knew of Baba, although this was the first time he had met him.

'Some say he's a saint. He lives in the forest and knows elephants better than any man alive,' said Mr Choudhury. 'He is the only person who knows the *Hastividyarnava* by heart.'

The *Hastividyarnava*, I knew from my reading, was the ancient Assamese treatise on elephants. It had originally been written down on strips of bark from the *agar* tree, and later versions were illustrated with exquisite miniatures. It sets out everything you might need to know about managing a *kunki*, giving numerous homeopathic remedies for typical pachyderm afflictions and tips on how best to look after the animals.

'It even gives details on how to judge an animal's character by looking for certain physical signs and attributes,' explained Mr Choudhury.

An elephant normally has five nails on each forefoot and four on each hindfoot, making a total of eighteen. Any animal with less is considered unlucky; those with more are deemed special.

'The tail is also considered very important,' he continued. 'One that touches the ground is unlucky. A good tail ends just above the hocks of the hind legs, has a glossy look and crescent-shaped hairs.'

One of the worst signs of all is a black tongue.

'I have noticed that the rogue has one. It is a very bad omen,' he said.

That evening the mahouts crouched round the campfire, their faces framed by the glow from the flames, as Mr Choudhury recounted our adventures with the rogue.

By his own admission, the hunter was not a natural narrator, nor was he one for theatrics. But his description of how the killer tusker tore his victims apart and trampled them into the earth captivated his audience, who listened with rapt attention.

He explained how the elephant had appeared in the darkness, how he had laid an ambush for the guards, and how he had half buried the farmer's body in the rain forest. He told them how the rogue had given us the slip and swum across the Brahmaputra. As he talked, not one of the mahouts or apprentices stirred. They sat with their mouths agape, listening intently to every word. Only Baba appeared indifferent to Mr Choudhury's narrative. Sitting on a grimy blanket, he smoked a *bidi* and gazed into the distance.

However, when Mr Choudhury had finished talking, the mahout made it clear that he had been listening to every word.

'The elephant is injured, is he not?' said the mahout in Assamese, Mole translating his words.

'Yes,' replied the hunter. 'He appears to have a bad leg.'

Baba cleared his throat and spat, the saliva landing on Rudra's boots.

'I know where he is going,' he announced with a flourish of his hands, his thick rings catching the light of the fire.

He was beginning to sound like a fortune-teller at a fair. And like all soothsayers, he made it clear that his services did not come free of charge. A small token would be required if he was to share his knowledge with us.

'The generosity of friends can make life so much easier,' he said, staring down at his filthy feet.

Mr Choudhury fished out a one hundred rupee note and handed it to the mahout. The money was snatched away and quickly disappeared down the front of Baba's trousers. The mahout drew on his *bidi* and exhaled, the smoke passing through the gaps in his rotting teeth. Then, with a sigh, he made his revelation.

'The elephant you are chasing is dying. He is going to the place where all elephants go when they feel the end coming near. He is going to the elephant graveyard.'

The elephant graveyard. Something in my memory stirred. Hadn't I heard the myth as a child? It was said to be a secret place of bleached tusks and bones where the animals went to die.

Sinbad, during his last voyage in *The Arabian Nights*, is taken by a herd of elephants to this cemetery, and in one of the Tarzan films, a group of evil white explorers try to find the sacred spot, hoping to cart off a fortune in ivory.

It was a wonderful legend, but surely there was nothing in it?

'Believe me, it exists,' continued the mahout, scratching his crotch. 'It is a sacred place, created by Brahma, the wisest of all gods.

'After creation, the god came down to earth in human form. He wanted to see the world for himself. Eventually he came to Assam and the banks of the Brahmaputra.'

According to local legend, the deity was reluctant to use his supernatural powers to cross the river, so he called upon the animals to help him. The monkeys were the first to offer their assistance, but they fooled around and accomplished nothing. Then came the bears, but they were too clumsy.

'Finally, the elephants came out from the forest and went into the river. They stood side by side, their backs forming a bridge. Brahma was then able to cross without getting his feet wet. The god was very pleased and, in return for their help, he granted the elephants three gifts.'

The mahout counted them on his fingers. The first gift, he said, was that the elephants would be the wisest of all creatures. The second was that they would know the time of their death. The third was a place, hidden from the eyes of men, where the elephants would be able to go to die in peace.

'Where is this place?' I asked Baba. 'How can I find it?'

His one good eye widened and stared at me.

'I'm not sure I can remember,' he said, stirring a stick in the fire. 'My memory is bad these days.'

This was obviously a hint that he wanted more money. The only question was, how much? As a white man in India, I was used to paying double the normal rate, so I took out two hundred rupees and handed them to him.

'When I was a young man,' continued Baba, his memory now much improved, 'I found the elephant graveyard.'

The other mahouts were clearly fascinated and moved closer.

'It is located on a barren hill where only one tree grows. At the summit, I found piles and piles of bones and tusks. They were lying about on the ground, carcass upon carcass, thousands of them. I could not believe my good fortune and decided to carry away as many tusks as I could manage.'

Choosing the best ivory, Baba made his way down the hill, his arms full. In his mind's eye, he saw himself rich beyond his wildest dreams.

'But the path only led back up to the top. Again and again, I tried to walk down, only to find myself where I had begun. I was trapped.

'I thought I would die from starvation or thirst. In the end, I had to put the tusks down. Only then was I able to leave. Later, I tried to find the elephant graveyard again. But it was not there. It was as if it had disappeared.'

A general murmuring broke out amongst the audience as

Baba rose and walked off into the darkness. While the mahouts chatted amongst themselves, discussing Baba's words as if there were knowledge to be gleaned from them, I asked Mr Choudhury and Churchill what they made of it all.

Churchill believed there might be such a thing as an elephant graveyard because, in all his time in the jungle, he had never come across the carcass of a *hathi* that had died from natural causes.

'I see many animal, no? Monkey, bird, snake. One rhino. But *hathi*, no. Where he go? Perhaps to elephant graveyard. Yes, it may be right, no?'

Mr Choudhury had never seen an elephant carcass in the wild either, but he refused to comment on whether or not he believed in the existence of the mysterious cemetery.

Badger didn't believe a word of it.

'It's absolute bollocks. This bloke's full of it,' he said.

Mole agreed.

'I've never heard so much baloney in all my life.'

A feast was prepared in our honour. Bamboo poles stuffed with rice and roasted over the fire and generous helpings of mutton stew were loaded on to dried tobacco leaves that served as plates. The mahouts ate with their hands, moulding the rice into sticky balls and shovelling them into their mouths. This was an art which I had failed to master, preferring instead to use a plastic fork that I carried with me at all times.

As Baba finished eating, he asked Mr Choudhury how we planned to find the rogue. The hunter explained that Amu, the ranger, had offered to place a team of guards at our disposal.

'That will take a long time. Kaziranga is a big place,' pointed out Baba.

He licked his upper lip, touching the end of his nose with his tongue. Clearly, he was leading up to something.

'I could help you find the elephant,' he said. 'You would know where he is by tomorrow morning.'

This was an interesting proposition. None of us relished the idea of traipsing through a hundred and sixty square miles of jungle and swampland. But how much was it going to cost? And, more important, how did Baba propose to find the elephant so quickly?

'That is easy. I will turn into a tiger,' replied the mahout nonchalantly. 'Then I will go into the jungle and find the tusker.'

His suggestion was made as casually as an Englishman might comment on the weather. Yet no one around the fire batted an eyelid. Apparently, there was nothing unusual in Assam about people turning into tigers. Such talk was not considered a sign of madness – or at least not by my present company. Even Mr Choudhury didn't flinch.

'How much?' was all the hunter asked.

This time, it was really going to cost us. Rupee signs were practically flashing in the mahout's one good eye as he named his figure.

'Five hundred.'

The hunter and Churchill shrugged. Clearly they did not have the cash. If I wanted to see someone turn into a tiger it was up to me to pay. I pulled out the cash.

Baba grabbed the notes, giving them only a cursory glance before thrusting them down his trousers. Then, he drew a cellophane packet from a string bag and opened it, emptying a dozen nutmeg seeds on to the palm of his left hand. Reaching into another bag behind him, he next took out a stone pestle and mortar and methodically ground the seeds into a fine powder before adding some tobacco and a resin-like substance that he had extracted earlier from the bark of a rare tree.

'Now, you must all form a circle around me. Whatever happens, you must not pull away,' instructed the mahout. 'If you do, it will have bad consequences.'

The others did as instructed but I hesitated. Ever since an incident over a ouija board at school, I had been wary of the occult.

'I'll give this one a miss,' I said.

But even Badger insisted that I join in, pulling me into the circle. 'Come on. This will be a laugh,' he said.

Once we were all in place, the mahout knelt in front of the fire in the centre of the circle.

'Do not touch me or try to wake me up. Do not be afraid. As long as you remain connected, you will not be hurt. Stay here until I am gone. Then you may go. You will have your answer by morning.'

With that, he placed the peculiar mixture on his tongue and closed his eyes.

'He go other place, no?' whispered Churchill.

'I think Baba's already in his own special place,' I commented. 'But when is he going to turn into a tiger?'

'Spirit taking over, tiger spirit. Very powerful, no?'

Baba's lower lip began to quiver as if he was about to burst into tears. The muscles in his face started to twitch. His breathing grew faster, a rasping sound emanating from his chest. His hands shook in time with his nodding head. He tensed his arms and the veins in his wrists began to bulge. His expression grew taut and strained.

Then, something very strange happened. The mahout started to make a truly eerie noise, as painful as the sound of nails being dragged across a blackboard. At first, I imagined he was grating his teeth together, but his jaw was not moving, and besides, Baba had few teeth left to grind. Gradually, the sound grew louder and louder, as if it was being amplified through speakers. Then he fell to his hands and knees and began to circle the fire. He scratched at the earth with his fingernails and bucked like a bull, throwing his head back and yowling.

Suddenly he froze, his fingers bent like claws. He opened

his eye, which was glazed over as if covered in a thin film. Foam oozed from his mouth. He curled up on the ground and rubbed his hands behind his ears. Then he sprang up and with a screech leapt out of the circle and scampered off into the darkness on all fours.

No sooner was he out of sight than Badger burst into laughter.

'That bloke is completely cracked,' he said.

'But where's he gone?' I asked.

'Cloud Nineteen is my guess,' said the Gurkha.

'He go into forest, Tarwin,' said Churchill. 'Find rogue.'

It was now well past midnight. The other mahouts made their way to their tents. Behind them, in the moonlight, I could make out the silhouettes of their elephants.

Mr Choudhury rose to leave.

'Aren't we going to wait for Baba?' I asked.

'We'll discover whether he's found our elephant tomorrow,' he said.

He sounded sceptical and somehow I could tell he didn't believe in tiger-men. But he wasn't about to say so in front of the others.

'Let's go back to the hotel.'

We said our goodnights and made our way to the Land Rover. Behind us, Badger made cat yowls and, as we drove away, we could still hear him laughing.

Back in the comfort of my room, I searched *Elephant Gold* to see if Stracey had written on elephant graveyards. Sure enough, I found various references to legends in Sri Lanka, where there is said to be a pachyderm cemetery near Adam's Peak; and in Mysore, in southern India, where the Kurabas, who have traditionally enjoyed a rich elephant culture, likewise believe in the existence of a sacred graveyard. The book also tells of the mythical land of Jambu-dvipa, home to the magical mountain Vinataka, which is shaped like an elephant and believed by many to be their final resting-place.

Indian mythology, it seemed, was packed full of legends about elephants. In ancient times, the animals were known as *hastin*, or the beast that has an arm, and it was believed that they could fly. According to one fable, they were grounded by a powerful wizard when they accidentally dropped a branch on his head.

Hindus believe that the eight points of the compass are each guarded by an elephant, while in Buddhism white elephants are considered auspicious, because the Buddha was reincarnated as one, albeit with a silvery trunk and 'six tusks of different hues'.

I closed the book and began to think over the events of the day, staring blankly at the revolving fan mounted on the ceiling.

Badger was right. Baba was as mad as they came. But I couldn't help wondering whether there might be anything in the myth. Had it, like so many others, developed from some basis of fact?

As I turned off the light, I remembered a saying that I had heard in Afghanistan some years earlier: 'The road to truth begins in the imagination of men.'

With this thought in mind, I closed my eyes, resolving to find out more about the legend of the elephant graveyard.

7

The Plot Thickens

'Life is infinitely stranger than anything which the mind of man
could invent.'

Arthur Conan Doyle, *The Adventures of Sherlock Holmes*

'HEY, BOSS! Vake up! It's late!'

The sound of this voice, together with the loud thumping
on my hotel door, made me sit bolt upright in bed as if I had
received an electric shock. I knew the voice only too well. It
belonged to Vipal Ganguly, my Calcutta cameraman.

'Vakey, vakey, Boss!' came his voice again. 'It is me. Your
best friend, Vipal! Open up!'

For a few groggy moments, I remained trapped between
dreamland and the conscious world, trying to figure out
whether I was hallucinating. A further knock on the door
confirmed that this was not the case. My nightmare was only
just beginning.

'Boss, you in there? It's six o'clock!'

The fact that Vipal was standing in the corridor filled me
with a sense of alarm. Like no other person I had ever met,
the Bengali had the capacity to drive me completely and
utterly round the bend. But on many occasions in the past, he
had done me enormous favours, twice helping me land scoops
that had furthered my career. As a result, I owed him a debt
of gratitude and, difficult as it often proved, went to great
lengths not to hurt his feelings.

Wherever Vipal went, he was always guaranteed to pick up a herd of lackeys, helpers and hangers-on, all hard-luck cases desperate to get a break in journalism. On several occasions when I stayed in Calcutta, he had brought his friends along with him and together they had drunk the hotel mini-bar dry. The likelihood that he was now standing outside my hotel door on his own was next to zero.

'Open up, Boss,' he screeched, banging on the door. 'Have no fear. Vipal is here!'

I lay on my bed, hoping he would go away. For a minute or two, there was silence, but then he started pounding on the door again.

'Shit, shit, shit,' I muttered under my breath, burying my head under the pillow. 'I don't believe this is happening.'

'Come on, Boss. Open up!'

With no apparent alternative, I made my way to the door. Reluctantly, I opened it. Vipal stood there, his face no more than a few inches from mine. He smiled at me like a mischievous imp.

'Hel-loo, Boss!' he shouted, straight in my ear. 'Surr-prrr-ise!'

He put up his fists like a boxer, playfully jabbing at my chest. 'Hey, Boss, nice place,' he said, straining to look over my shoulder.

Then, like an uninvited relative making an unannounced visit, he pushed past me. As I had guessed, he was not alone. This time, Vipal's entourage consisted of no less than seven meek-looking individuals who followed him inside, sheepishly filing past me. Before I could raise a word of objection, they settled themselves on various pieces of furniture around the room.

'Boss, this is Venky, Pratap, SP, Dalchan, Mister Jacob, Meraj and Supan. All my friends.'

They extended their hands towards me and I shook each one.

'What on earth are you doing here?' I asked Vipal, genuinely amazed and crossing my fingers that he didn't know
why I was in Assam. The last thing I wanted was the Bengali
muscling in on the elephant hunt.

Vipal was giddy with excitement. He liked nothing better
than a surprise. Stepping forward, he gave me an affectionate
hug.

'Ha, ha, ha,' he said, winking as he sat on the end of my
bed. 'I am here, Boss.'

'Yes, I can see that you are here,' I said, trying to remain
calm. 'But how did you find me?'

'Ha, ha, ha,' he repeated.

I could feel my nerves tightening. First he had woken
me at six in the morning, and now he was trying to be
clever.

'No, really,' I continued, 'how did you find me? No one
knows where I am. Not even the Delhi office.'

'Oh, Boss,' he said, grinning, 'I am saying to you *so* many
times, I am having fifteen *thousand* friend.'

It was true that Vipal seemed to have contacts everywhere
– he had an uncanny knack of getting to know people.
Apparently, his network stretched even as far as the North-
East Frontier.

'Well, it's great to see you, Vipal,' I said, trying to sound
enthusiastic but still concerned about his motives for being
there. 'So what are you up to? Here for a holiday?'

'No, no, no. I am hearing that you are with eleey-pant. I
love eleey-pant. So I made total journey from Cal to come
with you.'

'Over my dead body,' I blurted out.

Fortunately, my words were drowned out by the television,
which had suddenly been switched on. Grating South Indian
music blared out in stereo, accompanied by the sight of a
buxom, wide-hipped Tamil woman crawling across a daisy
field clad in a wet and clinging chiffon sari. Furious, I

snatched the remote-control from one of the lackeys and turned off the TV.

'Yes, I'm coming to hunt eleey-pant,' continued Vipal, pretending his fingers were a gun and play-shooting with them.

'Oh you are, are you?' I said, grinding my teeth. 'And what makes you think that?'

'Because I am always wanting to travel on eleey-pant,' he replied innocently.

I could feel the rage building up inside me. At any moment, I might erupt. I stalked off to the bathroom to cool down and emerged, several minutes later, armed with a plan.

'So, Vipal, you're coming with us. That's great. We'll have a lot of fun,' I said.

'Yes, yes. Eleey-pant is maximum fun,' he said, jumping up from the bed.

He pretended his arm was a trunk, dangling it from his face and making trumpet sounds. His friends joined in, mimicking him idiotically.

'The only problem is', I added, 'it's not up to me whether you come along. Only Mr Choudhury the hunter can give permission and he's not an easy man to convince.'

It was hard to keep a note of triumph out of my voice.

'Oh, don't worry, Boss,' said Vipal dismissively. 'I am talking with Choudhury. He is inviting me.'

'What? You spoke with him?' I spluttered. 'Who said you could do that? How do you know him?'

'I am knowing him maximum years,' replied Vipal, in a tone that implied this was common knowledge. He looked hurt by my outburst and pouted. 'I am doing total package on him many, many times back,' he added shyly.

I slumped on to the bed and shook my head in disbelief. Like it or not, it looked as if Vipal would be tagging along – unless, of course, I could think of another way out.

*

Having cleared the room of my unwanted and uninvited guests, I washed and dressed and then made my way down to the restaurant. Mr Choudhury and Vipal stood at the breakfast buffet, selecting their food.

Seeing the two of them together brought home Vipal's diminutive size. The Bengali measured no more than five feet, the top of his head coming level with my chest. He was scrawny and his clothes were far too large for him. His jeans, which hung about his legs in loose folds, were bunched up around his ankles, and the sleeves of his shirt were rolled up around his wrists.

Looking at him, it was difficult to imagine that for more than twenty years he had worked as a press photographer, and more recently as a video cameraman, spending his days battling it out in India's vicious press scrums. He had covered famines, riots and countless insurrections. On the day Indira Gandhi was gunned down by her own bodyguards, Vipal was in Delhi on the city's riot-torn streets taking pictures as angry mobs slaughtered thousands of innocent Sikhs.

'That was terrible time only. There was maximum bodies everywhere,' he once told me. 'I got the total coverage. I was sending too many photos, Boss. They were printed in maximum newspapers.'

'Wasn't it dangerous?' I had asked.

'Not for Vipal, Boss,' he'd replied. 'Maximum peoples are liking me.'

'I am from Brahmin caste, but I grew up in poor village only,' he told me humbly, the first time we met. 'No education. No money. Only little food. Maximum hardship. Even we are having none of the modern teengs.'

Considering his impoverished background and lack of formal education, Vipal had done extremely well for himself. His stories appeared regularly on the BBC's international satellite channel and, in his home city, he was something of a celebrity. Even in Bangladesh, where he had made several documentaries, he had become a household name, and recently he had been a special guest of the Prime Minister, Sheikh Hasina.

By Indian standards, he earned a fortune and his salary afforded him the luxury of travelling abroad. Only a month earlier, he had gone to France as the guest of Dominique Lapierre, author of *City of Joy*. The year before, he had stayed in Berlin with the Bangladeshi dissident Tasleema Nasrin.

'Soon I am going to United States of Amrika,' he said, as we sat in the restaurant eating breakfast. 'New York, San Francisco, Chicago, Los Angeles, the total cities. But Boss, I want to meet one man too much only.'

'Who's that?'

'I am *maximum* fan of Frank Sinatra. I love the song, "I am going it my way".'

He began to sing, but this was too much even for Mr Choudhury.

'Please, not at breakfast,' said the hunter politely.

Vipal looked a little hurt but soon recovered.

'So. You teenk I can see Meester Frank?' he asked.

From what I had read in the newspapers, Sinatra was on his deathbed. Still, Vipal had a knack of persuading famous people to meet him and his sheer stubbornness invariably paid off.

'Somehow I have a feeling you'll manage it,' I said.

'Yes, I'm sure you will too,' added Mr Choudhury, who seemed to find Vipal amusing, although I could tell that he was vaguely irritated by the Bengali's incessant chatter.

'So, will we shoot the total eleey-pant today?' asked Vipal.

'No, no shooting today,' replied the hunter. 'The rogue is in Kaziranga.'

I asked Mr Choudhury if he thought Baba had really turned into a tiger.

'No, I don't believe he turned into anything,' he replied. 'But sometimes these people can see things that we cannot.

They are in tune with nature and have certain powers which we do not understand.'

Did he think Baba would find the rogue?

'Perhaps,' replied Mr Choudhury. 'Stranger things have happened, is it not so?'

'Yes, very strange,' interrupted Vipal. 'Once, I saw one man turn into snake only.'

The Bengali paused, hoping one of us would press him for more details. But neither Mr Choudhury nor I took the bait and, having paid the bill, we made for the hotel's front door before Vipal had a chance to say another word.

The watchman who guarded Kaziranga's main gate was a lonely figure, armed with only a *lathi* which he tapped on the ground as he made his rounds. He hummed an Assamese folk-tune and rubbed his hands together, trying to keep warm, his boots splish-splashing through puddles of rain-water. He wore a dark green poncho, woollen mittens and a balaclava which obscured most of his face.

As we waited by the Land Rover on the far side of the gate for our rendezvous with Baba and the others, the guard sat down on his *charpoy* by the roadside. At his feet there burned a wood fire over which a whistling kettle was heating. He took off his mittens and warmed his hands over the flames. Then, once his tea was ready, he poured the liquid into a clouded glass and took a sip, the steam rising up around his face.

A piercing wind whipped across the stretch of no man's land on the edge of the park. I stuck my chin into my chest and tugged my coat collar over my ears. Grimacing at the sky, I tried to locate the sun, but it had vanished behind a canopy of brooding clouds which, even now, were preparing for another assault on the defenceless ground below.

To the south, the steep slopes of the Karbi Anglong hills

were lost in a bank of swirling mist, the tops of the fern trees reaching towards the sky like the arms of drowning mariners. To the north, the jungle looked drab and uninviting, all the colour washed out of its flora as if, overnight, it had been bleached by acid rain.

Even India's ever-present crows seemed depressed by the weather. A row of these ominous-looking birds sat huddled on an overhead telephone wire, silent and bedraggled. Rudra sat in the driver's seat of the Land Rover complaining that the damp was doing little to help keep his stash of betel-nut fresh and crunchy. And for once Vipal was subdued.

Only the hunter seemed to be enjoying what appeared to be the onset of winter. Standing on the edge of the road, wearing sandals with no socks, he surveyed the vast expanse of grassland that stretched out before us, breathing in the clean air with the bearing of a man who truly appreciates nature.

Now that the pressure was off, Mr Choudhury was visibly more relaxed. He and the rogue had both won a reprieve. Still, the hunter was not letting down his guard.

'We must keep a close eye on him. Who knows what he is planning? Perhaps he will stay in the park. Or perhaps he will go back across the river and make more mischief. We must be careful not to allow him to escape. If Baba is not able to help, then we must pick up his tracks from the river and follow them into the park using the *kunkis*.'

'Will you try and lure him out of Kaziranga?' I asked.

'No, no. Let him stay here. Perhaps he will reform.'

'But how long will you wait?'

'Let us see. This is like a game of chess. We will wait for him to make the next move,' he said. 'Then we will see what tactics are required.'

'So it's not over yet?'

'No,' replied Mr Choudhury. 'I'm sure we will be hearing from this elephant again. He is the most extraordinary fellow I have ever come across.'

As we waited by the gate, he told me about his time in Malaysia where he worked during the 1970s and of his passion for rifles.

'Have you ever been to Holland and Holland?' he asked. 'I believe it is in London. I have their catalogue – the most beautiful rifles in the world.'

'You should come to London to visit and I will take you there,' I suggested, expecting him to jump at the idea.

'I am not in any hurry to leave Assam,' said Mr Choudhury.

His brother, he pointed out, had emigrated to Kenya three years before and he had yet to visit him.

'This is my home. I am happy here,' he said. 'But one thing I would like is some back copies of *The Shooting Times*. It is impossible to get hold of it in India. If you could send some copies, I would be most grateful.'

A minute later two Maruti Gypsies pulled up packed with people. Faces peered out at us from the cloudy windows of the lead vehicle, their features warped by the glass. Even so, I recognized Churchill, Mole and Badger crammed into the front seat. The three of them had spent the night in the park and, given the sudden change in temperature, were none too happy.

'This weather really sucks,' complained Mole. 'We hardly slept a wink.'

'Very bad rain, no?' said Churchill as I introduced them to Vipal. 'Too much water coming. Even *hathi* not liking.'

'So what happened to Baba?' I asked Badger. 'Is he still a tiger? Or did he turn back into whatever he's meant to be?'

'Oh 'e's sleeping it off back at the camp,' laughed the Gurkha. 'He stumbled in in the middle of the night with scratches all over 'is face, muttering something about your elephant.'

According to Churchill, the old mahout had located the tusker at the far end of the park and had given us directions as to how to find him.

'He's marked the rogue's position on the map. But I'll believe it when I see it,' added Badger.

Mr Choudhury and Vipal climbed into the lead vehicle. Anxious not to have to spend the next few hours listening to the Bengali, I clambered into the back of the second jeep where I found four forest guards sitting face to face on narrow benches fixed to the jeep's outer walls. I squeezed in next to them.

'Hang on to this,' said one of them in English, indicating a leather strap attached to the roof support. 'It's a rough road and the driver doesn't use the brake pedal much.'

The driver turned the vehicle and floored the accelerator, heading back into Kaziranga, the radials slicing through shallow puddles and causing water to surge up against the windows. I peered out through the black smoke belching from the exhaust. The road behind us appeared to be alive with frogs, hundreds of them hopping around amidst the splattered remains of those unfortunate few who, just seconds earlier, had been flattened by our tyres.

Looking up, I spotted an eagle circling the sky, surveying the landscape. With wings stretched wide, he hung there, gliding on the thermals. Then, quite suddenly, he plunged to earth, only to rise again a few seconds later, a struggling kaleej pheasant pinioned between his talons.

The driver, who would have done well at Brands Hatch, sped through lush grassland where an Indian bison stood grazing. Startled by our engines, it turned and thundered off into the *tara* grass, disturbing a family of swamp deer who darted behind a wall of thorny rattan cane. Further on, we passed a lake where otters played in the water.

The grassland soon gave way to jungle. Moss-covered trees hung with sodden creepers lined the way. The road turned to liquid mud, and as we slid and skidded, the driver shifted into four-wheel drive. The tyres spun through the muck, splattering my knees and shoulders, while the jeep in front covered our windscreen with mud, the wipers smearing it across the glass.

Then, with a crash of thunder that sounded like Semtex exploding, the sky finally gave way. Hailstones the size and consistency of ball bearings bounced off the bonnet and smacked on to the muddy road. Huge raindrops followed, pummelling the foliage on either side of the road and humbling even the largest leaves which bowed under the onslaught.

'At least the rain's slowed down the driver,' shouted the oldest of the four guards over the sound of the downpour. 'We should be thankful for that.'

The guard's name was Dinesh and, like his namesake Mr Choudhury, he was in his mid-fifties. He had spent the past thirty-five years protecting the wildlife of Kaziranga and probably knew more about the park than anyone else.

'The rhino is very special to the Assamese,' yelled Dinesh over the roar of the motor. 'He was brought here by our god Krishna to fight against an evil king. Once the battle was over, the rhino decided to stay and make this his home.'

The guard wore an egg-shaped crystal around his neck. Like all Assamese children, he had been taken at birth to the sacred Temple of the Nine Planets in Guwahati, the only astrological temple in the world. There, the priests had drawn up his chart, predicting the course of his life. His family's astrologer had given him the crystal to help combat the negative influence of Saturn.

'Every Assamese has a chart. It has helped me make the right decisions throughout my life,' he told me. 'And this crystal has prevented destructive influences.'

Judging by the amount of action Dinesh had seen in Kaziranga, and the fact that he had emerged unscathed, his talisman seemed to work. However, some of his colleagues had not been so fortunate. Three months earlier, two of his closest friends had been shot dead by poachers during an encounter on the banks of the Brahmaputra. In that incident, the guard sitting next to me had been wounded. Proudly, he lifted his shirt and showed me the scar where the bullet had passed through his side, just missing his liver by a hair's breadth.

'Some poachers won't give up,' said Dinesh. 'They get about ten thousand dollars for each rhino horn. That's enough for them to retire on – if they survive.'

The road narrowed into a track, the trees closing in all around us. Low-lying branches brushed against the canvas roof. Thunder rumbled in the distance as flashes of lightning lit up even the darkest recesses of the jungle. As the jeep slid across the road, the back wheels going in one direction and the front ones in another, I began to feel sick.

'You know what makes lightning, don't you?' asked Dinesh.

'What's that?'

'Elephants,' said the guard.

'How?'

'Well, they say that when two tuskers fight, their ivory clashes together and it creates flashes of lightning.'

I asked Dinesh if he'd heard of the elephant graveyard.

The guard knew the Brahma legend, though in his version the deity was also assisted by a cow, to whom he gave the secret of immortality, and a chameleon, to whom he revealed the secret of prophecy.

So did he think the graveyard existed?

'Even in Kaziranga, I have never seen an elephant carcass,' he said, his voice wavering in time with the shuddering of the jeep. 'This has often struck me as strange. What happens to the bodies? How can such a big animal simply disappear? It is a great mystery.'

The guard knew of another legend, told to him by his grandfather: 'It is said that some elephants have pearls in their skulls. Even to this day, some poachers look for them. They are called *gaja-muktas*. They are said to be enormous and worth millions of rupees.'

'Have you ever seen one?'

'Oh no,' smiled Dinesh. 'They don't exist. Otherwise, the elephant would have been extinct a long time ago.'

The jeeps churned on, heading south according to Baba's directions. In places, torrents of water raged across our path; in others, the road disappeared into flooded gullies. Shortly after midday, as the rain began to slacken, I spotted a line of men tramping towards us, their rifles slung over their shoulders, their faces camouflaged with oil. As they drew nearer, I recognized them as Amu and his men, returning from their operation on foot.

Caked in mud, their uniforms soaking wet, the guards had spent the night in the park with only their ponchos to protect them from the elements. Yet their efforts had paid dividends and, once again, the lives of more innocent rhinos had been saved.

As for the poachers, they had met with a violent end. The limp bodies of a couple of notorious Nagas, allegedly responsible for numerous elephant and rhino killings, lay on two stretchers. One had been shot through the heart and his shirt was caked in blood. His colleague had been hit twice in the stomach and had taken nearly twenty minutes to die.

'We knew the route they would take. They had to pass over a certain bridge. That's where we laid our ambush,' said Amu, as he showed me their captured weapons, awesome-looking automatic things with telescopic sights and night-vision scopes. 'We ordered them to throw down their weapons, but instead they opened fire on us. That was a big mistake.'

The guards, conscious as ever of conserving their valuable ammunition, fired only six or seven times.

'We will take the bodies back to headquarters and make an exhibition of them there. It helps deter other poachers,' said Amu.

Looking down at the blanched faces of the dead men, I thought how absurd it was that they had lost their lives because of a few inches of rhino horn. After all, modern science has proved, beyond a shadow of a doubt, that the substance does nothing to increase man's virility. And yet millions of Asian men are still prepared to pay through the nose for just a few ounces.

'The poor rhino's cursed, man,' said Mole, as we stood in the drizzle. 'If it wasn't for that horn of his, everyone would leave him alone. Perhaps then he wouldn't be so grumpy.'

I wondered if Viagra would lessen the demand for rhino horn.

'Could be,' said Amu, as he and his men prepared to set off again. 'But I'm not taking any chances.'

An hour or so later, we pulled up next to a raised concrete platform that was used by tourists to spot animals. At last, we had reached the area where Baba said he had seen the rogue.

One by one, we climbed up the ladder. From the top, the view was breathtaking. Behind us, the jungle spread out towards the Brahmaputra, while to the north it gave way to a vast expanse of rugged grassland where a dozen rhinos were grazing. Like prehistoric tanks, they moved slowly yet purposefully across the terrain, lonesome animals that seemed to prefer their own company.

Mr Choudhury stood on the edge of the platform, searching the horizon through his binoculars. But there was not an elephant in sight.

'I knew it,' scoffed Badger. 'This is a wild-goose chase. There's no bloody way you're goin' to find the elephant with the help of that Baba bloke. Let's go to the river and we'll pick up 'is tracks there.'

'It's been raining,' pointed out Mole. 'They will have been washed away.'

'We stand more chance finding him my way than like this,' retorted the Gurkha.

'*Hathi* will come, no?' interrupted Churchill. 'Better to wait some time.'

The hunter decided to give it an hour and so we sat on the edge of the platform and tucked into some packed lunches prepared for us by the Wild Grass Hotel.

As I ate, I questioned Mole about Amu. Though most Indian institutions seem horribly inefficient, riddled with corruption and crippled by bureaucracy, the average Indian is generally unwilling to kick up much of a fuss. And yet, from time to time, I came across individuals like Amu who had taken matters into their own hands and wanted to make a difference.

'Yeah, you're right. Not a lot works around here because there's no accountability. Politicians can get away with murder, quite literally in some cases,' responded Mole. 'But some people are just different, I guess. They don't like things the way they are so they try changing them.'

'But most officials in India are corrupt,' I said. 'What's so different about the Assam Forest Department? You all seem to be very honest blokes.'

'Yeah. That's a funny thing, man,' smiled Mole, who enjoyed filling me in on how things worked in India. 'See, there are three sections in the Forest Department: Wildlife, Forests and Administration. Now there's plenty of money to be made in Forests, taking back-handers for turning a blind eye when someone hacks down the jungle. And Administration, well, those are the guys who control all the money, so all they have to do is skim off some for themselves. But the sort of men who go into Wildlife tend to love animals, so the department's pretty much clean.'

'So you have to care. Is that what you're saying?'

'I think so,' replied Mole. 'If you really care, you'll make a difference. Not enough people in this country care. Plus there are too many of us. What India really needs is three hundred million less people. Then it would be an okay place.'

An hour passed and still there was no sign of the elephant. Disappointed, we prepared to climb down from the platform. Mole went first, then Vipal. Badger was to go next. Mr Choudhury took a last look through his binoculars. Then, just as the Gurkha had started down the ladder, the hunter let out a cry. Much to everyone's amazement, he had spotted the rogue elephant.

'I don't believe it,' Badger blurted out, clambering back on to the platform. 'Let me see.'

He grabbed the binoculars from Mr Choudhury and held them up to his eyes. The tusker had emerged from the jungle about a mile to the north and was moving at a leisurely pace in an easterly direction.

'It's him all right,' said the hunter. 'I can tell by the way he's limping.'

Churchill poked the Gurkha in the ribs.

'See. Mahout is right, no?' he bragged, as giddy with excitement as a lottery-prize winner. 'Gurkha know nothing.'

'I don't bloody believe it,' repeated Badger. 'It's got to be a coincidence. Has to be.'

'Whatever you want to believe, there he is,' said Mr Choudhury. 'We've found him.'

The others came back up the ladder to take a look. Vipal peered through his telephoto lens and started clicking his Nikon F2. Mole squinted through a pair of opera glasses that he had pinched from a theatre in America.

'Hello, old friend,' said Mr Choudhury. 'Now, at last, I can get a good long look at you, is it not so?'

The rogue stopped by a stream to eat some aquatic weed, shoving the vegetation into his mouth with his trunk.

'This is interesting,' said the hunter, who had retrieved his binoculars from Badger.

'What's interesting?'

There was a pause.

'What's interesting?' I repeated, frustrated.

'Oh, he is a *koomeriah*.'

'What's that?'

'It means he is a high-caste elephant,' explained Mr Choudhury, 'a kind of Brahmin.'

As he explained, India's mahouts recognized an intricate elephant caste or *bandh* system, a form of classification laid down in one of the ancient books called the *Matanga-lila*, or *Sport of Elephants*. Long-legged pachyderms with small bodies fell into the *mreega* category and were considered common. But to the elephant connoisseur, the rogue was of a high caste. In the old days, had he been caught as a calf, he would have found his way into a maharajah's stables.

'Judging by the length of the tusks,' continued Mr Choudhury, 'I would say he is about forty years old. See how they are worn down at the ends.'

Borrowing the binoculars, I was finally able to get a close look at the elephant.

Even from such a distance, his tusks would have made a white hunter's mouth water. The slender ivory was sheer white, the tusks curved like two longbows, and his body was muscular and well-proportioned. But otherwise the rogue looked the worse for wear. His ears were frayed around the edges as if they had been rubbed thin with age. His trunk was scarred, several new gashes visible across the upper half. And he was still limping badly. What's more, he was filthy. His left flank was covered in mud, a sure sign that he had been lying down, something elephants rarely do, while his back was covered in twigs and leaves, as if he had attempted to camouflage himself.

'He is trying to keep the insects from biting him,' said the hunter. 'Do you notice anything else about him?'

I had another look but noticed nothing else of interest.

'Not really,' I answered.

'Look at his eyes, they are light-coloured. It is something that I did not see before,' admitted Mr Choudhury.

I was surprised that he could distinguish their shade at such a distance.

'What about them?' I asked.

White or yellow eyes, he explained, are anathema to the elephant connoisseur.

'It is a sign that he is dangerous,' he replied. 'Even though he is of a high caste, no *phandi* would ever capture him in the wild.'

The rogue laboured across the grassland, resting his trunk on his tusks. A crow landed on his back, hitching a free ride.

'Boss, I am seeing eleey-pant,' said Vipal, borrowing the binoculars. 'But I want to get closer. To get the maximum shot.'

'No, you can't do that,' I said.

'Why not?'

'Because the elephant will kill you.'

'Ah, okay,' replied Vipal. He sat down next to me on the edge of the platform and looked dejected. 'But Boss, I am not understanding one teeng. Why don't they just take him?'

'How do you mean? Take who?' I asked.

'You know,' continued Vipal, 'take him. With the streengs.'

I was tired of having to go to extra lengths to interpret Vipal's particular brand of English.

'Vipal, I don't understand you,' I said, trying not to be short with him but having to exercise a great deal of restraint in the process.

The Bengali tried again.

'It's no problem. I have seen it on BBC.' Vipal seemed to think that I was now following his train of thought.

Exasperated, I looked round to see if anyone might be willing to come to my aid. But everyone was preoccupied.

'What wouldn't be a problem?' I asked.

'To take him with the streengs!' he repeated.

It was Vipal's turn to look annoyed.

I sat on the edge of the platform, trying to make sense of it all.

'Do you mean why don't they capture him using ropes?'

'Yes, Boss. That is what I am saying for five minutes past!' His tone seemed to imply that I was being rather dim.

'Oh. Well, I believe it would be extremely dangerous to try capturing him. Even tranquillizing a rogue is no easy matter. If the elephant awoke and found himself tied up,' I elaborated, 'he might break free and kill people.'

I got up from where I had been sitting. Mr Choudhury was still watching his quarry. The elephant had moved on to a hillock. Until now, his legs had remained hidden in the grass, but at last Mr Choudhury was able to get a closer look at his injured ankle.

'I don't believe it!' he called out. 'Look at his lame leg, his ankle!'

I had never seen Mr Choudhury so animated. He sounded like a little boy.

'Do you see?' bawled the hunter, as I snatched Vipal's camera out of his hands. 'Look at his left ankle!'

I zoomed in as far as the lens would allow, adjusting the focus ring.

'Do you see? Do you see the chain?'

I squinted through the viewfinder. The image was grainy. But sure enough, I could make out something metallic wrapped around the elephant's ankle.

'Yes, I see it.'

Mr Choudhury lowered his binoculars and looked at me, his expression one of total puzzlement.

'What does it mean?' I asked.

'It means that he is a *bon-zharshia!*' breathed Mr Choudhury.

'A *bon* what?' I parroted.

'It means the rogue is a *kunki*, a domesticated elephant that has returned to the wild.'

8

The Pool of Ganesha

What boots their thirst, what boots the ravening fly,
The sun that sears their hide of wrinkles made?
Plodding, they leave a country parched and dry,
Dreaming of fig-tree forests and their shade.

Leconte de Lisle, *Les Éléphants*

THE FACT THAT the rogue had once been a domesticated elephant explained a great deal, or so Mr Choudhury assured me later that afternoon as we sat in the comfort of the Wild Grass Hotel.

'He must have been carrying that chain around for some years because it has become embedded in his skin,' said the hunter, as we sat drinking mugs of hot chocolate in front of a welcoming fire. 'The rust and friction have caused an infection. That is why he limps. No doubt it is also contributing to his vile temper.'

This new revelation also shed light upon certain aspects of the tusker's behaviour. The apparent ease with which he moved from one area of Assam to another, rather than sticking to one 'range', could be attributed to the fact that, as a calf, he had been taken from the wild and, consequently, did not behave like a typical male elephant.

Mr Choudhury also believed that something in his past, some terrible event or ordeal, had scarred him psychologically.

'I am not saying that he was a saint to begin with,' he said. 'But something has pushed him over the edge and he is wreaking his revenge. I believe he is trying to get back at humans for what they have done to him.'

I wondered whether there was anything in Baba's assertion that the elephant was dying.

'It is too difficult to tell from such a distance,' he said. 'Perhaps gangrene has set in. If it has, his days are numbered.'

'Why do you think most of his victims have been drunks?' I asked, as a waiter brought the hunter a sandwich.

'Who knows?' he replied. 'Perhaps he was badly treated by someone who drank. It is possible.'

Given this new development, it was now Mr Choudhury's duty to report his findings to the Forest Department in Guwahati. He was planning to leave for the capital within the hour.

'I would like you to stay here. I should only be gone for one day,' he said. 'There is a very slim chance that I may be able to persuade the department to revoke the destruction order because he is a *kunki* and not a wild elephant. Perhaps then they can send someone else to capture him, remove the chain and put him in a zoo.'

He also planned to look through the records and find out about the rogue's past.

'It would be interesting to know where he came from and the name of his owner and mahout. These men have a great deal to answer for.'

In the meantime, Mr Choudhury asked Amu to assign two guards, travelling with two mahouts and their *kunkis* and adequate provisions, to keep an eye on the animal and report his movements to the elephant squad.

'Is that a good idea?' I asked, thinking back to the death of the farmer in the rain forest. 'You know what happened last time you sent guards after him. Someone was killed.'

Mr Choudhury believed it was still worth taking the risk.

'This time it will be different,' he assured me. 'As long as the rogue remains in the park, there is no danger. I will be back by tomorrow night.'

He made his way outside where Rudra was waiting in the Land Rover. The driver had just purchased several chunks of fresh betel-nut from a vendor across the street.

'What about Baba?' I asked. 'How did he know where to find the rogue?'

The hunter shrugged his shoulders.

'Perhaps it was a calculated guess. That area where we spotted him is not far from the river. It was an obvious place to look. He was bound to be somewhere in that vicinity.'

Mr Choudhury got into the passenger seat and rolled down the window. Standing there in the driveway, I must have looked anxious, wondering what was going to happen and how long I would be left hanging around the hotel.

'Don't worry. This matter will be resolved soon,' said the hunter, before he drove off. 'That elephant will not stay in the park. He will head towards the villages. Just remember one of our Assamese sayings: *lahe lahe*, slowly, slowly. When it happens, it happens.'

The hotel restaurant was packed with Indian tourists from Delhi. Plump Punjabi aunties with flabby midriffs bulging from their polyester saris gobbled down *parathas* and butter chicken as their undisciplined children chased one another around the tables. Their husbands, who all sported black moustaches and large bellies, guzzled tumblers of Royal Challenge whisky, cracked jokes with each other and guffawed loudly.

Watching them from the sofa in front of the fire, I felt only pity for the over-worked Assamese waiter. Each time the young man brought another dish, the aunties gave him an earful, ticking him off for this and that, and telling him to hurry up. The men clicked their fingers in the air whenever they wanted a top-up. Not once did I hear any of them say thank you to the waiter.

'I am not liking Delhi people,' commented Vipal, who joined me by the fire. 'They have the maximum aggression.'

I had to agree. Although I had close friends in Delhi, people there were all too often rude and discourteous, which was not the general rule elsewhere in India.

'Okay, so vhat is your idea for tomorrow?' asked the Bengali, changing the subject.

'I need a rest,' I said wearily. 'It's been a long week.'

Concerned that Vipal might come knocking at my door at the crack of dawn, I asked him to allow me to sleep in.

'Don't worry, Boss,' he assured me. 'I have a total plan.'

With these words, he edged along the sofa and began to whisper conspiratorially.

'See, I am making contacts with …'

At that moment, a waiter approached. The Bengali began coughing loudly, apparently nervous that the man might be eavesdropping on our conversation.

'Yes,' he continued, once the waiter had withdrawn, 'I am making contacts with Bodo liberation peoples.'

By this, he meant the Bodo Liberation Front, one of Assam's principal insurgency groups, who were fighting for their own homeland within Assam. From what I understood, they were difficult to meet.

'Can I come along?' I asked eagerly.

His eyes narrowed and he nodded his head.

'Okay, Boss. I am making the total interview.' He looked over his shoulder to make sure no one was listening. 'Don't worry about a teeng.'

I rose from the couch, said goodnight and headed upstairs. Secretly, I was overjoyed at Vipal's latest plan. The prospect of interviewing the Bodos was an appealing one, but even more appealing was the fact that it would take time to set up a clan-

destine meeting. For tomorrow at least, it looked as if I would
be left in peace.

After breakfast the next day, the receptionist asked if I had seen
my companion. Vipal had apparently gone off in the middle
of the night, accompanied by two dubious-looking characters
– the receptionist described them as 'mischief-making men' –
who had arrived on bicycles. Since then, none of the hotel
staff had laid eyes on the Bengali, although the manager was
keen to have a word with him as some of his friends had run
up a substantial bill at the bar and he was anxious that the
amount should be settled.

Delighted that I was destined for a day of peace and quiet,
I returned to my room. An hour or so later there was a knock
at my door. I opened it to find Vipal standing in the corridor,
wearing a fake black beard and moustache, fighter-pilot sun-
glasses and an American baseball cap bearing the words WITH
AN OPEN MIND. He looked like a second-rate pimp.

'Vipal ...' I began, but before I could get any further he
waved his hands frantically in front of my face and rushed past
me into the room.

'No, no, no,' he stuttered. 'Don't be saying my name!'

Then he stuck his head out into the corridor, glanced left
and right and slammed the door behind him.

'See, I am in disguise!' he explained, adjusting his beard
which was slightly lop-sided.

'Some disguise,' I said. 'I recognized you immediately.'

He was crestfallen. His shoulders slouched and his head
drooped. Apparently, he had gone to great lengths to make
himself look inconspicuous.

'It is a maximum disguise,' he said weakly.

Vipal was extremely sensitive and I did not want to hurt his
feelings, so I tried backtracking.

'I only recognized you because I know you, Vipal,' I said,

sounding like a parent offering encouragement to an insecure child. 'No one else would see through your disguise. It's very good.'

As Vipal observed himself in the mirror, I had to fight hard to suppress my laughter – especially when his moustache began to part company with his upper lip.

'So why are you in all this get-up anyway?' I asked.

'Because I am meeting with Bodo liberation peoples,' he whispered, patting down his moustache.

Through a friend of a friend of a friend, he had arranged an interview with a Bodo commander 'in three days' time only'.

'But why the disguise?' I asked again.

'See, I am checking into another hotel under different name. So I am making the total arrangement from there.'

'What's your cover name?'

His eyes narrowed and, for a split second, he looked the part.

'I am Tagore. Mr R. Tagore.'

Rabindranath Tagore, Vipal's hero, was the Bengali poet and playwright who had won the Nobel Prize for Literature in 1913. But I still didn't quite understand the point of his elaborate arrangements for the rendezvous with the terrorists. I suspected they had more to do with my friend's compulsion to turn everything into a drama than with a genuine need for security. That aside, the news sounded encouraging and I congratulated him on his progress.

'Thank you, Boss,' he said, grinning beneath his thick poly-ester whiskers. 'So is there anyteeng new with the eleey-pant?'

Over breakfast that morning, I had chatted with the hotel manager who proved extremely knowledgeable about Assamese culture. When I mentioned my interest in elephant graveyards, he suggested I visit a nearby monastery inhabited by monks who were, he said, the custodians of Assamese culture.

The only problem was that Mole and the others were busy, so I didn't have an interpreter. I needed Vipal's help.

'I can do the maximum teeng,' volunteered the cameraman, who had now taken off his ridiculous disguise and was trying to remove a glob of stage adhesive from his upper lip.

'I don't think so,' I said, pointing out that he did not speak Assamese. 'I doubt the monks know much Bengali, either.'

'Oh, okay. I will bring some friends. We will go and see these monk mens together.'

I insisted that Vipal bring only one interpreter.

'One only?' he said, disappointed. 'But, Boss, I have the maximum number of friends.'

'Yes, I know. But I only want one.'

The man Vipal brought along was a young photographer who had taken only a few pictures in his life, knew nothing about his chosen craft and yet fancied himself as the next Cartier-Bresson. Still, Vipal assured me, he would be a 'tip-top' interpreter.

We rented a car from the hotel and drove east along Highway 37 to the Nowgong district, about an hour west of Kaziranga. Here, rapeseed grew in abundance, blanketing the landscape. Trucks carrying piles of hay chugged along in front of us, shedding their loads, the straw collecting on our windscreen.

As we turned a bend, a group of schoolchildren holding a rope across the road flagged us down, asking for contributions for Saraswati, the goddess of education. It sounded like a scam, but they assured me that the money would be used to buy school supplies. To prove it, they showed me their carefully maintained ledger accounting for all the monies they had received. Suitably convinced, I made a donation.

'Thank you, mee-ster,' they called out as we pulled away. 'Merry Christ-mast!'

Further down the road, next to a little-used railway crossing, a local quack was hawking panaceas to cure everything from AIDS to mental deficiency. We stopped to examine his curious assortment of bottles, which were laid out on banana leaves together with good-luck charms in the form of human teeth supposedly retrieved from the mouths of saints. The vendor showed me an incisor which, he claimed, had once belonged to the Buddha himself. Local legend has it that he received Nirvana, or enlightenment, not far from Guwahati.

Next door, another stall sold ice-cold Fruity Mango Drink, bunches of lychees and green coconuts. I asked the vendor whether he knew where we could find the monastery, but he simply held up an egg between his fingers and squinted at me.

'Egg,' he said, in English.

'Yes, that's an egg,' I agreed, asking our interpreter to translate my words. 'But do you know where the monastery is?'

He continued to hold up the egg.

'Egg,' he repeated, beaming proudly.

To keep him happy, I bought his egg and four of his coconuts. The vendor hacked off their tops with a machete and provided us with straws with which to suck out the milk. Once we had satisfied our thirst, he cracked open the shells and we scooped out the soft flesh.

Strolling across the railway tracks we discovered a bank that looked as if it had been gutted by fire.

'Maybe it was robbed,' I said, as we peeked through the windows. 'There's nothing left inside.'

Vipal had to stand on tiptoe to see through the window.

'You know, Boss, one time I was robbing a bank.'

'What?' I exclaimed, choking on a piece of coconut.

'It's true. I robbed the total teeng.'

Somehow, I found it difficult to picture the diminutive

Bengali bursting into a bank with a sawn-off shotgun and forcing everyone to hit the deck.

'Sure, tell us another one,' I said sarcastically. 'Next you'll be telling me you were a lion-tamer.'

'But it's true, Boss,' he objected.

There was something in his voice that was almost convincing.

'When was this?' I asked suspiciously.

'When I was young only,' he said. 'I was fighting Pakistanis.'

If he was to be believed, this had been in the early 1970s, when East Pakistan, now the independent nation of Bangladesh, was fighting for independence from Islamabad.

'I am becoming freedom fighter when I was seventeen years,' he said. 'I am not wanting to kill, not even a Pakistani. So I am joining one group and doing the maximum damages to infrastructures.'

His unit's main targets had been the country's bridges, power stations and national banks. The resistance movement required cash, and taking the Pakistani regime's reserves helped cripple their administration.

'Did you wear a mask and tell people to stick their hands in the air?' I asked, trying to picture Vipal in a bandanna, toting a six-shooter.

'No, we are robbing bank at night only, hitting the guards on the head. Then we are using dynamite and making maximum explosion,' Vipal told me.

'So how much did you steal?'

The Bengali shuffled his feet.

'How much did you get away with?' I pressed.

'Well, not so much, Boss,' he conceded. 'See dynamite is very strong. It did the maximum damage. The total money was blown apart.'

'So you didn't get a single rupee?'

'No, nothing,' confirmed Vipal, clearly embarrassed.

I was still laughing when we reached the car.

'But we made big problems,' he assured me. 'We were all total heroes.'

We carried on down the road, asking for directions from passers-by along the way. Typically, no one knew the monastery's exact location but everyone was keen to offer advice.

'Go down that road and you are bound to find it,' suggested one bicyclist.

'You will see it over there,' counselled a friendly buffalo herder, waving in the direction of a field.

'It is somewhere here,' said another. 'Turn around and head back where you have come from.'

When we stopped to ask directions from two vendors at a cigarette stand, one man pointed left and the other right.

Eventually, after asking the way from a travelling snake-charmer, a local madman, an auto-rickshaw driver who was also lost, a mendicant in the company of a five-legged holy cow and a dozen other people, we pulled up outside the entrance to the monastery.

Pushing past the rusting gates, we made our way on foot down a sandy lane cut through dense woods. Crimson flowers from silk cotton trees carpeted the way like confetti. Bulbul birds sat in the branches, puffing up their chests and calling to one another, as if warning their friends of our approach.

The lane brought us to the edge of a pond filled with giant turtles, their shells forming miniature islands amidst the water-hyacinths. One of these ancient creatures, which are considered holy by most Indians, surfaced near the water's edge, his toothless mouth nibbling on floating weed, before sinking back into the murky water.

On the far side of the pond crouched a figure wrapped in a length of white cotton. His chest and upper arms were only partially covered, revealing muscles as well developed as those of a body-builder.

When the man looked up, however, I noticed that his features were distinctly feminine. His lips were unnaturally pink as if he was wearing lipstick, his eyelashes were darkened with what looked like mascara, and his hair came down to his shoulders, the ends curled as if they had been professionally permed. At first, I assumed he was a *hijra*, a eunuch. But when he stood up and walked towards us, his hands crossed piously before him, I realized he was one of the monks.

'Welcome to our home,' he said. 'My name is Pitambar.'

Although it seemed that the monk had enjoyed little contact with the outside world and was somewhat shy, he was friendly and hospitable and offered us a guided tour of the *satra*, or monastery.

'Afterwards, I will take you to see the *satradhikar*, our master,' he said, smiling beatifically. 'It is he who knows about everything and will tell you all you need to know.'

Like the rest of the monastery's two dozen monks, Pitambar had taken a vow of celibacy. He and his fellow-ascetics lived in a row of bare cells constructed out of mud and bamboo. The entrances to their dwellings were only a few feet high and, as we walked past them, I had to bend down in order to look inside.

Crouched on the earthen floor, men draped in white cotton bent studiously over their scriptures. In one cell, a teenage monk was practising yoga-like contortions, his legs twisted behind his neck. Next door, a blind hermit with long silvery hair recited mantras, rocking back and forth on his haunches.

'Okay, Boss, let's go,' said Vipal, as Pitambar showed us around his cell, offering us handfuls of nuts and raisins and slivers of coconut. 'Now you have seen the total teeng. There is nothing more.'

'What do you mean? We haven't seen anything. We haven't

even met the head monk yet. You stay in the car if you like,' I told him. 'I'll be at least an hour.'

Sulking, Vipal followed several feet behind us as we approached the *satra's* main building, which was guarded by two clay lions gripping bunches of flowers between their teeth. Known as the *nam ghar,* or prayer house, it looked from the outside more like a village hall than a temple. Yet the interior was unlike any other Hindu place of worship I had ever visited.

Pitambar pushed open the heavy carved wooden doors and we stepped inside. The sanctum was dominated by a wooden pyramid twenty-five feet high and covered in garish red cloth. The base was decorated with carved wooden lions doing battle with ferocious elephants. At the summit of this strange edifice sat a copy of a leather-bound book which contained the cult's handwritten scriptures, dating back five centuries. In front of the pyramid stood two wrought-iron candleholders, their pinnacles crowned by brass peacocks.

Taking off our shoes, we followed Pitambar inside. Two kettle-drums were positioned on either side of the door next to a six-foot-high representation of Garuda, the mythical being who is said to be half man and half bird and is traditionally ridden by the god Vishnu. The only light in the room was provided by a clutch of candles and mustard-oil lamps which flickered in the gloom, lending the room a haunted atmosphere. Vapour trails of soot spiralled upwards, towards the elaborate red and gold awnings hanging from the ceiling.

'This is our place of worship,' explained Pitambar, as several local Assamese entered behind us and, with bowed heads, approached the pyramid where they made their offerings of fruit and nuts. 'This is the holiest place in all Assam.'

I had long found Hinduism, with its myriad cults, deities, incarnations, manifestations and interpretations, virtually impossible to grasp, so I took a deep breath before asking Pitambar which particular brand of Hinduism the monks advocated.

In the event, his explanation proved straightforward.

The monks were followers of a fifteenth-century saint called Shankaradeva, who had reputedly lived to the ripe old age of 120. Until his coming in 1449, Tantric cults that practised black magic and human sacrifice had predominated in Assam.

'One form of divination at the time was to examine a child cut from the body of a pregnant woman who had gone her full term of nine months,' said Pitambar. 'They were dark days.'

However, the country's Messiah preached against such horrific practices and also sought to unite the community by doing away with caste, dowries and idols, encouraging the people to worship one god, Krishna.

'Shankaradeva is the father of the Assamese nation,' said Pitambar. 'He made us one people and brought us together.'

As I was to discover during my travels, every Assamese village has a *nam ghar*, where the corpus of plays written by Shankaradeva to teach social rights and equality are still enacted during major festivals. Assamese Vaishnavism, the prophet's own brand of Hinduism, remains the predominant religion of the Brahmaputra valley.

'It is unique to Assam. You will not find it anywhere else,' said Pitambar. 'We are the guardians of his teachings and Assamese culture.'

But with the influx of hundreds of thousands of illegal Bangladeshi immigrants, not to mention the millions of *adivasis* brought by the British, Assamese culture was under threat.

'Now, more than ever, we must work to preserve it,' he said. 'Without our traditions, we are nothing.'

We walked around the back of the pyramid, where a small alcove housed another shrine containing a collection of relics of Shankaradeva. Vipal tried to take some photographs, but the monk asked him to desist.

'Boss, what about eleey-pant graveyard? They must be having the maximum information.'

I asked Pitambar whether he knew anything about elephants.

'Come,' he said, 'I will take you to the master.'

The master's only possessions were the length of cotton wrapped around his waist, a clay bowl and a rosary of *rudraksha* beads. His cell, which he shared with a diverse selection of Assam's insects, was cold, damp and unlit. A hole in the ground behind the cell served as a latrine. And yet, despite his poverty, the monk seemed serenely content.

I had expected the master to be older, but he could not have been a day over forty. Still, despite his comparative youth, he was considered by the other monks to be in possession of a third eye.

'I can see everything. I can see through you and inside you and beyond you,' he told me as we were introduced.

He was said to meditate for days at a time and to live on just milk and the occasional bowl of rice. Pitambar also told me that the master had committed all the Vaishnavite scriptures to memory, an undertaking he had begun when he was seven.

As we sat before him, crammed into the tiny room with our backs against the wall, the master leaned forward, and for the first time I was able to see his face clearly. Like those of his companions, his features were distinctly effeminate. His cheeks were heavily pockmarked, suggesting that at some stage he had suffered from smallpox. His eyes were sunk deep into his ascetic face, and nature had given him a pendulous lip.

Through the faint light of a slit window in the wall, the master stared back at me.

'The Western world is corrupting our culture,' he said. 'We must ensure that it is preserved. It is our most precious commodity.'

'How do you expect to stop the corruption?' I asked. Did he propose to smash television sets as the Taliban were doing in Afghanistan?

'No. We are trying other ways,' he explained. 'First, we have written to the President of the United States, asking him to stop exporting his culture to India. And second, we are spreading the plays of Shankaradeva, to enforce our traditions.'

'Did you get a reply from Washington?'

'No. But if they do not stop, we will take international legal action against them. In the end, our culture will predominate. It has survived for thousands of years and it will outlive America.'

Before I could ask him about elephants, he began to lecture us on the life of Shankaradeva and the miracles he is said to have performed. I sat patiently listening to him, partly out of interest, partly out of respect and partly to infuriate Vipal who, I could see, was growing increasingly impatient.

Eventually, however, I interrupted the master and asked whether he knew anything of the elephant graveyard.

'Yes, there is one legend,' he said, explaining that it did not exist within the Vaishnavite tradition but had been passed down verbally by the local Assamese.

'When an elephant knows that death is approaching, he goes to a pool. It is called the Pool of Ganesha. This pool is very deep. It is said to go down to the middle of the earth.

'When the dying elephant comes, he first washes himself in its holy waters and then, with his last breath, he plunges into the pool, disappearing for ever.'

'Do you know where this pool is?'

The monk shook his head. 'They say it is in the jungle not far from here in the Nowgong district. When I was a boy, one of my father's friends said he saw an elephant walk up to the edge of the pool and disappear into it. The elephant never came out.'

I asked whether he could give me more precise directions, but he was unable to do so.

'If this pool should ever dry up, then the race of the elephants will die out. We pray that this day will never come. For if the elephant dies, man will forever live in sorrow.'

Our conversation was interrupted by the sound of a monotonous clanging. It came from a cast-iron bell that hung from the branch of a mango tree by the edge of the pond. It was prayer-time. Our audience was over.

As we stepped outside, the other priests emerged from their cells, blinking in the afternoon sunshine. With solemnity, they filed towards the *nam ghar*, their master leading the way. At the steps of the temple, Pitambar invited us inside, but it was getting late, so I thanked him for his time and made my excuses.

We headed back down the lane to the car where the driver was waiting. Just as we were getting ready to pull away, Pitambar came running after us, carrying something in his hand which he gave to me. It was a cotton scarf, embroidered with a red geometric design around the edges.

'My master asked me to give this to you. It is a token of his respect. Wear it always and fortune will smile on you.'

During our visit to the monastery, Vipal had hardly said a word. Indeed, he had seemed threatened by the monks. His body language had said as much, as had his refusal to eat any of the sanctified food offered us by Pitambar.

As we drove back towards Kaziranga, I asked what was the matter.

'I am not liking these monk mens,' he sulked.

'Why not? They were very hospitable and kind.'

'No, they are not good,' he said with finality.

'All monks are a bit strange,' I remarked.

'No, you do not know,' he replied sarcastically. 'You are a foreigner. You are not understanding the total teeng.'

'What have you got against them?' I asked.

'They are maximum homosexual mens,' he said scornfully.

'Don't be ridiculous.'

'I am knowing.'

'They're not gay. And even if they were, so what?'

Vipal glared out of the window, flicking his hands at me in a dismissive manner.

'What have you got against homosexuals anyhow?' I demanded, the level of my voice rising.

'They are having AIDS!' he burst out. 'We can be catching it!'

'AIDS!' I snorted. 'You could only get AIDS by having sex with them. Or if you had a blood transfusion and they supplied the blood. Unless I'm very much mistaken, I don't remember having either sex or a blood transfusion while we were there.'

'You are eating their total coconuts,' he said. 'For sure, now you will be getting maximum AIDS.'

Neither of us said another word all the way back to the Wild Grass Hotel. Even so, the day had proved a tremendous success. I had discovered another legend about the elephant graveyard and had even been given some indication of where I might find it.

Back in my hotel room, I found a message under my door from Mr Choudhury. It read: 'Meet me at camp at four tomorrow afternoon. Have found out everything about the elephant.'

9

Death of a Mahout

'Elephants are continually being compared to man in favourable terms. This is supposed to be some great compliment. Yet surely to these extraordinary creatures, there can be nothing more demeaning.'

Bill Canning, *Elephant Days*

HUDDLED IN COARSE blankets, the members of the elephant squad and the Kaziranga mahouts were gathered in the dark around a smouldering campfire, playing a bastardized version of gin rummy with a dog-eared pack of British Airways in-flight cards.

Intermittently, as they drew burning twigs from the fire to light the ends of their cheroots, I caught glimpses of their faces. Shadows enhanced their features, accentuating hooked noses and cauliflower ears, while the combination of the smoke and the flickering light added to their sinister appearance.

The mahouts regarded one another with suspicion. Eyes peered cautiously over the tops of tightly clasped hands of cards. Scrutinizing his opponents for any sign of bluff or weakness, one man chewed on the cuticle of his left thumb. Another nursed his bottom lip and studied his cards intently as if the game were a matter of life and death.

In slow succession, each mahout picked up a card from the pile and added it to his hand. Bets of only a few rupees at a time were laid. This was no high-stakes game. Nonetheless, the oldest amongst them, a man whose eyebrows joined in the middle, was amassing a tidy sum. Each time he won a round, he let out a triumphant crow and gathered up his winnings with both hands like some greedy moneylender. The disappointed murmurs of his vanquished opponents suggested that unless their luck changed for the better, they would all soon be forced to fold.

I sat on a nearby tree-trunk cocooned in a sleeping bag, trying to stay warm and waiting for Mr Choudhury. Mole, Badger and Vipal sat chatting with Baba. Churchill, who apparently did not feel the cold and was wearing only a thin shirt and tatty trousers, sat by my feet with his back to the log. He was trying to tune his short-wave radio to the BBC World Service. He turned the knob and the speaker spat out a succession of whirrs and buzzes and snatches of foreign languages. I recognized many of the stations. First came the Americanized Eastern European accent of Voice of Russia, then the enthusiastic lilt of an Australian presenting a programme on pet-care for ABC. Next there was some ping-pong-sounding music from Radio China, and for a moment the mahout settled on Voice of America. Finally there came the comforting sound of the BBC: 'This is London.'

'BBC is best, no?' said the mahout, who had bought the radio years before on the Burmese black market. 'Very good English language. Make mahout international, no?'

I had noticed that Churchill was in the habit of listening to the radio whenever he was feeling anxious. It was his form of escape. On this occasion, he was growing increasingly uneasy about the rogue's latest movements.

'*Hathi* wants drink, no?' said the mahout. 'He has been on . . . how you say, cold chicken.'

'I think you mean cold turkey,' I replied.

'Chicken, turkey, duck, all same. *Hathi* want drinking. No drink in Kaziranga, I think, no?'

According to the guards who were following the rogue, he would reach the park's eastern perimeter in approximately thirty-six hours. That would put him within striking distance of a number of villages in the Nowgong district, not far from where we had visited the *satra*.

'Soon we must go,' he said. '*Hathi* is big danger.'

A presenter on the BBC introduced a programme about people obsessed with personal grooming. This seemed bizarre stuff to be broadcasting to an international audience, especially given my present company.

Churchill poked me in the leg, snapping me out of my daydream.

'How is hotel? Very nice, no?' he asked.

I nodded enthusiastically, wishing I was back in my queen-size bed.

'You like warm room and nice bath,' stated the mahout.

'Yes,' I said cautiously, wondering what he was getting at.

'Huh,' he said with contempt. 'You soft. No like life of mahout. Too hard for *firang*, no?'

It was true that I had found the squad's way of life hard going. Still, his comment hurt, even though I suspected his uncharacteristic severity had more to do with his concern over the rogue than with any real disapproval of my lack of fibre.

'That's not true,' I protested. 'I like camping out and looking after the *kunkis*.'

Churchill let out a loud tut.

'You like girl,' he said, 'very soft.'

He looked at his watch, holding the face up to the light of the fire.

'Where is Shikari?' he asked. 'Maybe he is stopping for drink. Just like *hathi*, no?'

It was well past eleven o'clock before the Land Rover's headlights were spotted along the Kaziranga road, making their way towards the camp.

As the vehicle approached, I felt a growing sense of anticipation. What dark secrets had been uncovered? Where did the rogue come from? Why were his victims mostly drunken men? And how had he escaped captivity? With any luck, all these questions – and more – were about to be answered.

Mr Choudhury was soon standing before us. Sipping a mug of tea, he stretched his legs and massaged his neck. The drive had been a long one. Judging by his haggard features, the hunter had had little or no sleep in the past thirty-six hours. The fact that he was still wearing the same clothes and had not shaved also suggested that his schedule had been a hectic one. Nevertheless, his eyes were twinkling with excitement. Clearly, things had gone well in Guwahati.

'I am sorry for being so late,' he began, as we all gathered round. 'Please bear with me a little longer. You will find that what I have discovered has been worth the wait.'

He stooped to pick up a kettle of tea which was boiling on the fire and refilled his mug.

'My trip was a success. I now know more about the rogue's past,' continued Mr Choudhury. 'It is one of the most astounding stories that I have ever come across. And one a journalist will love,' he added. He paused and nodded at me with a conspiratorial smile. 'I have brought with me someone who knows this story better than any other man alive.'

He turned towards the road where a Hindustan Ambassador was just pulling up next to the Land Rover.

'Mr Jain,' called out Mr Choudhury, 'please, come and join us.'

The car's headlights were switched off. A driver got out and scurried around the back of the Ambassador to open the door on the far side. We all strained to see who this mysterious guest could be, but the inside of the car was pitch black. Then one of the mahouts stepped forward with a hurricane lamp, illuminating the area where the vehicles were parked. A figure got out of the car, and as he walked towards us, we were provided with our first glimpse of the mysterious Mr Jain.

He was a stout gentleman with fleshy cheeks and an abundant waistline that stretched his belt to the limit. Indeed, the newcomer reminded me of an overfed cat, for his moustache stuck out like whiskers. Otherwise, however, I could see nothing remarkable about Mr Choudhury's friend – until, that is, he approached the campfire. For it was then that I noticed that there was something extraordinary about him. Mr Jain had no legs. He was walking with the aid of a cane on two aluminium prostheses.

'I am pleased to introduce you to the owner of the rogue elephant that we have been pursuing,' said Mr Choudhury, who was evidently developing a taste for theatrics.

The hunter helped Mr Jain to a place on the tree-trunk. With some difficulty, he sat down, his imitation legs sticking out in front of him. The mahouts brought their guest some betel-nut arranged on a lime leaf and then some tea. Their hospitality was touching, but I was growing impatient.

'Did he really own the elephant?' I whispered to Mr Choudhury. 'How did you find him?'

'Yes,' chipped in Churchill, 'tell us *hathi* story, no?'

The hunter raised his hands, appealing for quiet.

'I think it would be best if Mr Jain told you everything.'

Mr Jain leaned back on the palms of his hands to prevent himself from falling off the log. It was a cold night but he was sweating as if it was midday on the equator, beads of perspiration rolling down his neck. Before beginning his narrative, he took a crumpled packet of 555s from his suit pocket and lit one. Then, smoothing down the few remaining strands of hair on his otherwise bald head, he turned to Mr Choudhury and raised his eyebrows, as if looking for inspiration.

'I suggest you start at the beginning,' prompted the hunter.

Mr Jain nodded and drew hard on his cigarette.

'I am a businessman,' he began, licking the perspiration

from his upper lip. 'I own a transport company. Mostly, I deal with tea. From Assam we send it down to Calcutta and then ship it to the UK.'

Judging by his fair features and green eyes, I guessed that he was a Marawari, a term used to describe businessmen from the state of Rajasthan who are said to own half of India. The majority of Indians despise them as a class for their overt materialism and legendary stinginess. They are often referred to as the Jews of India.

'As a child,' he continued, 'I dreamed of owning my own elephant, but my father would never allow me to have one. He said the animals were dangerous and that I would get hurt . . . How right he was,' he added, exhaling a cloud of cigarette smoke.

'Many years later, in 1986, a mahout came to the door of my house where I live on the edge of the jungle outside Guwahati. He was travelling with an elephant, a beautiful creature with long tusks. The mahout said he wanted to sell the animal and I couldn't resist. As I said, I had always wanted an elephant. So, after some haggling, I agreed to buy it.'

Despite his enthusiasm for elephants, Mr Jain admitted that he knew nothing about the animals. In his excitement, he did not stop to ask where the tusker had come from, or about his past. Nor did he seek out an expert's opinion as to whether the animal was suitable as a domesticated pet.

'There was only one condition to the sale,' continued our guest, lighting his second cigarette. 'I could not buy him without hiring his mahout. But right from the start, I disliked and distrusted the man. At our first meeting, I could smell the stench of alcohol on his breath. I should have got rid of him immediately. He was always getting into fights and was rarely sober. Dev was his name, but I soon came to call him Devil.'

Mr Jain's business kept him travelling all over India and he spent little time at his house near Guwahati. Often, he would be away from home for weeks on end.

'One day, I returned from a trip to Delhi to find the animal in a terrible condition and all alone. He hadn't been fed properly and he looked emaciated. Also, he was tied to a tree with a chain which was too tight for his ankle and it had rubbed his flesh raw. Scars on the animal's back, legs and head suggested that the mahout had beaten the unfortunate animal with his *ankush*.

'But Dev was nowhere to be seen. I searched for him and eventually tracked him down to the local gaol where he was being held for fighting in a bar.'

Mr Jain made a fist with his left hand as he spoke, squeezing his fingers.

'I discovered that the mahout had been stealing the elephant's fodder allowance and buying arak and whisky, and gambling at cards.'

Churchill and the other mahouts were disgusted.

'If mahout steal food *hathi* know, no?' interrupted Churchill, who was clearly disturbed by the story and had been tutting throughout. 'That is making *hathi* most *very* angry.'

'So what did you do next?' asked Mr Choudhury, prompting the Marawari to continue.

'I fired the mahout. I told him to get out and never return. Otherwise, I would have him thrown in prison. He left and I soon found another man to look after the elephant.'

For some weeks, everything seemed to go well. The new mahout treated the tusker kindly, fed him properly and nursed him back to health. But then, one day, Dev came back. Drunk and cursing, he demanded money from Mr Jain which, he said, was owed to him.

'I told him to get out and went to call the police. I walked behind the house where we kept the elephant. The mahout followed me, shouting at the top of his voice. His presence had an instant effect on the elephant, who was in *musth* and already bad-tempered. The animal strained against his chain.

He kicked at the earth. He trumpeted. He wanted to break free and get at the mahout, who stood just out of reach. His eyes were wild. He was insane.'

Mr Jain's words began to flow more quickly.

'Even now, Dev jeered at him. He stood there laughing like a clown. Then, suddenly, the chain snapped. The elephant was loose. He charged at the mahout. Dev turned to run, but the animal grabbed him and hurled him to the ground. He lay there, putting up his arms in defence. He tried to order the elephant to stop, shouting out, "Stop! Kneel! Lie down!" But his fate was sealed. I could see the lust for revenge in the elephant's eyes.'

Mr Jain's hands began to shake and a muscle in his eye twitched involuntarily.

'The elephant picked up Dev and lifted him in the air. He was screaming for help, but there was nothing to be done. I stood there watching, horrified. Then the tusker slammed him down on the ground. I could hear the crunch of bones. He was not a strong man. He died immediately. He was lucky.'

The rogue hadn't finished with him, however. As with his other, more recent victims, he proceeded to batter the body.

'Finally, he ground the remains into the earth. The elephant was covered in blood. It was all over his tusks and all over his trunk . . .'

The Marawari's voice cracked as he paused to wipe the sweat from his brow.

'Next, he came for me. The last thing I remember, he was towering over me. Then I must have fainted. Either that or my mind has blanked out what happened next.

'When I came round, I was in excruciating pain. I was lying on the ground in a pool of my own blood. I sat up with great difficulty. Then I looked down and found that my legs . . . my legs . . .'

Mr Jain's voice broke as he lowered his head.

'My legs had been crushed,' he whispered. 'I believe the

elephant did this to me deliberately,' he said after a long pause, his voice now quiet and reflective. 'He wanted me to live in agony. He wanted me to remember him every day for the rest of my life. And so I have done for the past ten years.'

The Marawari did not see his condition as a misfortune. Rather, he believed it was punishment for some terrible sin committed, perhaps, in a past life.

'I must have done something very bad to deserve this,' he said. 'But what it could have been, I cannot imagine.'

A northerly wind had begun to blow across Kaziranga, pitching up leaves and loose bits of straw from the ground and throwing them across the landscape. The embers in the fire stirred, red-hot coals revealing themselves beneath the grey ash. The mahouts drew their blankets ever tighter around them.

Mr Choudhury sat down on the log next to Mr Jain and continued the story where his guest had left off.

'The elephant made his escape and was declared a rogue,' he said. 'After a few days, another hunter, who is now retired, went after him. The rogue escaped across the Brahmaputra. Eventually, he went into Arunachal Pradesh.'

The hunter took a deep breath and exhaled.

'History has a way of repeating itself, is it not so?'

We sat pondering over the story for a few minutes before I asked Mr Choudhury whether he had had any luck with the Forest Department. Had they revoked the destruction order?

The hunter shook his head regretfully.

'I'm afraid not,' he said. 'The elephant has killed too many people. He is too dangerous. He must be destroyed.'

'What about you, Mr Jain?' I asked. 'Do you want to see him killed?'

The cripple nodded his head.

'I'm not interested in revenge,' he insisted. 'I do not blame him for what he did to me. I blame myself for not taking proper care of the animal. And I feel responsible for what he has done.

'If you can shoot him,' he continued, looking Mr Choudhury in the eye, 'you would be ending a lot of pain and misery. Most of all his.'

Mr Choudhury nodded.

Mr Jain raised himself from the log. 'By coincidence I was coming this way for a meeting and I was happy to accept Mr Choudhury's invitation to tell my story. But now I must get going if I'm to make my appointment. Let me wish you good luck.'

We shook hands and then he made his way to the car. Mr Choudhury gave him a helping hand as the rest of us followed behind.

'Just one more thing before you go,' I said, as he squeezed into the back of the Ambassador. 'What's the rogue's name? He must have a name.'

'Yes, he does,' he replied. 'He is called Phandika.'

10

A Rendezvous with Terrorists

'When you have got an elephant by the hind leg and he is trying to run away, it is best to let him run!'

Abraham Lincoln

AT FOUR-THIRTY the next morning, I tiptoed past Vipal's room and made my way down to the lobby with my bags. Mr Choudhury was waiting for me by the front desk.

'Where is Vipal?' he asked, as I settled the bill. 'Is he coming?'

'He'll catch up with us later,' I said, not entirely truthfully.

In fact, the Bengali and I had stayed up late the night before. I had bought a bottle of Old Monk rum from a local off-licence and, while I hadn't touched the stuff, Vipal had had seven or eight glasses. It wasn't long before he began to sing Frank Sinatra hits in a voice that would have been considered distasteful even in a karaoke bar. Shortly after midnight, he launched into an ear-splitting rendition of 'New York, New York', and as he finished the last verse, reaching a shrieking crescendo that threatened to perforate my eardrums, he keeled over on his bed and passed out. I was fairly sure he would not wake up before lunch, by which time we would be well on the trail of the rogue elephant.

'It will be up to him to find us later,' said Mr Choudhury, as we loaded our bags into the back of the Land Rover. 'But I won't wait around for anyone. This isn't a Cub Scout outing.'

The hunter was in no mood for complications. The rogue elephant, who was still on the move, was expected to reach the park's perimeter the next morning. Mr Choudhury planned to cut him off by heading east along the highway which ran around the edge of the park. Then, once we reached the Nowgong district, we would head south into the rain forest.

'If we leave now with the elephants, we will reach the edge of the park as he comes out,' said the hunter, as we drove to the squad's camp. 'There are no villages in that area, so we will not be endangering anyone's life.'

There was just one problem.

Assam's main insurgency group, ULFA, had declared a day's *bandh*, or strike, to protest against the arrest of a member of their high council. The militants had ordered the entire population, with the exception of those working in the emergency services, to remain at home from six in the morning until six in the evening. All shops would remain closed, all factories would shut down. No tea would be picked, no oil would be pumped and no planes would land at Guwahati airport. Vegetables would decay, fish would go bad, meat would turn rotten. Not a single government office would function – not even the Chief Minister's. In short, the entire state of twenty-three million people would come to a grinding halt.

'How can that happen?' I asked Mole when we reached the squad's camp inside Kaziranga, where Churchill and the others were packing up their tents. 'A bunch of thugs can't just close down the place.'

'Sure they can. It happens several times a month,' said Mole nonchalantly. 'It costs the government and business millions in lost revenue. But there ain't nothing they or the army can do about it, man.'

'Doesn't anyone stand up to them?' I asked.

Mole looked at me.

'Would you?'

'Sure I would.'

'Well then, you're stupid and you'd get shot, man. ULFA kills anyone found outside during a *bandh*.'

'Okay, so I'd stay at home,' I conceded. 'But I wouldn't be happy about it.'

'You're not Assamese, man,' pointed out Mole. 'We're a lazy people and most of us love the strikes. As a matter of fact, ULFA usually calls them on a Friday or a Monday which gives everyone a nice long weekend to sit at home and watch videos.'

Given ULFA's track record, didn't he think it was a bad idea to travel along the state's only highway? 'We'll be spotted in a heartbeat. Can't we go through the park?' I asked, concerned that we might end up dead. 'Surely that would be safer. There aren't supposed to be any militants in Kaziranga.'

But there was no choice. Travelling through the park would take too long.

'Relax,' said Mole, 'it'll be fine.'

'You just said I'd get shot if I went outside!'

'Don't worry about it, man. I know these guys. They won't touch us. They're probably all at home watching videos too.'

We set off under a blood-red sky, waving farewell to Baba and the other Kaziranga mahouts who came out of their tents to give us an enthusiastic send-off.

Sitting astride Raja, I was happy to be back on the road again. As much as I had enjoyed the comforts of the Wild Grass Hotel, I had come to realize that there is nothing to compare with the thrill of travelling on elephant-back. The leisurely pace made me appreciate the beautiful countryside far more than if I had been in a coach or a car. It also gave me a sense of freedom and timelessness which, for all the tension of the hunt, I found relaxing. Somehow, moving about on an animal rather than in a machine made the whole endeavour of travelling seem more worthwhile. With each mile came a growing sense of achievement that I had not experienced before.

Jasmine followed behind us, pulling up clumps of juicy green grass from the verge. After bashing them against her knee to remove the dirt, she stuffed the clumps into her mouth and seemed to wink at me as if to say that I didn't know what I was missing. The Land Rover brought up the rear, packed with Badger, Mole, Rudra and two forest guards provided by Amu for our protection.

Raja, who during our time in Kaziranga had been carrying on with an attractive young female, was in high spirits. Indeed, had it not been for the fact that he weighed seven tons, I would have sworn that there was a spring in his step. Repeatedly, from inside his chest, he emitted a deep, satisfied rumbling noise. It sounded like a bad case of indigestion, but according to Mr Choudhury it was the skin over his nasal passage vibrating like a drum and creating the sub-sonic wave that could travel twelve miles and be understood by all other elephants.

'It is a far more sophisticated form of communication than anything we humans are capable of,' said the hunter, who was sitting behind me. 'If we want to talk with someone over that distance, we have to use a radio.'

I wondered if Raja was chatting to his girlfriend back in Kaziranga. For all I knew, at that very moment he was wooing her with some choice pachyderm poetry. Then again, perhaps he was warning the rogue of our approach. Did his loyalties lie with the tusker or with his human masters?

My thoughts were interrupted by the thudding sound of helicopter rotor blades. Looking up at the sky, I soon spotted a camouflaged army Chinook skimming across the tops of the Karbi Anglong hills and then swooping over the road half a mile ahead where it hovered like a bird of prey searching for its breakfast. The force of its blades stirred up a whirling dust storm, beating back bushes and bending over trees. Then, from the middle of this whirlwind charged two formations of Black Cats, India's Special Forces, armed with machine guns. Zigzagging across the road in neat formation, they took up positions along the hedgerows, the officers scanning the countryside with their binoculars.

Then more army personnel came into focus. Soldiers marched along the verge, bristling with grenades, bayonets, pistols, knives and machine guns. Jeeps sped past. Troops manoeuvred across paddy-fields, gesturing to each other with hand signals. The Chinook veered off to the south, climbing into the sky where it hovered high above the ground.

Evidently, we had walked straight into the middle of a major operation.

'ULFA killed two soldier yesterday,' said Churchill, who hated the omnipresent Indian army, likening them to an occupation force. 'Now they search. Take revenge.'

It wasn't long before we were stopped at a checkpoint manned by a group of thuggish-looking, plain-clothed Assamese. Their commander, who wore a uniform, was a cocky Punjabi badly in need of a lesson in public relations.

'Hey, you ugly *jungleys*,' he called out to Churchill and the others in Hindi, spitting at the ground. 'Where the hell do you think you're going?'

The mahout tried to explain our mission, but the Punjabi only sneered and spat again.

'Shut your mouth, *jungley*,' he shouted aggressively. 'Get down from the elephant. Give me your ID.'

Fortunately, despite the soldier's insulting language, Churchill kept his cool and ordered Raja to sink to his knees. Mr Choudhury, the mahout and I slid down the elephant's side on to the road, the commander looking at Churchill with contempt.

'Your ID, now!' he barked, snatching away Churchill's identity card.

I knew from past experience that the Punjabi's attitude was typical of many soldiers and officers based in troubled states such as Kashmir and Assam. Mostly, these men hail from elsewhere in India and they tend to regard the Kashmiris and the Assamese as troublemakers. Indeed, at checkpoints, they generally show disdain for the locals, an attitude that does little to endear them to the population.

'Hey, you, foreigner,' the officer cried in English when he spotted me. 'What the hell are you doing here?'

He swaggered over to where I was standing between Raja and Jasmine.

'I'm on my way to Nowgong,' I replied.

'Where are you from?' he demanded, standing inches from my face.

'I'm British,' I told him.

He held out his hand.

'Passport.'

'How about a "please",' I said, irritated by his tone.

'Passport!' he spat.

I handed it over. He grabbed it and, turning the pages, scrutinized every single visa and stamp. The names of the countries in it read like the United States' list of terrorism-supporting nations: Afghanistan, Sudan, Iraq, Iran, Algeria. All I was missing was Libya. Finally, he came to a green sticker printed with an Islamic crescent and read out the word emblazoned across the top: 'Paa-kee-stan.'

I could almost read his mind as he jumped to all sorts of convoluted and paranoid conclusions. As far as he was concerned, the fact that I had visited India's arch-rival condemned me as a dangerous terrorist. After all, I might be an agent of ISI, Inter-Services Intelligence, Pakistan's secret service, who are known to aid Assam's militants, or maybe a gun-runner, supplying arms to the various insurgency groups.

'I'm taking you in for questioning,' he said, grabbing me by the shoulder. 'You come with me.'

I tried to explain that I was a journalist but he wouldn't listen. While Mr Choudhury protested, he began to lead me across the road.

Just then, Mole, who had been slow at getting out of the Land Rover, intervened, saying that he was a senior officer with the Forest Department and that I was a fully accredited journalist and his guest in Assam.

'Well, what are you standing around here for? Go on! Get out of here or I'll have you all arrested!' He stomped off to the other side of the road as we climbed up on to the elephants.

Churchill nestled his feet behind Raja's ears and, with a shout, the *kunkis* lurched forward.

Curling his lip, the Punjabi saluted me with a quick flick of his hand to his forehead and, hawking, spat a gob of phlegm on to the road.

Only when we were out of earshot, did Churchill start cursing.

'Bastard mens, no?' said Churchill. 'They are mating with buffalo.'

The soldiers were soon far behind us. However, the incident had left the squad feeling angry and unsettled, and for some time they talked to one another in Assamese in raised voices, leaving me out of the general conversation.

Mole had switched places with Mr Choudhury and was now sitting behind me. When he and the others had cooled down, I asked him about the plain-clothes Assamese that we had seen at the checkpoint.

'They didn't look like soldiers,' I said. 'Why weren't any of them in uniform?'

'They're what we call SULFA, ULFA militants who have surrendered and are now on the army payroll,' he said. 'They're used to hunt down their former comrades. They're a *very* dangerous bunch, man.'

These so-called 'surrendered militants' are allowed to retain their arms and are encouraged to police certain territories. The policy has proved effective at weakening ULFA but has also given SULFA units *carte blanche* to set up protection rackets and terrorize the local people. Anyone standing in their way is fingered as a militant and arrested or gunned down during so-called 'encounters'.

'The government just wants the militants under control and out of the headlines, and they don't care how it's done,' said Mole. 'But it's a sick, cowardly policy. It leaves the local people at the mercy of these thugs. They've created a monster and it's going to come back and bite them on the ass.'

The road was deserted thanks to the strike. So, too, were the few villages scattered along the way, save for a few defiant souls who emerged from their homes to give presents to the *kunkis*.

'Blessings upon you,' called out one slim Assamese woman who dashed out into the road with a banana for Jasmine before quickly scampering back inside her house.

'God protect you,' beamed a toothless old man who brought Raja some lychees, allowing the elephant to take them from the palm of his hand.

In the next village, the head of the local *nam ghar*, or prayer house, came out on to the highway and invited us to stop and share some tea.

'You are my guests. Please stop and honour my home,' he implored.

But there was not a moment to lose and Mr Choudhury, thanking the man for his kind offer, urged the squad on towards Nowgong.

By midday, however, everyone was in need of a break, especially the elephants, and when we came upon a garage and café, we padded into the car park. A sign over the petrol pumps read: SWASTIKA SERVICE STATION. Next to it hung a swastika, the arms pointing anti-clockwise, a sign that figures in nearly all of India's great religions. In the Buddhist tradition it represents the Buddha's footprints; to the Jains it is a symbol of their seventh saint; while to the Hindus it is simply an auspicious sign and is often found on the front door of people's homes.

We dismounted in front of a squat concrete building that housed the café. Much to everyone's surprise the place was open. When Churchill pushed through the doors, two muddy-faced boys carrying wooden boxes bursting with pots of polish and brushes ran out shouting, 'Shoeshine! Shoeshine!'

They pointed at my sneakers.

'Shine good!' they both screeched. '*Panch ruppeea!* Five rupees!'

I pointed at my Nikes.

'You can't polish these,' I said. 'They're made of foam and rubber.'

'Yes, yes,' cried the boys. 'Shining!'

I shook my head apologetically.

'Why don't you do their shoes?' I said, pointing to Raja and Jasmine's enormous feet.

The two boys looked at one another in confusion and then up at the elephants, cocking their heads like puppies reacting to an unfamiliar sound. Then they both screeched 'Okay!' and ran over to the mahouts to plead to be allowed to polish the *kunkis'* feet.

The rest of us walked into the dingy café where our nostrils were assaulted by the powerful smell of rancid butter. Fans hung from the ceiling covered in cobwebs thick with decomposing flies. Behind the cash register, the proprietor, a man with a larcenous face and greedy, bloodshot eyes, sat counting a wad of dirty banknotes. A toothpick protruded from between his stained teeth, the end gnawed like a dog's bone. Narrowing his eyes, he motioned us to a table on one side of the room under a sign that announced: 'CAUSE NO NUISANS'.

A waiter brought us each a metal cup brimming with tap water. Thirsty, I lifted one to my lips, only then noticing the bits of finely chewed meat swimming about at the bottom. After that, I settled for a bottle of warm Thums-Up cola and a packet of stale Hombre nacho chips. I was still suffering from the after-shocks of the meal at the AßBA Restaurant and wasn't going to take any more risks.

My companions were equally decisive when it came to giving their orders. The day's menu offered yoghurt and rice, and nothing more. It took less than five minutes for their food to arrive and when it did, I couldn't help looking down at their plates in disgust. Even the smell made me feel nauseous.

The only other customers in the Swastika café were four men dressed identically in white cotton *kurta* pyjamas. With their yellow skin, wiry beards, oriental features and blue turbans, they looked like Hazaras, a people who inhabit central and western Afghanistan and are reputedly descended from the hordes of Genghis Khan.

Curious, I went over to greet them. However, as I drew nearer, I noticed that their turbans were not Afghani, they were *pagris* or Indian turbans, tied like a Sikh's.

'We live in a village called Barkola,' said the youngest of the group in English when I asked them where they were from. 'Our car broke down early this morning and now we are stuck here until the *bandh* is over.'

They might have looked and even dressed like Sikhs, but they were spindly individuals compared to those I had seen in Amritsar. There, the men sported great black beards and ceremonial daggers tucked into their belts.

'You are thinking that we are not like the Punjabi Sikhs you have seen in north India,' he said, evidently guessing my thoughts. 'This is because we are Assamese Sikhs. My name is Gurudutt Singh.'

Shaking me by the hand, the young man invited me to sit down next to him. Intrigued, I drew up a chair.

'Our forefathers came here in 1824,' he continued. 'They were sepoys in the British army and fought against the Burmese. After many battles, they decided to stay. They fell in love with the Brahmaputra valley and the beautiful local girls.

'When our forefathers settled here, they retained no links to their home. Their children were born Sikhs, but over the years our traditions were mostly forgotten. Because of our Assamese blood, we grew only short beards.'

Finally, in the 1970s, the village elders decided to take action to save their traditions. They raised funds to send a representative to Amritsar to establish links with their past and bring back a copy of the Sikhs' holy book, the Guru Granth Sahib.

'When he arrived at the Golden Temple in Amritsar, our most holy shrine, the other Sikhs laughed at him. They said, "What kind of a Sikh are you? You do not speak Punjabi or even Hindi. And you cut your beard off which a Sikh must never do."'

With difficulty, the envoy established his credentials and, eventually, he was able to return to his village with a teacher, who helped the Assamese Sikhs to re-establish their traditions and learn Punjabi.

'Now we are knowing our religion well, except the old men are a bit slow,' he said, laughing. 'They are taking their lead from us.'

Glancing over Gurudutt's shoulder, I noticed that Mr Choudhury and the others were paying for their food at the cash register and making for the door. But before I left, I asked the Sikhs whether they knew anything about elephant graveyards.

They shook their heads.

'We do not know anything about elephants,' Gurudutt said. 'But I know one man who may be able to help you. He lives in a village not far from here. You should visit him. He will be able to tell you about many things.'

The Sikh jotted down the man's name and address. Thanking him for his time, I followed the elephant squad out into the sunshine. Back on top of Raja, I recalled a conversation about Sikhs that I had had with a friend in Delhi.

'Sikhs are like potatoes,' he had commented one evening over a beer, 'you will find them growing everywhere! Once my uncle was in the Himalayas. He went high, high, high up. Really high, you know. There was nobody around, not even a goat. Only snow and the wind and the mountains and all. Finally he came to a remote cave. And in that cave do you know who was sitting there?'

'Who?'

'A Sikh! Even *there* in the mountains my uncle found one. I'm telling you, these Sikhs are everywhere only.'

I made a mental note to tell my friend of my meeting with Gurudutt and his friends. No doubt, he would be amused to know that there were Sikhs to be found even here on India's North-East Frontier.

It was late afternoon by the time we reached the Nowgong district. Here, by the roadside, the *kunkis* were fed and watered, while essential items such as tents and cooking equipment were loaded on to the animals' backs. Leaving the rest of our gear in the Land Rover – which Rudra was to drive to the nearest Forest Department outpost where he would await further instructions – we set off on foot. Only Churchill and Chander rode on the elephants.

We had gone just a couple of hundred yards when a car

came screeching to a halt on the road behind us and Vipal jumped out, bouncing down the embankment like a coiled spring.

'Hey, Boss! Vait up!' he shouted.

He came running through the fields, waving to me enthusiastically. Apparently, the effects of the Old Monk had worn off.

'Hi, Vipal,' I said, doing my best to look pleased to see him. 'It's good you were able to find us. But what about the strike? It's dangerous to be outside today.'

'No problem,' he gasped, trying to catch his breath and speak at the same time. 'I am driving at the maximum speed. You must be coming with me.'

'I can't. We're going after the elephant. Mr Choudhury is planning to shoot him tomorrow.'

Impatiently, the Bengali took me aside and began to whisper conspiratorially.

'But I have arranged the total teengs.'

'What teengs – I mean things?' I asked.

'The meeting with the Bodo liberation peoples.'

'I'm sorry, Vipal, but I won't be able to make it. I have to stay with the elephant squad.'

His face fell, his eyes drooping like those of an unloved hound.

'You do the interview. I'm sure it will be very good. We'll meet in a couple of days.'

The Bengali shuffled his feet from side to side and looked down at the ground dolefully. I began to weaken.

'Look, once this is over, we'll do a journey together. I want to visit Majuli, the largest river island in the world. Perhaps we could go together.'

His face brightened up.

'Okay, Boss,' he said. 'We will have maximum fun.'

The squad began to move off. Mr Choudhury reminded me that there was not a moment to lose.

'I'll meet you back at the Wild Grass Hotel in a day or so,' I said. 'We can make our plans then.'

'Great, Boss!' cried the Bengali. 'You are my best, best friend in the whole world. I am really loving you.'

He gave me a hug, his short arms not quite managing to embrace my frame. And then I turned and jogged after the others, trying hard to quell pangs of guilt.

The countryside was deserted. Islands of trees, which Churchill said were sacred groves that nobody dared chop down for fear of enraging the gods, were the only infringements upon the otherwise flat landscape. Narrow paths hreaded their way between paddy-fields. On any other day there would have been farmers at work, but as we headed south-west towards the rain forest that loomed in the distance there was not a person in sight.

At regular intervals, Mr Choudhury used his walkie-talkie to check on the progress of the guards tracking the rogue in Kaziranga. According to the latest report, the tusker was still heading east at a slow but steady pace.

'As long as we do not dilly-dally, we will be in a position to stop him early tomorrow morning. If we fail, he will go on another killing spree. By lunchtime, it must all be over,' he said.

The elephant, Mr Choudhury reminded me, had been given ample opportunity to reform. This time, there would be no reprieve. I felt his words were as much for his own reassurance as mine.

'There is something I did not tell you last night,' he continued, as we marched behind Raja and Jasmine. 'I looked up the rogue's records in the Forest Department. What I read convinced me, once and for all, that this elephant must be destroyed.'

'What did you find out?' I asked.

'A few years ago, in Arunachal Pradesh, another hunter was assigned to shoot him. It took him several days to track down the elephant. On the fourth night, he camped inside a forest, not far from where the animal had been spotted. But the rogue struck first. He went into the hunter's camp, pulled down his tent and then trampled him to death.'

Mr Choudhury was clearly troubled by this story and, for the first time, I detected a hint of anxiety in his voice.

'Tonight, we will post a guard just in case the elephant gets any ideas,' he said. 'We wouldn't want to be taken by surprise.'

'How do you scare away a rogue elephant?' I asked. 'Are they afraid of mice?'

Mr Choudhury laughed.

'No. That's one of those old wives tales,' he said. 'They're frightened of horses and fire – and hunters like me. So to-night it might be a good idea to light a few campfires around the tents. It is better to be on the safe side, is it not so?'

By the time we reached the edge of the rain forest, dusk was falling. A general calm had settled over the countryside as the day's heat began to dissipate and the first bats flitted across the burnished sky. Hidden insects whirred in the undergrowth, accompanied by crying jungle mynahs and moorhens hurrying back to their nests before nightfall.

Inside the forest, it was dark. We picked our way through the brambly undergrowth. Gnarled tree trunks towered above us, the twisted knots in their bark forming demonic faces. Creepers brushed against our backs as if they were alive, while branches creaked in the breeze blowing in from the fields.

Badger and Mole turned on their torches, the beams reflecting in the eyes of a dozen jackals who lurked in the bushes and thickets. Wings flapped invisibly above us. A wildcat screeched. Something to my right hissed its disapproval of our presence. Then, from up in the trees, came the haunting hoot of an owl.

'One hoot good sign, no?' commented Churchill, as we headed deeper into the forest.

The owl called out again.

'Oh dear, that is two hoot,' said the mahout. 'That is not good sign.'

'So does two hoots mean we'll have bad luck?' I asked, glancing around nervously in the gloom.

'Means the owl's horny, if you ask me,' interrupted Mole.

The bird hooted a third time.

'That's three. What do you make of that?' I asked.

'It means the owl doesn't know what the bloody 'ell 'e's talking about,' joked Badger. 'I say we shoot the bastard.'

Soon, we came across a path that led to a clearing complete with a brook. Mr Choudhury decided to camp for the night.

'Let us be early to bed and early to rise,' he said. 'We will set off again at dawn.'

Exhausted after the long day's march, we unloaded Raja and Jasmine, who drank their fill from the stream. We lit fires to ward off unwanted visitors, fed the elephants, erected our tents, and then prepared our evening meal. *Bhindi*, or okra, were fried with onions, spices and lashings of ghee, while handfuls of coarse, locally grown rice were boiled in a large sooty pot. Dessert consisted of juicy tangerines grown in Churchill's native Cherapunjee hills – 'the most delicious in the world, no?'

As we finished eating, there was a sudden rustling in the bushes on the far edge of the clearing. It was followed by the sound of a branch snapping. Someone – or something – was moving through the undergrowth less than a hundred yards from the camp.

Startled, we froze, our eyes fixed on the trees as we watched for any movement and listened for further sounds. Very slowly, Mr Choudhury reached for his Magnum rifle, slipping the weapon out of its case. The forest guards cautiously picked up their machine guns and pulled back the loading mechanisms. Another branch snapped. Badger switched on his torch, directing the beam to the edge of the clearing. I caught a brief glimpse of a figure darting behind a tree.

Mr Choudhury and Mole whispered to one another. Then the forest officer called out in Assamese. There was no reply. The guards, now lying flat in the grass, trained their machine guns on the trees, squinting through the sights. The forest officer called out again in a loud, authoritative voice.

This time a man answered. Mole stood up and announced himself. There was a pause. Voices whispered in the woods. Then came another brief exchange. Mole relaxed his shoulders. Mr Choudhury sighed and lowered his weapon. The guards followed suit.

'There's nothing to fear, man,' Mole reassured me. 'It's just a couple of ULFA guys.'

'ULFA!' I gasped, my heart still racing. 'I thought you said they were dangerous!'

'I know these two, man. We went to school together. They don't want their faces seen, so they won't step out into the open. I'm going to go and say hello. Come over if you like.'

Mr Choudhury was against the idea. He said it was dangerous to fraternize with the militants and warned me not to go.

'Who knows what it can lead to?' he pointed out. 'These men are trouble, is it not so?'

However, Mole assured him that there was no harm in a quick chat.

'I told you, I know them. They won't harm us.'

'What if you're wrong? It might be a trap.'

'I tell you, there's nothing to fear. Come on.'

He started across the clearing. Armed with my torch, I followed him, promising the hunter that I would return within a few minutes.

We found the two ULFA men crouched behind a tree, sharing a cigarette. They wore baseball caps, the sun visors pulled down over their noses so that I could only make out their mouths and chins. They were dressed in jeans and T-shirts and could have blended in anywhere. However, the pistols that protruded from the back of their waistbands left me in no doubt as to the nature of their business.

'We are always on the move. We never sleep in the same bed twice,' said the older of the two, Mole translating his words. 'It is dangerous for us to spend too long in one place.'

The two men, who I guessed were in their early twenties, had been living rough for three years. They had trained in ULFA camps in Bhutan and now organized terrorist attacks on 'legitimate targets' in Assam, travelling mostly at night.

'We have one main objective. That is to rid Assam of the millions of Bangladeshis and *adivasis* on our land. We want Assam for the Assamese.'

The two men spoke bitterly of India's politicians who, they claimed, exploited the North-East. The region produced half the country's oil and a large proportion of the world's tea.

'But what does the government give back? Nothing! We have no roads or schools. We do not even have drinking water.'

During my short time in Assam, I had heard a similar refrain from dozens of people. Clearly, there was no love lost between the Assamese and New Delhi's politicians. What's more, few people I spoke to living in the Brahmaputra valley considered themselves to be Indian.

'When I go to Delhi,' a senior newspaper editor told me gloomily, two weeks later in Guwahati, 'it is as foreign to me as Rome. Because I look oriental, everyone thinks I am a Japanese tourist and tries to rip me off. I am unable to communicate with anyone except in English, and no one knows anything about my homeland.'

The editor told me that a combination of corruption, neglect and a stagnant economy have created resentment and unemployment, all of which has helped swell the ranks of the various insurgency groups. Each new day sees fresh outbreaks of violence and killings.

'The only way to get New Delhi to take notice is to use the gun,' said the older ULFA man. 'Violence is the only thing they understand.'

ULFA, I knew, stood accused of thousands of murders and kidnappings, and of running an extortion racket that milked the state of millions of rupees every year. I asked the two militants how they could condone such actions.

Muttering something unintelligible, they chose not to answer my question. Instead, they stood up, exchanged a few hasty words with Mole and then slipped away into the forest. Apparently, the interview was over.

'I'm sorry. I hope I haven't got you into any trouble,' I said, as we walked back to the camp.

'Don't worry about it, man,' chuckled Mole, giving me a light slap on the back. 'Look, I've known these guys all my life. We were childhood friends. If we didn't share that history, I'd turn them in, man. They're not solving anything. In fact, I can't work out who I dislike more, the Indian army, the politicians or ULFA. They're all as bad as each other.'

'But don't you sympathize with their cause?'

'No way, man. We're a part of India whether we like it or not. Don't believe a word ULFA has to say. Like I told you before, they're just in it for the cash.'

We returned to the camp. Mole and the elephant squad turned in, leaving Mr Choudhury on guard by the campfire. Rather than going straight off to sleep, I sat down across from him. The hunter was sharpening a piece of wood with the blade of his Leatherman.

'Have you ever killed anything?' he asked me, looking up.

His question took me by surprise and I had to think hard. Only one incident came to mind. I had been driving through Kent when a rabbit ran under my car.

'I had to put it out of its misery using a tyre iron,' I said.

'So you have never had to kill something to eat?'

'No, never. It's always been done for me.'

Mr Choudhury smiled. He had been taught how to kill animals from an early age. It was second nature to him.

'Killing for the pot brings you closer to nature,' he said. 'But elephants are different. An elephant's life is like that of a human being. It should not be taken.'

He looked up at the sky. Clouds drifted past the sickle moon. A cold front was moving in from the north and the wind was beginning to buffet the tops of the trees. The hunter pulled a blanket around him and stoked the fire with a length of bamboo.

'I remember the first time I had to shoot an elephant,' he said. 'He was a *makhna*, a tuskless male. He had killed half a dozen people, but I could see that he was in *musth*. I decided to spare him, knowing that after some time, he would return to the forest. But just to be sure I kept an eye on him.

'Then, one morning, as I was watching him from a distance, the sun broke through the clouds behind me. My shadow fell on him and he turned and charged. I had no time to get out of the way. Instinctively, I raised my rifle and fired. He was dead in an instant.'

The hunter looked down at the fire. For a moment, he seemed almost overcome with sadness and I felt tempted to walk over and offer reassurance. But Mr Choudhury was someone who kept people at a distance, and I knew any sympathy on my part would make him feel uncomfortable. So I sat quietly, saying nothing.

Eventually, he looked up again.

'It's getting late. You had better get some sleep. You must be up by four.'

It was obvious that he wanted to be left alone.

'What about you?' I asked.

The hunter shook his head.

'I won't be able to sleep tonight,' he replied.

I I

The Rogue's Last Stand

'Most men who have shot elephants come afterwards to regret having done so.'

J. H. Williams, *Elephant Bill*

MR CHOUDHURY UNZIPPED his leather rifle-case and carefully eased the .458 Winchester Magnum from between its folds, laying the powerful weapon across his lap. In the light cast by a hurricane lamp, he inspected it, his hawkish eyes examining the hair trigger and the black metal barrel before settling on the finely polished butt.

Like a mother cradling a young child, he gently turned the rifle over on to its side and ran his hand over this, his most prized possession. Noticing a blemish in the varnish near the join with the magazine clip, he wet the end of his index finger with some spittle and rubbed it into the walnut.

For a minute or two, as he sat on a log outside his tent, the hunter stared blankly at his weapon, seemingly unaware of the elephant squad, who were busy preparing the *kunkis* for our imminent departure. Closing his eyes, he slouched forwards and sighed deeply, his shoulders rising and falling awkwardly, as if they were rusty and in need of lubrication.

Watching him from the other side of the camp, I began to wonder if, perhaps, Mr Choudhury had lost the strength and determination to carry on with the dangerous task that lay ahead of him. But somehow, in the coming minutes, he was able to rally himself and, sitting up straight and stretching his back, he lifted the rifle to his shoulder and peered down through the sights.

Satisfied that all the parts were properly oiled, he removed a circular piece of cork that had been jammed into the muzzle to prevent insects from crawling inside. Then he reached into his knapsack and pulled out a small packet wrapped in plastic. Inside were several sachets of silicon gel, used to keep out the damp, and a small cardboard box printed with the words 'WARNING: KEEP AWAY FROM CHILDREN'. Cautiously, as if he was handling unstable dynamite, Mr Choudhury took off the lid, revealing a row of brass bullets. Each one was as thick as a man's index finger, their shiny metal cones nestling innocently in their styrofoam packaging.

Choosing one from the middle, the hunter held the deadly object up to the light, turning it round in his fingers, like a jeweller appraising a rare gem. Then he inserted the bullet into a slot at the bottom of the rifle and, once it was in place, pulled back the weapon's iron bolt with a clunk–click, thereby loading the round into the chamber.

'I will only have the opportunity for one shot,' he said to me as I approached his tent. 'But to be on the safe side, I had better keep a few more up my sleeve. It is always better to be safe than sorry.'

So saying, he extracted four more rounds from the box of ammunition and pushed them into the magazine clip, which he then attached to the bottom of the rifle.

'Here, take it,' he said, holding out the weapon to me.

I hesitated.

'Don't worry,' he prompted. 'The safety catch is on. It cannot be fired. See?'

He pulled the trigger and, sure enough, nothing happened.

Cautiously, I took the rifle from him and held it in both hands. I had handled a diverse assortment of weapons, everything from pistols to rocket-propelled grenades. But the Magnum was in a class of its own.

'Come over here, I'll show you something,' said Mr Choudhury, leading me to the edge of the clearing where dawn was just breaking over the tops of the trees. 'See if you can do this.'

He unclipped the magazine and ejected the bullet from the chamber, putting it in his pocket for safe-keeping. Then, holding the rifle to his shoulder as if to fire the weapon, he pointed the barrel at the ground at an angle.

'Take this coin and balance it on the end,' he said.

He handed me a rupee and I did as he instructed. Then, once the coin was in place, he gently raised the rifle until it was level with his chin and shoulders, keeping the weapon steady. Squinting down the barrel, he squeezed the trigger. Amazingly, the coin remained in place.

'Now you have a go,' he said, flipping the rupee up into the air and catching it with his left hand. 'You have a steady hand, is it not so?'

'Quite steady, although a cigarette and a scotch wouldn't go amiss at this stage.'

Holding the rifle as Mr Choudhury had done, I attempted the same exercise. But my hands trembled, causing the coin to fall to the ground.

'It is a good job you are not the one shooting the rogue today,' laughed the hunter, reloading the rifle. 'You'd probably miss his temple by a few inches and that would be the end of you.'

We strolled back to the camp. The apprentices were busy tying sacking to the *kunkis'* backs, while Churchill, Mole and Badger sat around the main campfire, bolting down a meagre breakfast of cold *rotis* with bright, radioactive-looking jam. The mahout offered me a plateful, but I was suffering from nerves and the most I could manage was some tea.

Filling up his mug, Mr Choudhury called everyone into the middle of the camp where he outlined his plan.

'Prat and Sanjay, you are to stay here and guard the camp. Keep in radio contact,' he said briskly. 'Report anything strange immediately. If the rogue should get past us, he will come for you. So be prepared.'

The two apprentices nodded solemnly.

'I will ride with Churchill on Raja. Badger, you and the guards are to stay on the ground. I will need you to work as scouts. Don't shoot at the rogue unless he leaves you with no choice. But if he attacks you, aim for his knees. That's the only way you'll bring him down. Mole, you ride on the back of Jasmine with Chander.'

Mr Choudhury took out his good-luck charm, his silver rupee coin, which he turned around in his fingers.

'What about me?' I asked.

'I was just coming to you,' said the hunter. 'Tarquin, you ride on Jasmine with Mole and Chander. But remember, if the rogue attacks us, do not dismount under any circumstances. You will be safest on her back. It is very rare that an elephant will try to pull someone off a *kunki*.'

'Yes, it is true,' interrupted Churchill. 'Mahout and *hathi*, they have smell same, no?'

'If the rogue should attempt to pull you off,' continued Mr Choudhury, 'spit at the end of his trunk. Elephants detest that. It should help deter him.'

He paused, looking at each of us in turn.

'Any questions?'

On any other day, Churchill, Badger or Mole would have cracked a joke or two to help ease the growing tension. But now the three of them looked deadly serious.

'Churchill, are you ready?' asked the hunter.

'We are always ready, no?'

'Badger?'

'Yes, mate. Ready.'

'Good,' said Mr Choudhury, wishing us all luck. 'The rogue is only a few miles ahead. Let's get this over with.'

The hunter put on his baseball cap and climbed up on to Raja's back, his rifle held across his chest. Churchill took his position on the *kunki*'s neck.

'Forward!'

Raja moved out of the clearing, heading east towards Kaziranga and our final showdown with the rogue elephant.

Something was troubling Jasmine. At feeding time earlier that morning, she had eaten little of her rice and drunk only a small quantity of water. Now, as we followed a narrow path through the jungle, she stopped every few hundred yards and refused to budge, infuriating Chander, her mahout. Only the sternest of reprimands persuaded the elephant to move on, and even then she did so grudgingly.

Could this sudden change in her behaviour have anything to do with the hunt, I wondered. Was she, like me, dreading the thought of watching the elephant being gunned down? Or was she simply feeling under the weather as Churchill had suggested.

Whatever the case, Jasmine was not her usual self. When I offered her a packet of *paan*-flavoured Polo mints, which she had never refused in the past and which she usually gobbled down wrapping and all, she turned her trunk up at them. And as we plodded along the path, she trumpeted continually, the squeaky notes coming out in rapid succession.

Unfortunately, as I soon discovered, Jasmine's trunk was not the only part of her anatomy through which the *kunki* was inclined to blast hot air. Periodically, from the centre of her great sagging buttocks, a series of low-pitched, reverberating sounds erupted which rivalled, in both their duration and intensity, the kettledrum crescendos in Sibelius's *Finlandia*. These outbursts were invariably followed by an intense hissing sound and then a pungent, fermented-cabbage smell that lingered long after the accompanying thunder had died down, causing me to lift my shirt up over my mouth and nose and breathe through the cotton.

In the meantime, Jasmine's stomach rumbled loudly. Every so often, she would lift her tail high in the air and push out great clods of dung. These thumped to the jungle floor where they lay steaming in the cold morning air.

'That flippin' elephant's got more wind than a bloody force nine gale,' said Badger who, on foot, was trying his best to stay ahead of the *kunki*. 'There's no need to shoot the bloomin' rogue, we'll just get Jasmine to gas 'im.'

But it wasn't long before we came across something that rivalled even the *kunki*'s suffocating emissions. It was the sweet yet sickly stench of decomposing flesh, a disgusting smell that made my eyes water as I tried to prevent myself from retching. Soon, we discovered the rotting remains of a pi-dog strewn across the path. The creature's throat and stomach had been ripped out, its assailant's teeth marks clearly discernible in the remaining flesh. A few yards on, we spotted its half-eaten intestines hanging from the low-lying branch of a tree where some large cat must have crouched.

Further on, however, the awful odour was replaced by a pleasanter autumnal smell of compost, the result of an overnight downpour that had left the jungle fresh and glistening. By now, the sun had climbed high into the sky, flickering behind the canopy of emerald-green leaves like a strobe light. Crystal-clear beads of rainwater dripped down from branches, bouncing off the plants below and pitter-pattering on to the carpet of decomposing leaves that lay in a thick layer upon the earth.

The elephants padded across this soft, organic carpeting, brushing against freshly spun spider's webs that had caught only raindrops in their intricate patterns of silk thread.

After a while, Mr Choudhury turned on his walkie-talkie

and called the two guards who had been trailing the elephant through Kaziranga.

'Elephant squad to team two,' he called. 'Come in, team two.'

The hunter released the talk button. The speaker hissed static.

'This is elephant squad calling team two. Come in, team two,' he repeated.

But there was no answer.

I exchanged an anxious look with Badger, who was walking alongside Jasmine. Mr Choudhury looked concerned.

'Maybe there is something wrong with my radio,' said the hunter. 'Mole, you have a try.'

The forest officer switched on his own walkie-talkie and repeated our call signal. But still there was no reply.

A chill ran down my spine.

'Pray that it isn't true,' said Mole, who was sitting behind me. 'I know those two guards. They were – *are* – good guys, man.'

'Come on, now. Don't jump to conclusions, mate,' said Badger. 'They could be out of batteries, or anyfink. They might be takin' a piss.'

'He's right. Let us not assume the worst,' said Mr Choudhury.

However, given the elephant's history, it was difficult to think otherwise. Time and again, the rogue had proved himself both cunning and deadly, and now, it seemed, he had struck again. In doing so, the elephant had relieved us of our advantage. Without Amu's guards, there was no way of knowing the tusker's exact position. Mr Choudhury could only hope that we were following the right course.

For the next ten minutes, hardly a word passed between us. Everyone stared stoically ahead, lost in their own private thoughts, their faces rigid with tension.

Continuing east, we passed an illegal still built out of termite-ridden planks of wood and corrugated iron, its roof patched with plastic bags. A faint trail of wood smoke together with the smell of fermenting sugarcane rose from the rusting, cock-eyed chimney. If anything was going to attract the rogue's attention, I thought to myself, it was this place.

Over the next mile or so, the path grew gradually narrower and the jungle pressed in around us. Little light penetrated inside this shadowy world where snakes slithered through the undergrowth and lizards with beady eyes regarded us suspiciously. Churchill pulled out a machete from the sheath hanging around his *kunki*'s neck and began to hack away at low-lying branches and springy bamboo.

Then, quite suddenly, for no apparent reason, Raja and Jasmine stopped. Simultaneously, they raised their trunks in the air, bending the ends forward ninety degrees and moving them from side to side like submarine periscopes searching the surface of the sea for enemy ships. Churchill held up his hand, indicating that everyone should remain still. Badger crouched down, like a cat ready to spring. Mr Choudhury held his rifle at the ready. The guards slipped their machine guns off their shoulders and levelled them at the undergrowth. The rest of us sat completely still.

Bizarrely, the jungle had fallen silent too, as if the animals and birds also sensed something up ahead. Indeed, the only sounds audible were those of Raja's ears beating against his sides and Jasmine's tail whisking away flies.

Seconds later, however, the jungle was rent by the blood-curdling sound of a woman's scream. A desperate cry of sheer terror, it first stunned me and then sent my heart racing. Instantly, the jungle broke into uproar, hundreds of animals and birds calling out all at once, their screeches and cackles, squawks and squeals panicked and confused.

The woman screamed again – and then again. It seemed as

if she might be close by. But with all the racket that had broken out around us, it was impossible to gain a fix on her position.

She screamed a fourth time.

'Quick! Over there!' bawled Mr Choudhury, throwing out his arm to the right. 'She is over there!'

Churchill pummelled the backs of Raja's ears with his feet, shouting out urgent commands. The mahout turned the *kunki* off the path and into the dense jungle. Like a tank, the animal's immense body drove through the vegetation, crushing plants and flattening saplings.

Badger and the guards charged after Raja, with Jasmine close on their heels. Trying to grip with my legs and hold on tight to the ropes drawn across the elephant's back, I rose and fell in time with the *kunki*'s great shoulders as thorns and twigs lashed out at my face and hands. Low-lying branches threatened to sweep us from Jasmine's back, but somehow we stayed on, soon emerging, eyes blinking, into a wide clearing bathed in sunshine.

Once again, the *kunkis* came to an abrupt halt. The guards blew on their whistles in an effort to attract the woman's attention.

'Where the hell is she, man?' murmured Mole as he glanced around him, blocking out the sun with the backs of his hands. 'She's got to be here somewhere.'

But the screaming had ceased and the woman was nowhere to be seen.

Mr Choudhury slipped down the side of Raja and walked cautiously into the middle of the clearing, his rifle held across his chest. Then, from in front of us, a woman came stumbling out of the woods. Whimpering pathetically and glancing fearfully over her shoulder, she ran towards the hunter, flailing her arms in the air. Twice, she tripped, falling flat on her face, but each time she managed to scramble to her feet and run on.

Mr Choudhury rushed towards her and saved her from falling a third time. Badger reached the spot and, together, the two men helped the woman back to where the elephants were standing on the edge of the clearing.

The terrified woman clutched at her legs which were badly cut and bruised. Her clothes, too, had been shredded. Blood ebbed from a wound on the bottom of her left foot.

Mr Choudhury stooped down next to the distraught woman, offering her a sip of water from a flask as he tried to comfort her. All the while, she gasped and sobbed to herself, trying to articulate what had happened.

'What's she saying?' he asked Churchill.

The mahout's eyes were fixed on the jungle. When he replied, they did not move.

'*Hathi* attack her,' said Churchill rapidly, half under his breath. '*Hathi* chase. Just behind. There in jungle, no?'

Mr Choudhury stood up. Removing his waterproof coat, he laid it on the ground like a matador preparing to face the bull. He pushed back his glasses until they sat firmly on the bridge of his nose and switched off the safety catch on his rifle. Instructing us to stay put, the hunter walked back into the middle of the clearing. There, he knelt down, his eyes scanning the line of trees that rose up in front of him, some thirty feet away.

The *kunkis'* chests began to rumble, sounding their in-built elephantine early warning system. Jasmine took several steps backwards as if she was considering making a run for it.

'*Hathi* is here,' whispered Churchill. 'Now he come.'

To the right of Mr Choudhury, trees began to shake as if an earthquake had struck. The hunter turned, still kneeling, and raised his rifle. With the butt held firmly against his shoulder, he inclined his head, rested his right cheek on the Magnum's neck and aimed through the sights.

From the jungle came a drawn-out creak as the branch of a tree snapped and crashed to the ground.

Mole's hands clutched my shoulders, his fingernails digging into my skin. I found myself shivering and realized I was suffering from *hathi jokar*, or elephant shivers, a term used by the mahouts to describe how it feels to come face to face with a wild rogue.

Then suddenly, with a loud crunch, the rogue appeared on the edge of the jungle, just behind a copse of trees, his head obscured by some bushes. He trumpeted furiously and I caught a glimpse of his tusks which, for a split second, were thrust through the bushes, snow white against the green foliage. The end of his trunk followed, writhing like an angry python.

Mr Choudhury curled his index finger around the trigger and lowered the rifle by several degrees. He stiffened, preparing for the rogue to reveal himself.

The elephant took another step forward. I could make out the nails on his front feet. His moment of retribution had finally arrived. Yet even now, despite everything I had seen and knew about him, I found myself urging him to make his escape. 'Go back. Go back!'

Then, as if he had heard my words of warning, the rogue retreated. We caught glimpses of his massive frame as he walked to the left just behind the perimeter of trees. Mr Choudhury kept his rifle trained on him, but the tusker disappeared from view.

Two or three minutes passed. The hunter remained crouched on the grass, his Magnum still levelled at the rain forest. He moved the rifle from left to right and back again in one fluid, steady movement.

The rest of us remained frozen, eyes staring forward, ears straining for the slightest sound. Behind us, a monkey's screech made us start, sending our hearts pounding ever faster. Another minute passed. The hunter relaxed his pose and lowered the rifle. Nothing stirred. He stood up, his eyes still fixed on the trees. Cautiously, he began to walk backwards towards the elephant squad.

It was then that the rogue launched his surprise attack. Squealing furiously, he came crashing out of the forest in a last desperate attempt to rid himself of the hunter. The elephant was crazed and defiant. His ears were stretched wide, his trunk held rigid like a spear, his tusks scything through the air like scimitars. He tossed his head from side to side. Every fibre in his massive body was set on one thing and one thing alone: murder.

The rogue lowered his head, his eyes turning wildly in their sockets. He was preparing to charge.

But that moment never came. Even now, when confronted with this demonic elephant no more than a hundred yards away, Mr Choudhury's nerve held. Once again he kneeled on the ground and raised his rifle. He inclined his head and squinted down the sights. He took aim. For the last time, the tusker trumpeted defiantly. And then the hunter pulled the trigger.

I watched as the powerful weapon kicked hard against his shoulder. A deafening thunderclap ripped through the jungle. And then a deathly silence fell over the place, and time seemed to slow down.

The elephant's head jerked back as the high-velocity bullet penetrated his temple. I could see clearly the spurt of blood that gushed out on to his ear and dripped down his cheek. His trunk whipped back in the air. His mouth opened wide, revealing his writhing black tongue. He reared up on his hind legs, kicking out defiantly.

Then the fight went out of him. His ears fell to his sides. His trunk flagged. His head slumped as if he was overcome with fatigue. Like a disgraced child who only now understood that he had misbehaved, the rogue tried to turn and walk away, almost apologetically.

Then, in one violent movement, he reared up once again, his trunk reaching for the sky as if he was trying to clutch at his departing soul. He let out a tortured, rasping noise. Then his legs buckled. His body slumped forward. And he dropped to the ground with a thud, his tusks driving into the soft earth.

I felt nauseous and disorientated, as if I had been in a car accident or near a bomb blast. A numbness came over me. I lost all sense of touch and smell. All I could hear was a ringing in my ears, together with the sound of my heart pounding. It was as if I was no longer a part of the events taking place around me, but just a ghost who could only watch silently.

Looking down, I saw Mr Choudhury place his rifle on the ground. Still kneeling, he lowered his head.

No one else moved or said a word.

At least five minutes passed, each minute like an hour. Then, gradually, I felt reality taking hold once more. I found that my mouth was wide open and my hands were frozen around one of Jasmine's ropes. All at once, the adrenalin that had been coursing through my veins ebbed away and a feeling of total exhaustion swept over me. All I wanted to do was lie down, go to sleep and have nothing further to do with the world.

Then my eyes fixed on the elephant. He was slumped on the ground, his trunk curled up around him, his legs tucked in underneath his belly and his ears draped over his cheeks. He looked peaceful. Even now, it was difficult to picture him tearing people apart.

Somehow, I found the strength to climb down from Jasmine. Mr Choudhury was still kneeling on the ground, his head lowered as if in prayer. I walked past him and, folding my hands in front of me, approached the elephant.

I could have sworn that he was watching me. His left eye, which had glazed over, all the malice driven from it for ever, seemed to follow me as I walked up to him.

Standing there, I reached out with my hands and touched his head. The skin was still warm, the hairs soft to the touch.

I noticed a tear roll down the rogue's left cheek and fall into the grass. Choked with emotion, I felt my own tears well up and fall from my eyes, splashing on to his ear.

Mr Choudhury walked up behind me and placed his hand on my shoulder. He kept it there for some time, patting me reassuringly. Then, bending over the tusker, he drew the palm of his hand over the elephant's eyes, closing the lids shut.

12

To the Elephant Graveyard

'What happens to beasts will happen to man. All things are connected. If the great beasts are gone, man will surely die of a great loneliness of spirit.'

Chief Seattle of the Nez Percé, 1884

AN ELDERLY COUPLE stepped shyly into the clearing and, with heads bent low, made their way over to where the elephant lay inert upon the ground. Dressed in filthy, tattered clothes, their faces worn by years of hardship, they both walked with pronounced limps. The woman's left hip appeared to be deformed, while the man's right foot was twisted at a sharp angle.

They must be bonded labourers, I thought. Like millions of other Indians, they probably spent their days breaking rocks on the roadside or baking bricks in inferno-like kilns – only to watch their children grow up trapped by the same unscrupulous trade. Even so they had walked barefoot for more than five miles to reach this spot, bringing with them handfuls of blossom picked in the jungle along the way.

Unwittingly, they stopped at precisely the spot where Mr Choudhury had pulled the trigger and stared, transfixed, at the rogue's head, reverence and disbelief written large across their faces.

In the few hours that had passed since the hunter finally brought the animal's murderous rampage to an end, the forest guards, using an axe, had hacked out the tusks, slicing away the flesh at their roots in order to remove every last inch of ivory. Since then, a pool of blood had formed around the body, gallons of the dark liquid seeping from the wounds on to the grass.

Confronted with this gory spectacle, the couple were overcome with emotion. Shuffling forward, the husband clasped his hands to his head and began to wail. His wife, shaking with grief, fell to her knees, the tears coursing down her face. Then, together, they began to pray, placing their blossoms on the animal's head and raising their eyes heavenward.

News of the shooting had spread far and wide, drawing hundreds of people from a radius of seven miles or more. Some came because they had nothing better to do and spent their time crouched on the edge of the clearing, watching the comings and goings as they might at any other public event. Others had come to pray for the rogue's soul.

The elephant squad, too, was in a sombre mood. Even Churchill was quiet. He sat on his own on a grassy bank, watching with a sorrowful expression as the locals filed past the dead elephant. Periodically, he glanced down at his feet and rubbed at the patches of calcified skin on the bottoms of his toes, lost in thought.

Raja and Jasmine also seemed subdued. Their ears hung down the sides of their bowed heads, slack and listless. Remarkably, Jasmine had not regained her appetite and didn't touch any of the fruit that had been placed by the mourners next to the tusker's head. Raja stood just a few feet from the dead elephant, running the tip of his trunk over the body and sniffing at the carcass.

Mr Choudhury had clearly been deeply affected by the morning's events. The recent lack of sleep had caught up with him and he looked tired and pale, dark bags etched under his eyes. Far from being relaxed now that the ordeal was over, he seemed tense. As he sat on a log at the end of the clearing, he watched the locals warily.

'The Assamese believe each elephant is a manifestation of Ganesha. When one is killed, it is very upsetting for them,' said Mr Choudhury, as I sat down next to him. 'A few years ago, when I shot another dangerous rogue who was terrorizing southern Assam, the local people tried to lynch me. They said I had brought misfortune upon them. It was only thanks to the local forest officer, who dispersed the crowd by firing his pistol over their heads, that I was able to escape.'

'Do you think we are in any danger?' I asked.

'So far, these people do not appear to be angry, only upset. But if a crowd should gather ... well, we must keep an eye out, is it not so?'

Just then, a group of tough-looking characters armed with pickaxes walked into the clearing. I shrank at the sight of them. But I soon realized that they were only day labourers, hired by Mole to dig a grave for the rogue elephant.

'I've taken on twelve men for the job,' said the forest officer, who had brought them from the nearest village. 'I'd still prefer to cremate the elephant, but there's no way we'd ever get him up on a funeral pyre.'

It surprised me to learn that Mole was going to the trouble of burying the elephant. After all, in most parts of India dead animals are traditionally left out in the open and nature is allowed to take its course.

'What's different about an elephant?' I asked.

'If we leave him here, do you know what's going to happen?' he countered.

'He'll start to smell incredibly bad?'

'Yes. But also the local poachers will cut off his feet just above the ankles and make them into genuine "foot" stools. If we allow that to happen, it will help increase the appetite for elephant trophies.'

'Is that why you cut off the tusks?'

'Exactly, man. Stop the bastards getting at them.'

'So are you going to mount them over your fireplace?'

'You must be kidding, man. That's illegal. No, they'll be kept under lock and key at the state repository in Guwahati. They'll be in their own box, which will be sealed with wax. And that's where they'll remain.'

Mole picked up a stick from the ground and used it to mark out an area in the middle of the clearing roughly fifteen foot long and ten foot wide. Stripping down to their waists, the labourers set to work, driving their pickaxes into the earth and gouging out great chunks which they shovelled to one side.

Mr Choudhury watched their progress for some minutes and then headed back to the camp where we had slept the night before to take a nap. Once he was out of sight, I sidled up to Mole, who was overseeing the digging.

'So did you manage to get me some?' I asked him.

'Yeah, I remembered,' he said reluctantly. 'But I don't approve, man. These things are bad for you.'

So saying, he reached into his pocket and drew out a packet of Indian cigarettes. Normally, I would never have smoked such a low-quality brand, but I was craving nicotine.

Thanking him, I tore off the cellophane wrapping and pulled out a cigarette, lighting the end with a match. I took a long, hard drag, allowing the smoke to slip over my tongue and down into my lungs.

'That's absolutely disgusting,' I said, 'but I can't tell you how good it feels.'

Mole watched me exhale the smoke and then reached for the packet.

'I think I need one too.'

He pulled out a cigarette, lit the end and took a drag.

'I've got some good news,' he said. 'The guards who were tracking the rogue weren't killed after all. It turns out one of them accidentally dropped the walkie-talkie into a stream. That's why we couldn't reach them.'

'Thank God for that,' I said.

'Let's celebrate.'

So saying, he reached into his rucksack and pulled out two bottles of Tipsy 1000 beer. They were wrapped in a plastic bag along with half a dozen chunks of melting ice. With a wink, he tugged off the caps and handed me a bottle.

I hesitated. As much as I was dying for a drink, it seemed inappropriate to be celebrating so soon after the elephant's death. Didn't he think we should wait?

'Probably. But after what we've been through, I think we deserve it.'

He pushed the bottle into my hands and raised his in the air.

'Cheers.'

Vipal Ganguly did not learn about the shooting until the following morning, but he wasted little time in travelling to the scene. He arrived in the clearing shortly after midday, when the labourers had almost finished digging the grave.

Characteristically, he brought with him no less than eleven friends. They immediately gathered for a group photograph in front of the elephant, thereby offending the crowd of mourning locals.

'Hey, Boss,' he shouted, spotting me on the other side of the clearing where I sat chatting with Mole and Churchill. 'I am here!'

Seeing the Bengali, I felt a further twinge of guilt at having left him behind at the hotel, but at the same time I was kicking myself for having suggested that we travel together to Majuli, the river island.

'Hi, Vipal,' I said as he approached. 'How are you?'

'Great! I am making the total arrangements for nice journey

to Majuli,' he replied. 'We will be having the *max*imum fun. Two of my friends, they are coming with us. Okay?'

'Fine,' I said wearily, realizing that I would have to hatch another plan to escape from the Bengali. 'So how did it go with the Bodos? Did you meet them?'

Vipal waved his hands frantically in front of my face and emitted a loud shush, which only succeeded in attracting the attention of everyone standing within a hundred-yard radius. Taking me by the arm, he led me to one side.

'Not to be saying so loud, Boss,' he said. 'I can be in total trouble with police peoples.'

The thought of this rather appealed to me, but I kept my voice down.

'So did you meet the insurgents?' I whispered.

Vipal narrowed his eyes and, for a moment, he looked really angry.

'Bodo peoples are maximum idiots!' he spat.

'Why? What happened?' I asked.

'Last night, they are coming to my hotel. There I am waiting in my total disguise. But the Bodo peoples are making the maximum mistake. They are going to reception and asking for Mister Tagore. That is me . . .'

'Your assumed name,' I added.

'Correct, Boss. So Bodo peoples are being told room fourteen and then they are going and knocking on door!'

'What was so wrong with that?'

'I am not in fourteen! I am in seventeen!' he said, raising his voice.

'So who was in room fourteen?'

'One army man. He is called Tagore, also. But he is not wearing uniform. So the idiot Bodos are introducing themselves and being arrested – on the spot.'

Unable to control myself, I burst out laughing. But Vipal saw nothing amusing in what had happened.

'Boss, why you laugh? This is not so funny. I am having to

make the total escape from the hotel. Probably the Bodo peoples are looking for me! They are thinking I am arranging the total teeng.'

Here was a golden opportunity to persuade Vipal to go back to Calcutta.

'Just think what they might do to you if they caught you. You should lie low, perhaps go home,' I said.

Unfortunately, the Bengali did not seem at all concerned. He had been in far stickier circumstances, he assured me – like the time a group of Naxalites, Communist militants renowned for their violent ways, held him hostage for two days and threatened to slit his throat.

'Don't worry, Boss,' said Vipal, regaining his sense of humour. 'Like I am telling you always, I have fifteen thousand friends! Here, meet two more.'

Two of his new hangers-on stepped forward.

'These are my friends, Tinu and JJ,' he said. 'They are coming to Majuli.'

I shook them each by the hand.

'So, Boss, when we leave?'

'I'm not sure,' I said, hesitating. 'I'm still trying to find out more about the elephant graveyard. Some Sikhs I met a couple of days ago told me about a man who might be able to help and . . .'

Vipal waved his hand in the air dismissively. Right from the start, he had been sceptical about the legend and had wasted no opportunity in patronizing me as an ignorant foreigner.

'This is total bullshit, only,' he said in exasperation. 'Why you are wasting your time with the maximum garbage?'

'I like the legend and I'm sure there has to be something behind it.'

Only that morning, I explained, I had interviewed various locals who had heard of the Pool of Ganesha, the place described by the head monk at the monastery. However, I had to concede that no one seemed to have any idea how to find it.

'See!' jibed the Bengali. 'Hindustan has one millions of these legends. People are believing the total teengs they are hearing. They will be telling you what you want to hear only.'

'Be that as it may, I am going to continue looking for it.'

I suggested we meet up in two days' time in Guwahati where I hoped to visit the university and see if the folklore department might be able to help.

Hundreds of farmers gathered in the mild afternoon sun to watch the rogue elephant's last rites. Some had waited since dawn for the proceedings to begin, sitting patiently for up to seven hours while the labourers worked tirelessly to extract the large pile of dirt that now lay to one side of the pit.

There were representatives of all ages and castes. Faces squinted in the sunlight: toothless crones with wrinkled features, black *adivasis* with caste marks daubed on their foreheads, rosy-cheeked children with slanting eyes and high cheekbones, and wives with red powder rubbed into their scalps, indicating that they were married.

Crouching on their haunches, shoulder to shoulder, they chatted to one another while they waited for the proceedings to begin. Women bedecked in bright reds and yellows and jangling bangles clucked like broody hens. The men, mostly farmers, chewed *paan* and kept up a running commentary as the elephant squad made preparations for burying the dead animal.

By mid-afternoon, the grave was finished and the squad, having tied two thick ropes to the elephant's ankles, were at last ready to proceed. Raja and Jasmine, ridden by Churchill and Chander, took up their positions in front of the rogue while four labourers, standing on the other side of the grave, took hold of the ropes.

At Mr Choudhury's signal the mahouts shouted a string of commands, working their feet behind the *kunkis'* ears. Obediently, the animals lowered their heads and began to nudge against the carcass. Seeing this, the crowd rose to their feet and fell silent, watching, fascinated, while the mahouts urged the elephants to push harder.

With a great bellowing, trumpeting and snorting of air, Raja and Jasmine leaned forward, pushing for all they were worth, their legs straining as their feet slipped on the grass. Directly opposite them, the labourers pulled hard on the ropes, their muscles taut and glistening with sweat, grunting and groaning in unison.

Gradually, the body inched towards the grave, feet first, blood still ebbing from its wounds. The rogue's trunk dragged behind him, bouncing along the ground as if he was still alive and was trying desperately to grab hold of something.

Soon, the legs drooped over the edge and, inevitably, gravity took over. The earth beneath the elephant gave way and he tumbled to the bottom, his great trunk arching through the air before it slammed to the ground with a muffled thump.

The crowd rushed forward, brushing aside the guards who tried, in vain, to hold them back. In the confusion, two men fell into the grave, but they quickly scrambled out for fear of being tainted by the animal's bad spirit. Some of the women started to cry and wail, throwing blossoms into the grave. One woman fainted and had to be carried out of the crowd. For a time, Mr Choudhury was worried that, in such a hysterical state, the crowd might turn on us. But in time they calmed down and the funeral continued.

Stepping up to the grave, Churchill lit some incense-sticks, which he stuck in the ground. Muttering something in Khasi, his native language, he then split open a coconut with his machete and sprinkled the milk over the body.

'What did you say?' I asked him, when he had finished.

'Just few words, no?' replied Churchill. 'There is no tradition burying *hathi*. But Hindu peoples, they love the ceremony. That is why we do this, no?'

Next, six barrels of diesel, which had been carried to the clearing by the *kunkis* earlier that morning, were rolled forward by the labourers and positioned by the graveside. One by one, these rusting metal containers were opened and the contents were emptied into the grave – a final deterrent to poachers who, it was feared, might strip the carcass of its flesh and sell the meat in the market.

The contents glugged from the containers and splattered down on to the animal. Inch by inch, his dusty grey skin was covered, pools of the liquid bubbling up around him as it seeped into the earth.

As the last drops dripped from the barrels, Mr Choudhury stepped forward, holding a garland of marigolds in both hands. Solemnly, he knelt at the foot of the grave and slowly lowered the flowers on to the rogue's body. Then he stood up and, turning away, instructed the labourers to start shovelling in the earth.

With the rogue finally buried, Churchill, Mole and the apprentices were anxious to return to their respective homes on the north bank of the Brahmaputra. Back at the camp after the funeral, they wasted little time in packing up their belongings.

'Mrs Mahout, she will be wanting money for food. She eating very much, no?' joked Churchill.

Mr Choudhury and I accompanied the squad to the edge of the jungle where Rudra was waiting for us with the Land Rover. It was here that we finally went our separate ways.

'Tarwin, I not like say goodbye,' said Churchill. 'So I not say anything, no?'

Instead, the mahout handed me a gift wrapped in a page of the *Assam Sentinel*. Tearing open the newspaper, I discovered a bracelet made from thick, wiry hairs plucked from Raja's tail. It was a replica of the bands worn by the mahouts and their apprentices. I slipped the gift on to my wrist.

'Tarwin, now you part of elephant squad,' pronounced the mahout. 'Don't forget. I am teaching you many thing. When you go London, ride *hathi*. Very much cheaper than car, no?'

I thanked the mahout for his touching present and he shook me warmly by the hand. Then, without another word, he mounted his elephant.

The others stepped forward. Badger, who had decided to remain with the squad for the foreseeable future, wished me 'the best of luck, mate', and Mole invited me to visit his head-quarters 'any time, man. It'll always be a pleasure.'

Last but not least, I bade farewell to the *kunkis*, presenting each of them with a tin of travel sweets taken from the depths of my backpack. Greedily they ate the contents, coating the tips of their trunks in powdered sugar, so that they looked like junkies snorting cocaine.

'Okay, now we go,' said Churchill.

The squad moved off in the direction of the Brahmaputra River and the Tezpur suspension bridge. From the tops of the *kunkis*, Mole, Badger and the others looked back, waving to me, while the elephants saluted with their trunks.

I waited by the Land Rover, watching them trudge towards the horizon, overcome by a sense of loss and sadness. Standing there, I realized that after my travels with Churchill and the team, work was going to be more tedious than ever, and I felt the urge to run after the *kunkis*, climb up on Raja and continue my adventures with the inimitable elephant squad. But I knew that, before too long, I must return to my job in Delhi.

Reluctantly, I turned and climbed into the Land Rover. Rudra shifted into four-wheel drive and headed across the fields towards the nearest dirt road. The car shook and the engine strained. But when I closed my eyes, I could still sense the gentle rocking motion of Raja beneath me.

I had hoped to try to find the man mentioned by the Assamese Sikhs and ask him about the Pool of Ganesha. But Mr Choudhury wanted to head back to Guwahati. As Rudra gunned the Land Rover east along the highway, I sat in the front seat and Mr Choudhury reclined in the back, pleased at last to be heading home.

The elephant 'season', harvest time, when the herds caused the most havoc in the fields, was over, he explained, and he planned to spend the next month with his family. His eldest daughter's birthday was only a few days away, and shortly after that his brother was arriving from Kenya.

'Life goes on, is it not so?' he said.

However, before returning home, the hunter wanted to make a short detour.

'There is someone you must meet. He is very special to me and I am sure he will be able to help you,' he said.

'Help me? How?'

'His name is Geala. He knows everything there is to know about elephants,' said Mr Choudhury. 'I feel sure that he will be able to help you find the elephant graveyard.'

I sat up straight and turned around in my seat to face the hunter.

'Really? That's wonderful,' I spluttered. 'Why didn't you mention this before?'

Mr Choudhury shrugged his shoulders.

'If I had told you, then you would not have bothered trying to find out for yourself. Knowledge is useless without effort.'

'So who is this person?' I asked.

'He taught me everything I know about elephants. For want of a better term, he is my guru. But professionally, he is

– or was – a *phandi*, probably the greatest elephant-catcher that ever lived, and one of the last now alive.'

Mr Choudhury took out his Survey of India map of Assam and spread it out, pointing to where the *phandi* lived for Rudra's benefit.

'His home is on the edge of the Karbi Anglong hills. It is in an area cut off from the rest of the world,' said the hunter. 'Let us hope he is at home. He still keeps one or two elephants and sometimes he goes off with them for weeks at a time.'

It was mid-afternoon as we turned off the highway. In the distance, steep slopes rose above the tea gardens, the tops of the green hills lost in low cloud. A dusty dirt track led through a pine forest, planted in regimented rows for miles at a stretch. Emerging on the other side, Rudra shifted once again into four-wheel drive and headed cross-country along a grassy riverbank lined with fishermen.

At the foot of the hills, we stopped in front of a compound surrounded by a high bamboo wall. Two Assamese girls sat outside the front gate combing each other's hair, while a small boy played with the metal rim of a bicycle wheel, rolling it along the ground like a hoop. All three of them took one look at the Land Rover and began squealing Mr Choudhury's name, running over to the vehicle and clamouring for the hunter's attention.

'This is Panipat, Baman and Hema,' he said, scooping the two girls up in his arms. 'They are just a few of the *phandi*'s grandchildren. As you will see, he has a very large family.'

With the girls clinging to him affectionately, Mr Choudhury pushed open the gates and we walked inside. Four mud and straw huts were arranged in a circle around a stone well. Over the well a wooden bucket hung from a winch, dripping water on to the sun-baked earth. Ducks and chickens pecked about in the shadow of a hutch used to store rice, which stood on stilts to prevent rodents from getting inside.

Sitting on a flagstone, positioned outside the door of the smallest of the four huts, two women sat scouring pots with coconut husks. A young boy swept around them, using a brush made from stiff reeds, a cloud of ochre-coloured dust forming at his feet.

On the opposite side of the compound, an elderly elephant, a *makhna* or tuskless male, stood tethered to a post munching on a banana tree, bunches of leaves protruding from his mouth. With rheumy eyes and a wise, furrowed brow, he was a distinguished-looking animal. His ears were great floppy affairs that had lost much of their shape, and his jowls sagged in great folds below his chin as his few remaining teeth worked on his afternoon snack.

To the right of the elephant crouched the *phandi*. He was busy chopping up a pile of fodder with a machete. As we approached, he looked up and his face immediately broadened into a wide smile. Then he leapt up and gave the hunter a hug, lifting him off the ground with his arms.

'This is Geala,' said Mr Choudhury, introducing us. 'He is my best friend in the world.'

The *phandi* bowed to me gracefully, his eyes not leaving my face, and then he shook my hand enthusiastically.

'Welcome to my home. Come and meet my elephant Toomai,' he said, Mr Choudhury translating his words. 'He is almost as old as I am.'

We walked over to the *kunki*'s area of the compound, where the old boy was now tucking into a bucket of millet.

'He is much smarter than me,' continued Geala. 'Lately, he has learned to unfasten his chain by undoing the nut and bolt with the tip of his trunk. Of course, he does not run away, but he likes to wander off.'

Leaving us to become acquainted, Geala went over to one of the huts and soon re-emerged with a plate of coconut *ladoos*.

'You must be hungry,' he said, offering the plate.

Then he hurried over to the well, where he quickly filled a bucket of water and carried it to Toomai.

For someone in his seventies, the *phandi* seemed to have boundless energy. But unlike his *kunki*, he did not look his age. Indeed, far from being old and wrinkled, his skin was supple and he was also remarkably fit.

'I caught Toomai in 1942,' said our host, as we admired the elephant. 'He put up a great fight and it took me many hours. He was very hard to train. It took me weeks to convince him that his wild days were finally at an end. At the time, I knew this was a good sign. If an elephant struggles during the breaking period, then he will make a good *kunki*. So it was with Toomai, who has been a faithful companion – and friend – ever since.'

I worked out that the elephant was at least sixty years old.

'That's about right,' replied the *phandi*. 'He can expect to live for another ten years. Elephants have roughly the same lifespan as humans, although their memory lasts to their dying day.

'Last year, I fell from him and was knocked unconscious in the forest many, many miles from here. He picked me up, laid me over his back and then, in the middle of the night, carried me for over thirty miles until he reached our home. Placing me by the gate, he roused everyone from their beds and waited outside my door until I was better.'

The *phandi*'s wife, a happy woman who giggled almost continuously, called to us from the middle of the compound where wooden stools had been arranged around a fire. We sat down and she and two of her grandchildren served us tea in shallow clay cups, together with *muri ladoo*, puffed rice balls, and *tilar ladoo*, sesame balls.

I was anxious to ask the *phandi* about the legend of the elephant graveyard. However, before an opportunity presented itself, our host, at Mr Choudhury's instigation, began to tell us about his experiences catching elephants in Assam's now depleted jungles.

'I am a Khamati, from the Sadiya district of Upper Assam. We have always owned many elephants, supplying them to kings, princes and armies across India for thousands of years,' he began proudly. 'I was only a young boy when my father took me to see elephants being caught for the first time. Dozens of mahouts and *phandis* had congregated in the jungle. They were tough, colourful men, and at times they could be a rough lot. But they lived for their trade and knew no other way.

'In the middle of the jungle, they had built a huge stock-ade, made of giant bamboo. I will never forget standing there and hearing the words *hathi porise* – the elephants are coming. Suddenly, from out of the trees, I heard a great crashing and rumbling, and the ground seemed to shake. Then a herd of forty or more elephants stampeded into the stockade, chased by a team of expert *phandis* on their *kunkis*.

'Quickly, the gates were closed behind them and the animals were trapped. The elephants realized this and tried to smash their way out. Amongst them, there was a huge Ganesha, a male elephant with only one tusk. He battered his great head against the door, pounding and pounding, desper-ate to escape back into the jungle. The other elephants trum-peted, bellowed and roared. I thought I might go deaf listening to them.'

'What happened next?' I asked.

'Given time, the animals grew tired and calmed down,' continued Geala. 'Then, the *phandis* started to rope the younger elephants that they wanted to keep and led them away to the training depot, the *pilkhana*. The other elephants were set free and returned to the jungle. The mahouts were always careful never to deplete their numbers and of course, in those days, the herds were free to wander virtually wher-ever they liked.'

As Geala explained, there were four acceptable ways of catching elephants in India, all of them laid down in ancient texts. The first method, which he had already described, had been developed by the Aryans and was called *khedda*, or stockade, a Sanskrit word derived from *khet*, meaning to drive.

The second, which originated in southern India, made use of a pit and was considered the most primitive and potentially harmful technique. The third involved laying a noose on the jungle floor and then waiting for an elephant to put its foot in the right spot.

'And the last was developed by the Assamese. It is called *mela shikar*,' he said proudly. 'Using tame elephants, two *phandis* would isolate a calf from the herd and lasso the animal with ropes made of jute. This could be very difficult because usually the wild ones would run away and you had to chase after them. Sometimes, the older elephants came after you, too, and many times *phandis* would be killed.'

Mr Choudhury explained that Geala had been apprenticed as an elephant-catcher while still a teenager, working his way up to *bor phandi*, or great catcher. Over the years, he became something of a legend, catching more elephants than any other *phandi* of his generation and working with the likes of P. D. Stracey and A. J. W. Milroy, British former heads of the Forest Department. During various periods of his career, he was employed in Burma and Sumatra, which used to have sizeable elephant populations, as well as on the Andaman Islands, in the Bay of Bengal, where the British transported *kunkis* in the 1940s.

'Geala is the only *phandi* who has ever lassoed two wild elephants at once,' said the hunter. 'It is a feat that has never been repeated, although many have tried.'

'Now, all the *phandis* are gone and most of the mahouts along with them,' said Geala sadly. 'All those days are at an end. Nothing will bring them back.'

Our host suddenly appeared subdued. Silence fell over our small company, broken intermittently by the sound of twigs crackling in the fire and Toomai munching behind us.

Quietly, I waited, staring into the flames, longing to ask the *phandi* about the elephant graveyard but not wanting to be the one to interrupt his quiet reflections.

Eventually, however, I could wait no longer and, speaking in a voice just above a whisper, I asked our host whether he could help me find the fabled cemetery.

Mr Choudhury translated my words.

'Do you *really* want to find this place?' asked the *phandi*.

'Yes,' I replied, 'very much.'

For a minute or so, he considered my request, consulting with Mr Choudhury. Then he looked me straight in the eye.

'I know its location,' he said at last. 'I know it only too well.'

I felt a rush of adrenalin. The elephant graveyard was real after all, I thought.

'Would it be possible to go there?' I asked hesitantly.

'Oh, yes, I will take you there. But first, let us eat. My wife has prepared a meal in your honour.'

Mrs Geala had made her speciality, *patat diya mas*, fish cooked in a banana leaf with mustard seeds. This and other dishes were laid out on the floor of one of the huts where we gathered after washing our hands at the well. Fragrant rice seasoned with cloves and cumin was heaped on to my plate, along with pungent, spicy chicken cooked with papaya. Afterwards, *kheer*, or rice pudding, was served in tiny steel bowls.

But the food was wasted on me. Throughout the meal, all I could think about was finding the elephant graveyard, but I had to bide my time until our plates were taken away. Then the *phandi* jumped up from where he had been sitting.

'There are only a couple of hours of daylight left,' he said. 'If you want to see the graveyard, then we must hurry.'

Picking up my camera bag, I followed him out of the door. Mr Choudhury was just a few steps behind me. We crossed the compound, pushed through the gates, ran up a grassy bank and then crossed a rickety rope bridge that spanned the river.

Once on the other side, Geala marched barefoot along a pathway that led through the jungle and up into the hills. Gradually, the terrain grew steeper and steeper, and soon I found myself clambering along on all fours, completely out of breath. Two or three times, I stopped to rest. But the *phandi*, who did not falter once, kept up his relentless pace.

'Once it is dark, you will not be able to see it,' he said. 'There is no time to waste.'

Mustering the last of my strength, I stumbled on, with Mr Choudhury bringing up the rear. Sweat streamed down my face, soaking my shirt and trousers, and stinging my eyes. The muscles in my legs began to stiffen and weaken. By the time I got to the top I was completely exhausted.

For several minutes, I lay on the ground, trying to catch my breath, my heart pounding against my chest. When I sat up, the *phandi* was standing on the edge of the hill, which afforded a panoramic view of the Brahmaputra valley below.

'There it is,' he said, indicating to the south. 'There is the elephant graveyard.'

With wobbly legs, I managed to rise to my feet and walked unsteadily over to where the *phandi* stood.

Far below, the Brahmaputra, like a thread of mercury, snaked its way through the lush valley. From this vantage-point, I could see how little of the rain forest remained. Most of the landscape was covered in a patchwork of tea gardens and paddy-fields. Black tarmac roads and steel railway lines cut across the land. Cities and towns, with their cars and power stations and oil refineries, all belching smoke into the air, stood like blemishes on the site of what had once been uninterrupted forest and ancient elephant migratory routes.

Just a few miles from where we stood, on the site of a new housing development, bulldozers carved into the side of a hill, gouging out great chunks of red earth with brush and saplings still clinging to them. Trees fell to whining chain-saws, while nearby, fires burned away the undergrowth, leaving a black scab upon the landscape. But, as hard as I looked, I could find no sign of a graveyard.

'Do you see it?' the *phandi* asked me. 'It is there, right in front of you.'

Again, I gazed out over the valley, searching for a lake or pool, like the one described by the monk; or a hill littered with bones and tusks, as described by Baba. Still I could see nothing.

'Where is it?' I asked the *phandi*.

He looked at me with a half smile on his face.

'Until recently,' he said, 'this valley was home to thousands and thousands of elephants. Now, there are only a few hundred left. The rest have all died or been killed. Their bones and tusks lie strewn across the land.'

He paused, looking to see if I understood his meaning. But by now, I was completely confused.

The *phandi* pointed again at the valley.

'This, my friend, *is* the elephant graveyard.'

Mr Choudhury, the *phandi* and I sat down on the edge of the hill, watching the sunset.

Though I knew my quest was at an end, I did not feel disappointed. The *phandi*'s words had made a strong impression on me, and suddenly finding the fabled graveyard seemed like a foolish exercise.

'Your time would be better spent writing about the plight of the elephants,' said Mr Choudhury. 'Make no mistake, they are facing extinction. But here in Assam, no one is doing anything to save them.'

There was an urgency in Mr Choudhury's words that I had not heard before.

'Our government does not care. They have done nothing

to help save the elephants,' he said. 'We desperately need international support to set up sanctuaries. Otherwise, the elephants will simply die out.'

The *phandi*, too, was desperate to prevent such a tragedy and launched into a rousing appeal for help.

'Many times, I have travelled from village to village, imploring people not to cut down the jungle. I tell them about the elephants and about our heritage. But they do not listen,' said Geala. 'We Hindus are hypocrites. Every day, we pray to animals and Mother India, and even to Ganesha. Yet at the same time, we are destroying the very earth that we hold so sacred.'

With dusk creeping over the valley, the glow of electric lights became more visible in the gloom below. Car headlamps bobbed along the roads, while in the villages, figures crouched around smoky evening fires.

'Our priests say that this is Kalyug, the Age of Kali, a time of decline and degeneration,' continued the *phandi*, relighting his pipe. 'But that has become an excuse to do nothing. The fact is, people are selfish and lazy.'

It was clear that Mr Choudhury and the *phandi* expected me, as a foreigner, to mobilize the outside world into action. But as a journalist, the most I could promise was to write about my experiences.

'That is all we are asking,' said Mr Choudhury, as we stood up and headed down the hill in the receding light. 'Publish what you have seen and maybe people will take notice. Who knows, perhaps the elephants will yet be saved. Great things have small beginnings, is it not so?'

I spent the next three weeks on India's North-East Frontier, travelling the length and breadth of Assam and visiting Majuli – without the company of Vipal Ganguly, although how I managed to avoid him is a tale for another time.

Unfortunately, I was unable to make the pilgrimage to Kohima, where Charles had fought against the Japanese, because the Indian government refused me a travel permit to Nagaland, a restricted state for foreign journalists. Instead, I journeyed to Churchill's native Cherapunjee, the so-called Scotland of the East, which until recently boasted the highest rainfall in the world; and to Shillong, the old British hill station, with its quaint bungalows and narrow, winding streets.

Soon, I was back in Guwahati, making preparations for my return to Delhi. On the morning of my departure, Mr Choudhury insisted on taking me to the airport in the Land Rover. Along the way, he asked Rudra to stop and pointed out some elephant tracks in the muddy fields on the side of the road.

'During harvest time, they come down from those hills and raid the fields,' he said, pointing to a distant range topped with rain forest. 'Next time you visit, I will bring you here. I have a pair of night-scope goggles and this is the perfect place to watch the elephants.'

We piled back into the Land Rover and sped on to the airport. In the car park, the hunter and Rudra helped put my bags on a trolley.

'Send me good British magazine,' said Rudra, winking at me. 'I like looking at girl with lovely mangoes.'

I agreed to send him what I could.

'Take this now,' he said, handing me several chunks of betel nut wrapped in a grimy cloth which he'd used to wipe the windscreen. 'When you eat this, think of me!'

Rudra stayed by the car while Mr Choudhury helped me wheel the trolley over to the departure terminal. At the door, a security guard checked my ticket but barred Mr Choudhury from entering. It was here that we said goodbye and I thanked him for all he had done.

'By the way, I was called by the Forest Department this morning,' said the hunter, shaking my hand. 'They have asked me to travel to Upper Assam. Apparently, there is another rogue on the loose. They want me to appraise the situation.'

'Will you go?' I asked.

'Yes, I must,' he replied. 'He has killed many people. A warrant has been issued for his destruction.'

For a moment, I couldn't think of anything to say. The two of us stood looking at one another while passengers pushed past, cramming through the narrow entrance to the terminal.

'Why don't you come with me?' said Mr Choudhury. 'It will be an interesting time.'

I felt tempted, but I couldn't justify delaying my return to Delhi.

'I don't think I want to see another elephant die,' I said.

'Neither do I', sighed the hunter.

The final check-in announcement for my flight sounded over the loudspeakers. I held out my hand and Mr Choudhury shook it warmly. Promising to visit Assam again, I said one last goodbye and watched as the hunter turned and headed back to the Land Rover.

Author's Note

DURING RESEARCH for this book, I learned that there is no such place as an elephant graveyard – at least in the sense that elephants do not migrate to a single, secret location in order to die. Still, the legend is not so far-fetched.

According to the experts, elephants, like most animals, need to be close to water when they sense death approaching, and during their last days they remain by a favourite river or lake within their own 'range' or territory. Eventually, when they finally keel over, their bodies simply fall into the water, sink down into marshy ground or are washed away entirely. This may explain why so few carcasses are discovered in the wild.

It stands to reason, therefore, that over tens of thousands of years, countless generations of elephants, whether African or Asian, have laid down their bones and tusks in the same locations. Over time, rivers have shifted course and swamps and lakes have dried up, revealing the bones and tusks. Who could be blamed for stumbling across one of these sites, littered with ivory and the remains of thousands of elephants, and mistaking it for an elephant graveyard?

Today, in India, *Elephas maximus* is under greater threat than ever. Despite the fact that its African cousin receives most of the world's attention and aid, the plight of the Asian elephant is far worse. Already, its population has dwindled to just ten per cent of the African species, placing it perilously close to extinction. Most official figures put the wild elephant population in India at between 20,000 and 25,000, and in many parts of the country, the animals have disappeared altogether.

In recent years, poaching has increased at an alarming rate. Poachers use any and all means available to slaughter their quarry. Elephants have been killed using pits lined with sharp stakes, electrocuted by cables powered by overhead pylons or simply shot. Meanwhile, the elephants' habitat continues to be chopped down, leaving the herds isolated in ever-shrinking islands of forest. Who knows how much time is left for the elephants of India?

Bibliography

Anderson, K., *Nine Man-Eaters and One Rogue* (George Allen & Unwin, London, 1954)

Barkataki, S. N., *Tribal Folktales of Assam* (Publication Board, Guwahati, 1970)

Barker, G. M., *A Tea Planter's Life in Assam* (Thacker, Spink, Calcutta, 1884)

Barpujari, H. K., *The Comprehensive History of Assam*, 5 vols. (Publication Board, Guwahati, n.d.)

Barua, B. K., and Sreenivasa Murthy, H. V., *Temples and Legends of Assam* (Bhavans Book University, Bombay, 1988)

Bedi, R., *Elephant, Lord of the Jungle* (National Book Trust India, New Delhi, 1969)

Bertrand, G., *The Jungle People* (Robert Hale, London, 1959)

Bishop, S. O., *Sketches in Assam* (Thomas Smith, Calcutta, 1885)

Bloomgate, A., *The Plain Narrative of the Doings and Destruction of the Most Murderous Rogue Ever Known* (n.p., 1895)

Cantlie, A., *The Assamese* (Curzon Press, London, 1984)

Carrington, R., *Elephants* (Chatto & Windus, London, 1958)

Chadwick, D. H., *The Fate of the Elephant* (Viking, London, 1993)

Choudhury, P. C., *Hastividyarava* (Publication Board, Guwahati, 1976)

Das, J., *Folklore of Assam* (National Book Trust India, New Delhi, 1972)

Douglas-Hamilton, Iain and Oria, *Among the Elephants* (Harvill Press, London, 1975)

Bibliography

Dubois, A. J. A., *Hindu Manners, Customs and Ceremonies*, third ed. (Rupa and Co., New Delhi, 1996)

Dutta, A. K., *Cha Garam: The Tea Story* (Paloma Publications, Guwahati, 1992)

Dutta Barooa, B. N., *The Red River and the Blue Hill* (Lawyer's Book Stall, Guwahati, 1954)

Edgerton, Franklin, *The Elephant-Lore of the Hindus* (Yale University Press, Princeton, 1931)

Eliot, Sir Charles, *Hinduism and Buddhism* (Edward Arnold, London, 1921)

Eltringham, S. K., *The Illustrated Encyclopedia of Elephants* (Salamander Books, London, 1991)

Evans, G. H., *A Treatise on Elephants* (Government Publication, Rangoon, 1901)

Fraser, W. M., *The Recollections of a Tea Planter* (The Tea and Rubber Mail, London, 1935)

Gait, E., *A History of Assam* (n.p., 1905)

Getty, A., *Ganesa* (Munshiram Manoharlal, New Delhi, 1971)

Goodwin, Jason, *The Gunpowder Gardens* (Chatto & Windus, London, 1990)

Hanley, P., *Tiger Trails in Assam* (Robert Hale, London, 1961)

Hastings, J., *Encyclopaedia of Religion and Ethics* (T. & T. Clark, Edinburgh, 1921)

Hazarika, S., *Strangers of the Mist: Tales of War and Peace from India's Northeast* (Viking India, New Delhi, 1994)

Holder, C. F., *Ivory King* (Samson, Low, London, 1886)

Izzard, R., *The Hunt for the Buru* (Hodder & Stoughton, London, 1951)

Karotemprel, S., and Dutta Roy, B., *Tea Garden Labourers of North East India* (Vendrame Institute, Shillong, 1990)

Kingdon-Ward, J., *My Hill So Strong* (Jonathan Cape, London, 1952)

Knight, M., *How to Keep an Elephant* (Wolfe, London, 1967)

Lindgren, O., *The Trials of a Tea Planter* (privately published, 1933)

Masson, J. M., and McCarthy, S., *When Elephants Weep: The Emotional Lives of Animals* (Jonathan Cape, London, 1994)

Moss, C., *Elephant Memories* (Elm Tree Books, London, 1988)

Muirhead Thomson, R. C., *Assam Valley* (Luzac & Co., London, 1948)

Bibliography

Nugent, R., *The Search for the Pink-Headed Duck: A Journey into the Himalayas and Down the Brahmaputra* (Houghton Mifflin, New York, 1991)

Orwell, George, 'Shooting an Elephant', *New Writing*, 1936.

Ramsden, A. R., *Assam Planter* (John Gifford, London, 1945)

Sanderson, G. P., *Thirteen Years Among the Wild Beasts of India* (W. H. Allen, London, 1890)

Sarma, S. N., *The Neo-Vaishnavite Movement and the Satra Institution of Assam* (Department of Publication Gauhati University, Guwahati, 1966)

Schilling, T., *Tigermen of Anai* (Allen & Unwin, London, 1957)

Shand, Mark, *Travels on My Elephant* (Jonathan Cape, London, 1991)

——*Queen of the Elephants* (Jonathan Cape, London, 1995).

Shoshani, J., *Elephants: Majestic Creatures of the Wild* (RD Press, Sydney, 1992)

Sillar, F. C., and Meyler, R. M., *Elephants: Ancient and Modern* (Studio Vista, London, 1968)

Slym, M. J., *Treatise on the Treatment of Elephants in Health and Disease* (n.p., Maulmain, 1873)

Stracey, P. D., *Elephant Gold* (Natraj Publishers, New Delhi, 1991)

——*Reade: Elephant Hunter* (Robert Hale, London, 1967)

Sukumar, R., *Elephant Days and Nights* (Oxford University Press, New Delhi, 1994)

Temple-Perkins, E. A., *Kingdom of the Elephants* (Andrew Melrose, 1955)

Ward, S. R., *A Glimpse of Assam* (Thomas S. Smith, Calcutta, 1884)

Weatherstone, J., *The Pioneers* (Quiller Press, London, 1986)

Williams, Heathcote, *Sacred Elephant* (Jonathan Cape, London, n.d.)

Williams, J. H., *Elephant Bill* (Hart-Davis, London, 1950)

Wise, M., *True Tales of British India* (In Print Publishing, Brighton, 1993)

Yule, H., and Burnell, A. C., *Hobson-Jobson* (John Murray, London, 1903)